Collected Works of Sebastian Kappen

Volume III

Jesus and Cultural Revolution
and Related Essays

Collected Works of Sebastian Kappen
Volume III

Jesus and Cultural Revolution and Related Essays

Compiled and Edited by

Sebastian Vattamattam

2021

Collected Works of Sebastian Kappen, Volume III: Jesus and Cultural Revolution and Related Essays, Ed. Sebastian Vattamattam — published by the Indian Society for Promoting Christian Knowledge (ISPCK), Post Box 1585, Kashmere Gate, Delhi-110006.

© ISPCK, 2021

All rights reserved. No part of this book may be reproduced or transmitted in any form or by any means, electronic, mechanical, photocopying, recording, or by any information storage and retrieval system, without the prior permission in writing from the publisher.

The views expressed in the book are those of the author and the publisher takes no responsibility for any of the statements.

Online order: http://ispck.org.in/book.php

Also available on amazon.in

ISBN: 978-81-947592-6-3

Cover image: C F John

Laser typeset by

ISPCK, Post Box 1585, 1654, Madarsa Road, Kashmere Gate, Delhi-110006 • *Tel:* 23866323

e-mail: ashish@ispck.org.in • ella@ispck.org.in
website: www.ispck.org.in

Sebastian Kappen (1924 - 1993)

Sebastian Kappen, an Indian Jesuit theologian, doctored in 1961 from the Gregorian University, Rome, with a thesis on 'Praxis and Religious Alienation according to the Economic and Philosophical Manuscripts of Karl Marx.' His subsequent studies had been geared to the requirements of transformative social action in India. This led him to an investigation into the liberative and humanizing potential of the original teachings of the historical Jesus as well as of Indian religious traditions, particularly the tradition of dissent represented by the Buddha and the medieval Bhakti Movement. He wrote and lectured extensively on the cultural restructuring of Indian society.

In 1977 appeared Kappen's major work in English, *Jesus and Freedom*. It was followed by *Marxian Atheism* (1983), *Jesus and Cultural Revolution - an Asian Perspective* (1983), *Liberation Theology and Marxism* (1986), and *The Future of Socialism and Socialism of the Future* (1992). His posthumous publications are *Tradition Modernity Counterculture* (1994), *Hindutva and Indian Religious Traditions* (2000), *Divine Challenge and Human Response* (2001), *Jesus and Society* (2002), *Jesus and Culture* (2002), *Towards a Holistic Cultural Paradigm* (2003), *Marx Beyond Marxism* (2012), *Ingathering* (2013), *What the Thunder Says* (2013). His books in Malayalam are *From Faith to Revolution* (1972), *A Sexual Morality for Tomorrow* (1973), *Ecology and Culture* (1988), *An Introduction to the Philosophy of Marx* (1989), *Prophecy and Counterculture* (1992), *In Search of the Non-Christian Jesus* (1999), *Liberation of Jesus from the Churches* (2012), and *Death of God and the Birth of the Human - tr. of Marxian Atheism* (2015)

Sebastian Kappen had been visiting professor to the Pontifical Seminary (Pune), Vidyajyoti (Delhi), The Catholic University of Louvain (Belgium) and Maryknoll Seminary (New York). Mother Earth called him back on 30 November 1993.

Contents

Introduction

In Jesus and Freedom, Fr. Kappen Goes back to Jesus of Nazareth and re-discovers his revolutionary message. Based on that, in *Jesus and Cultural Revolution*, he elaborates on the prophetic role of Jesus in human history and deals with the relevance of the historical Jesus for India today.

In the last two decades of his life, Fr. Kappen lived in rented houses, outside the Church institutions, to be with the common people. Among the intellectuals and social activists in India and abroad, he had a large number of friends and collaborators. In 1970s, there was in Bangalore a meeting of social activists, to reflect on the theme, 'Faith and Social Action', and Fr. Kappen was a resource person. As requested by the participants, he started publishing a series called Anawim, of tracts recapturing the liberating message of Jesus for contemporary humans. In the second part of this volume III, chapters 7 to 26 are taken from Anawim. The next two chapters are taken from *Ingathering* and the last from *What the Thunder says*. Chapter 29 was originally published in 'Socialist Perspectives', an occasional publication, initiated by Fr. Kappen, for promoting independent socialist thinking. It was edited and published by Ajit Muricken, Centre for Social Reconstruction, Madras.

Let me express my gratitude to Mercy Kappen, and artist C F John, both closely related to Fr. Kappen, for their consistent support and encouragement in completing this volume. The cover image of this book is John's artistic creation.

Sebastian Vattamattam

PART - 1
JESUS AND CULTURAL REVOLUTION

Foreword

In the history of peoples, there are peak moments when their spiritual energies concentrate and come to a head, be it in a person or an event. Conditions are then ripe for a historic mutation, for a qualitative leap forward in the direction of a fuller humanity. Such moments constitute the real origins of human communities. But, in course of time, the emergent forces of re-creation either die out or become debased and denatured. Then follows a period of cultural decadence and stagnation. A fresh start is possible only if men and women return to their origins and drink straight from the primal sources of their historical existence.

So in an earlier work, *Jesus and Freedom* (Volume I, Part 1), I tried to go back to Christianity's origin which is Jesus of Nazareth, and reconstruct his revolutionary message. The present work builds on it while at the same time going beyond it. It seeks to relate the life and teaching of the Galilean prophet to the genuinely original forces of self-transcendence within the religious-cultural tradition of India. My main concern is to show that the point of insertion for Jesus in our cultural history is not the *Brahmanic Sanskritic* tradition of the Vedas, Upanishads, Epics, and *Puranas* but the socio-religious movements of dissent, originating from the repressed culture of the downtrodden and the marginated. I have also tried to show that the Jesus tradition can make a significant contribution to that revolution of consciousness required for the restructuring of Indian society.

Originally the work consisted of the lectures given at the "Third-world Theologians in Dialogue" held in New York, in 1979. I have since given courses on the theme at Vidya Jyothi, Delhi, and the Jnanadeepa Institute of Religious Studies, Poona. I used the same material for the "Joshi Memorial Lectures" for the year 1982, sponsored by the Bombay Industrial League for Development (Build).

I am grateful to Build, Bombay, for undertaking to publish the book. My thanks are also due to the friends who have gone through the manuscript and suggested corrections and improvements, and to St. Joseph's Press, Trivandrum, for their neat and expeditious printing.

S. Kappen

Madras, March 1983

1

The Dialectic of Culture and Prophecy

What is the relevance of the historical Jesus for India today? Every question emerges from a specific standpoint. And the standpoint from which the present question is raised is that of commitment to the creation of a new society based on justice and freedom. The standpoint is further narrowed down to the concern for *freedom from* inherited cultural bondages and *freedom for* fashioning a new, humane and humanizing culture. Hence the question boils down to this: What is the relevance of Jesus to the efforts being made for a culture that affirms genuine values? For an answer we need to have some knowledge of Jesus' stance in relation to his own cultural context and of the new vision and values he stood for. But before grappling with that, let me make a few observations on cultural change in general in order to place Jesus in the broader historical framework.

Culture may be described as the organic whole of ideas, beliefs, values, and goals which condition the thinking and acting of a community or people. Understood thus, culture finds conceptual expression in ethics, philosophy and law; symbolic expression in art, literature, myth and cult. It is also embodied in economic, social, political, and cultural institutions and structures. It is equally enfleshed in the psycho-structure of individuals - in their reflexes, reactions, sensuousness, expectations and hopes. Even ordinary artifacts and products are bearers of culture. The beliefs and values of a people can be read from the kind of houses built, dress worn, food eaten and implements used. Culture is thus an all pervasive reality and goes to form an integral element of any social system. However, the relation between culture and social institutions is not only one of identity but also of difference, even to the point of contradiction. Contradiction arises when social institutions have developed along lines which render them incapable of bearing the values which they were meant to realize, or when the development of culture is at variance with existing institutions. This shows that culture is not a static reality given once and for all, but something which is caught up in the overall process of historical change.

Culture in Crisis

Even in periods of relative equilibrium, each culture contains itself the seeds of crisis and dissolution. The eruption of crisis depends on the interplay of many factors. I have already indicated one important factor leading to cultural crisis, namely, the unequal development of culture and social institutions. Uneven development may be due to the advance made in science and technology or to contact with other cultures or to subjugation by a foreign power or, again, to the self-criticism initiated by creative individuals. The most important cause of crisis, however, is the class character of culture. Here Marx's dictum that the ruling ideas of any age are the ideas of the ruling classes is of crucial relevance.[1] Those who own the means of production and control the levers of power are in a position to project their class culture as universally valid and impose it on the common man. This they can do easily since, as owners of the means of material production, they also control the production and circulation of cultural goods. Over time, the oppressed classes internalize, and identify themselves with, the culture of their masters. With that the sense of being dominated recedes into the collective subconscious. The disprivileged may even use the tools provided by the dominant culture to legitimize their own condition. The ruling classes thus find an accomplice in the false consciousness of the ruled. This is one way in which the dominant culture develops internal mechanisms for its own reproduction and perpetuation.

In proportion as the oppressed classes realize that the prevailing culture is one that their masters have created for promoting their own class interests - a realization which will be hastened by the convergence of the historical factors mentioned earlier - there is an upsurge of mass discontent. Such discontent seething beneath the surface will naturally seek an escape by rupturing the cultural integument imprisoning people's consciousness. The agents of this rupture are prophetic individuals and groups. The prophet appears on the scene as the focus of concentration of the crisis of consciousness affecting the masses as a whole.

The Prophet and His Project

If it is true that it is the crisis that creates the prophet, it is equally true that it is the prophet who creates the crisis. Having emerged on the scene, he acts on the people helping them articulate and make explicit their implicit critique of the prevailing society and culture. He identifies himself with their longings for a new social order, in which they will live their own thoughts, values, norms, and hopes. He is in actuality what every member of the community is potentially. The structure and dynamics of his consciousness set the pattern for that of the community as a whole. He sums up in his own person the past, the present, and the future of the culturally disprivileged.

The prophet is not only the point of *eruption* for the repressed longings of the masses but also a point of *irruption of* the Divine. He is essentially one who has been called and taken hold of by God, not by God as he is in himself but by God as *the answer* to the collective aspirations of the people. He is called to announce the new-found answer to his fellowmen. It is to this experience of being called that he appeals when, challenged to legitimate his claims. However, the eruption of popular aspirations and the irruption of the Divine are not two distinct realities which happen to converge and coincide. Rather, they are one and the same reality. Or, more precisely, the latter is the depth dimension of the former. Just as the seed buried in the ground bursts the crust of the earth and sprouts into the light of day, the Divine - the beginning, the middle and the end of all that is - that was silently at work in the community of the oppressed unveils itself in the word and deed of the prophet. In the latter the God who calls becomes the man called. Through him the community achieves a breakthrough into the ultimate horizon of human destiny.

I have already stated that it is as the answer to the mute longing of the disprivileged that the Divine appears on the horizon of prophetic consciousness. Therefore, the point of arrival of the prophetic breakthrough is neither God nor man but *God-in-man* and *man-in-God*. The goal is a theandric community of justice, love and freedom. Prophecy thus takes the form of an ultimate project of hope. Clearly, the project of freedom from all alienation is not a mere product of creative imagination, nor a child of morbid phantasy. For, in projecting such a horizon, the prophet is also projected (propelled) by it. His prophetic consciousness is at once the cause and the effect of the project. If he fashions the project, so does the latter fashion him. While it is true that it is the experience of alienation - his own as well as that of the community — that enables him to envision a future of integral freedom, it is also true that it is the vision of the theandric community that attunes his soul to a deeper awareness of human alienation. In other words, the prophet and the project stand in a relationship of reciprocal conditioning and creation.

The project of hope, which is the central theme of all prophetic preaching, should not be understood as a conceptual model of an ideal world order extrapolated on the basis of any scientific criticism of existing conditions. The ultimate destiny of mankind is ineffable. Our one-dimensional concepts prove inadequate when it comes to describing it. Better suited to the purpose are myths and symbols whose meaning is multidimensional. Hence every prophetic movement tends to throw up its own array of myths. That they seek symbolic, mythical expression is not their weakness but their strength. Consider, for instance, the classless society envisaged by Marx. If it is capable of eliciting heroic commitment on the part of millions, it is not because it is a scientific concept but because it has deeper significance as a myth.

From Project to Praxis

The project demands to be realized. And it cannot be realized without praxis i.e. without action aimed at self-transformation through world-transformation. The *no* to human alienation, implicit in the project, must now become explicit and assume the form of collective commitment on the part of the prophet and the people to overthrowing the prevailing culture. Where it does, prophecy becomes subversive praxis. But the subversion of the existing culture and of the institutions in which it is embodied has for its reverse side the creation of a counterculture in tune with the project of hope. For, every negation is an affirmation. When the sculptor chops off pieces from his block of wood he is performing an act of negation, but by the same process he is creating something new, a work of art. So it is with the subversion of a culture. What Kenelm Burridge says of millenary movements holds true also of all authentic prophecy:

> "The hypothesis that millenary activities predicate a new culture or social order coming into being... is a fair one. Certainly it is more scientific to regard these activities as a new-culture-in-the-making, or as attempts to make a new kind of society or moral community, rather than as oddities, as diseases in the body, social or troublesome nuisances to efficient administration - though of course they may be all of these as well."[2]

In initiating a counterculture the prophet also brings into existence a new dissenting community.

Countercultures, however, are not created out of nothing. The prophet and his community of dissenters can fashion the new only by drawing upon the wealth of tradition.

> "Men make their own history, but they do not make it just as they please; they do not make it under circumstances chosen by themselves, but under circumstances directly encountered, given and transmitted from the past."[3]

Old myths and symbols are taken over but given a new content, a new meaning. There may emerge also new myths and symbols. But even they must have some affinity with the inherited structures of feeling and thinking if they are to grip the imagination of men and women. Whatever is true and worthwhile in the past is preserved to be realized on a higher level, that is, without the limits and constraints imposed by tradition. In this sense, what prophetic praxis aims at is the dialectical supersession of the past involving the three moments of abolition, preservation and sublimation.

It can happen that the project of hope fails to issue in appropriate praxis due to the immaturity of either objective conditions (lack of means of communication for disseminating the counter-culture, dispersal of the enslaved classes over a wide area, absence of any economic crisis and so forth) or subjective conditions such as the failure of the prophet to identify himself with the people and lack of organization. Under such conditions, the creative energies released by prophetic proclamation seek compensatory outlets. Chief among these are vertical escape into an illusory heaven above, inscape into one's own isolated self, orgiastic cults issuing in a paroxysm of emotion, and nostalgia for death and dissolution. These ways of finding compensation pose no threat to the Establishment and may even serve to reinforce it. Hence they will be tolerated, if not encouraged, by the dominant classes. Where, on the contrary, prophetic enthusiasm leads to revolutionary praxis, the prophet and his followers will be exposed to ruthless repression.

The dialectic of culture and prophecy, whose basic structure and movement I have tried to explain, is constitutive of man's collective historical existence. In the light of the perspectives opened up by this somewhat theoretical discussion, let us now consider the prophetic mission of Jesus.

2

Jesus: The Prophet
of a Counterculture

In the time of Jesus, the mass of people in Palestine were under twofold cultural domination. The first had its source in foreign rule. From as early as the third century B.C., a process of cultural symbiosis had been at work between Judaism and Hellenism. Greek customs and way of life had been introduced into Palestine, along with the Greek method of education. Subsequently, Hellenization was carried out by force when Palestine came under Syrian rulers.

> "The walls of Jerusalem were torn down and a fortress was built on the hill of the ancient city of David (the Acra). The Jews were forbidden on pain of death, to keep the Sabbath and to circumcise their children... In Jerusalem, a pagan altar was erected on the site of the altar of burnt offering, and sacrifices were offered there to the supreme God, the Olympian Zeus." (167 B.C.)[1]

Significantly, this cultural invasion was welcomed by a small section of the indigenous population, by "the relatively narrow, but normative stratum of the priestly and lay nobility and the prosperous city population."[2] The common people, on their part, clung to the faith of their fathers and resisted the alien culture, as is clear, above all, from the support they gave to the Maccabean struggle. Later, when the Romans established their rule in Palestine, the mass of people protested whenever the colonial rulers did anything that offended their religious sensibilities.[3]

What weighed still more heavily on the masses was the oppressive character of Judaism itself in the form it had assumed since the exile. I shall refer to specific instances when I discuss the prophetic role of Jesus. Here I shall do no more than comment on some major trends. Jesus lived at a time when cult, law, and apocalypticism had supplanted prophecy. This meant there was none to defend the cause of the poor and the oppressed. The priestly aristocracy allied itself with the lay nobility and lived affluently on the profits they made by exchanging the grace of God for money. In the absence of genuine prophecy, the apocalyptic movement came to the fore. Whereas the prophets had announced a future age of justice whose realization depended on the free initiative of God and the equally free response of man, the apocalyptic seers viewed history as following a predetermined course: an intensification of misery in the present age followed by a new eon of freedom and happiness. Though meant to console the people in a period of intense tribulation,[4] these visionary writings also served to legitimize the ills of society in so far as these were conceived of as inevitable and divinely ordained.

The same period witnessed an overgrowth of legalism and casuistry originating in Pharisaic and Scribal circles. Knowledge of the Law gained ascendancy over love. Underlying this development was a change in the class basis of the Jewish religion. Love can be practiced by all whereas knowledge is non-democratic. Only the educated and the wise could grasp all the implications of the written and the oral law. No wonder the vast majority of people in the time of Jesus failed to observe the details of the Law. What was originally a religion of the common man thus became a religion of the elite that set itself apart — that is what the word Pharisee means - from the masses. The only religious-cultural movement that was close to the people was Zealotism. The Zealots had popular support for their policy of using force to throw out the Romans.

A New Horizon of Hope

The time was thus ripe for a prophet to arise who would help the poor and the disinherited to shake off their cultural shackles and march forward to new frontiers. And a prophet did emerge. He was Jesus of Nazareth.

As one who encountered the God who is to come, Jesus lived from the future. He was gripped by the vision of the human-Divine community of the end-time. In itself, such a vision was nothing new. Ever since the prophets of old, the Jews had nursed the hope in the dawn of a new age of peace and abundance. What marks Jesus out from his forebears and contemporaries was the way he understood the realization of that goal which he called the reign of God. He did not coin the word. Its roots go back to the Old Testament and were very much in vogue in current literature. But what he meant to convey burst all earlier moulds of thinking. He announced that the future reign of God was already germinating in the present.[5] And thereby he showed a way out of the gloom and pessimism which apocalypticism inspired. More, he rejected the prevailing view that human action was of no avail in determining the course of history. He required of his disciples to seek the kingdom of God and its justice even to the point of inviting persecution.[6] His vision of the future was also free of every particularist, nationalist overtone. True, the prophets before him had envisaged a new humanity encompassing all nations. But theirs was a universalism that continued to see Israel and the temple as the centre of the universe. In the perspective of Jesus, on the contrary, the new humanity will have no centre other than God. The sole condition for entry into it will be preparedness to do the will of God,[7] which for him meant loving one's fellowmen. The same universality distinguished him from the Zealots who looked forward to the restoration of the Jewish monarchy. In short, the message of Jesus marks the emergence of a radically new vision of the ultimate possibility open to mankind.

But one might ask, What has the hope of the reign of God to do with Jesus' attitude to Jewish culture? Very much indeed.

The ideas, beliefs, values, and norms which go to make up culture are not so many disparate elements somehow juxtaposed. They are held together by a common primal focus which is none other than the ultimate goal of individual and collective existence, whether it is called *Mukti* (Hinduism), *nirvana* (Buddhism), or the reign of God. This primal focus is the light in which meanings are grasped, values are perceived, hopes crystallize and norms are framed. A radically new vision of the ultimate goal of life, therefore, will call for a radical questioning and reinterpretation of the prevailing culture. Conversely, a radical critique of culture involves a reinterpretation of the ultimate goal. Then, hope in the reign of God was of crucial significance for the concrete practice of Jesus concerning the cultural universe of his contemporaries. No less significant is it for his disciples today. For, as we shall see, it is the loss of this hope that reduced Christian faith to an ideology of legitimation.

The Subversion of Jewish Culture

That Jesus translated his hope in the reign of God into subversive praxis is clear from every page of the Gospels. I shall here limit myself to the rupture he effected with the prevalent system of values. This does not mean ignoring the other elements of culture. For in any organic culture, a part is, in a sense, equal to the whole. Any value presupposes certain ideas and beliefs and gives rise to norms, customs, and expectations. Therefore, the subversion of existing values is equivalent to the subversion of the entire cultural universe. In this context, it should also be kept in mind that, in dealing with traditional cultures, it is not possible to make a clear distinction between religion and secular society because the former determined every aspect of the latter. Secular terms such as the poor, justice, law, and earth have in the Bible also a religious meaning. Hence Jesus' critique of the Jewish religion is at the same time a critique of Jewish society and *vice versa.*

Now to return to the question of values: For Jesus, the reign of God constituted the Value of all values, that universal value in the light of which the value of everything else was measured. Compared with it, all else was of secondary importance. This is the import of the saying,

"The kingdom of heaven is like a treasure hidden in a field, which a man found and covered up; then in his joy, he goes and sells all that he has and buys that field. Again, the kingdom of heaven is like a merchant in search of fine pearls, who on finding one pearl of great value, went and sold all that he had and bought it."[8]

In the perspective of God's impending rule, what was valued high by his contemporaries appeared to him of little value, while what the former held in contempt became invested with value. The last became the first, and the first the last. The new way of evaluating things, persons, events, customs, and actions shaped his social praxis. He became a contester of the polar social relation into which the traditional perception of values had crystallized: rich versus poor, great versus least, man versus woman, parents versus children, Jew versus Gentile, wise versus simple, pure versus impure.

The Rich Versus the Poor

The dominant ideology attached supreme value to wealth, projecting it as a concrete sign of divine favour. Poverty was held to be a punishment for sin. This suited very well the interests of the rich, who could nurse the comfortable feeling that they were close to God and that they were not exploiting the poor. Jesus shattered their complacency by proclaiming the incompatibility of the pursuit of mammon and the service of God.[9] He went further and taught that the blessings of the new age belong only to the poor.[10]

But to qualify what Jesus effected as a reversal of values is misleading, if not incorrect. He did not set more value on poverty than on wealth taken abstractly. Were it the case, the reign of God would be characterized by indigence. No, he spoke of the future as one of abundance, material as well as spiritual.[11] Nor did he mean that the exploited of his day would be exploiters in the age to come and vice versa. That would only have amounted to a reversal of roles, not to the definitive transcending of all exploitation. If he opted for the poor, it was because they were the exploited and, as such, were open to the future, God had in store for them, whereas the rich tended to hold fast to the conditions which made and maintained them rich, thereby shutting out the prospect of a radically new order of things.

The Great Versus the Least

This value polarity concerns the social distribution of power, the relation between the rulers and the ruled. At issue is the political master-slave relationship which obtained in contemporary Judaism. It conferred on a privileged few the right to impose their options on the rest. Jesus could not but repudiate such domination of man by man, believing as he did in the prospect of total freedom open to all human beings. He would have nothing to do with a social order in which the rulers loaded it over their subjects and made them feel the weight of their authority.[12] His call, "whoever would be great among you must be your servant, and whoever would be first among you must be the slave of all", should not be interpreted away as mere advice to use power as a means to service or to use service as a means to power; it must rather be understood as a call to radically renounce all exercise of power. Those who aspire to be great (to have slaves under them) must retrace their steps and seek to be slaves to others. Those who aspire to be the first must seek the lowest place. And in a social order in which all are slaves to one another, none is master over others. Rather, each man will be master and slave in one: slave, because he recognizes each member of the community as an absolute value, not a mere means to his personal ends; master, because he, in turn, is recognized by all as an absolute value. In this sense, the future community is the dialectical supersession of mastery and slavery, a supersession which preserves on a higher level the truth of both, namely, *being-for-oneself* (mastery) and *being-for-others* (slavery).[13] Jesus not only rejects the division of society into the great and the least but also repudiates the very standard by which the worth of a person was determined. Not command over, but service to, others is, for him, the true measure of greatness.

Here too Jesus favours the least, the powerless, not because the ruled of today are to become the rulers of tomorrow but because the former are more open to the new humanity in which there will be neither rulers nor ruled. It is against this background, we must understand his saying,

"But many that are first will be last, and the last first."[14]

The last will be the first not in terms of power but in terms of love. In contrast, the first of today, were they to continue to lust for power and satisfy the itch for domination, would be the last in respect of the Kingdom. They would represent man's fall from authentic existence.

The Wise Versus the Simple

In all societies based on the division of labour into intellectual and manual, there gradually emerges a class of people who claim the monopoly of knowledge. As they do not have to work for a living, they have ample time to create illusions, myths, and theories to promote the interests of the dominant classes from whom they usually stem. Living on the margin of history, they naturally tend to develop eternal and immutable ideas. So long as the consciousness of the masses could find a voice in prophetic teaching, such a class could not arise in Israel. But with the death of prophecy, there arose the Scribes, the official interpreters of the Law. True, the majority of them were poor and had to engage in a craft to make a living. But where knowledge becomes *class-ified*, it is itself power over human beings. That is how the Scribes came to occupy a privileged position in Jewish society. They were the originators of the apocalyptic movement with its penchant for secret revelations from God concerning the future of mankind.

The emphasis on legal and esoteric knowledge involved a devaluation of that knowledge of God which is gained through the practice of love and justice, the only knowledge of God recognized as valid by the prophets.[15] Jesus, on his part, rejected the wisdom of the wise.[16] Instead, he reaffirmed the common man's way of knowing God through love. This is the gist of his saying,

"Blessed are the pure in heart, for they shall see God."[17]

The purity of heart he inculcated meant not harbouring evil intentions against one's neighbour. Positively, it called for an attitude of universal compassion and empathy.

Man Versus Woman

The third point of crystallization of the values of Jewish society concerned the relations of reproduction comprising the two pairs of opposites: man and woman, parents and children. As is the case with all patriarchal societies, Judaism set a high value on man and relegated women to an inferior position. The latter were considered a source of moral danger, forbidden to move about freely in society, assigned an inferior place in the temple, and, if married, liable to be sent away for good under any silly pretext. Seen against this background, Jesus' teaching is truly revolutionary. In contravention of the written law,[18] he taught the indissolubility of marriage[19] until the dawn of the new age when the *two-in-one-fleshness* of marriage will yield to the *all-in-one-fleshness* of a new communion of men and women.[20] In applying the same yardstick of doing the will of God to man and woman, he affirmed their fundamental equality.[21] His preaching was matched by his practice. He associated freely with women,[22] cultivated their friendship,[23] allowed a retinue of them to accompany him in his journeyings and support him out of their means.[24] He thus defied the prevalent social taboos governing man-woman relationship. Marcion might well have been right when he wrote that Jesus' free dealings with women was one of the accusations brought up against him at his trial.[25] In short, the Galilean prophet sowed the seeds of a liberating sexual culture, which, unfortunately, was smothered in course of time.

Parents Versus Children

In assessing Jesus' stand on the parents-children relationship, it is necessary to keep in mind the sanctity traditional society attached to kinship. Among the early Hebrews, the father had absolute right over his children, including the right to life and death.[26] Ex. 21:7 presupposes the right of the father to sell his daughter into slavery. Striking one's father deserved capital punishment.[27] Though these rights were never exercised at the time of Jesus, the parental authority still held supreme. All decisions were taken by the father of the family. Jesus, on his part, would repudiate the perverted sense of values which legitimated the domination of children by parents, of the young by adults. He came out with the, to his contemporaries, startling and audacious teaching that the reign of God belongs to children.[28] To understand what he meant, we must go back to the famous saying where he thanks the Father for hiding 'these things' — the things concerning the reign of God to come - from the wise and revealing them to the young. As the contrast clearly shows, he thought the young better disposed to receive the knowledge of the Kingdom, because they were uncorrupted by the wisdom of the wise. After all, their hearts were not hardened by the ideologies of the status quo. No wonder he devalued parental rights to the point of sanctioning revolt against them where the superior claims of the Kingdom demanded it.[29] The Gospel evidence seems to suggest that he himself was rejected by his kinsfolk who took him for a mad man and that it was outside the family circle that he found his true mother, brothers, and sisters.[30]

The Pure Versus the Impure

Finally, let us consider the valuational aspect of the polarity, pure-impure. I shall dwell somewhat longer on it, because it is central to all religions and because it is here that the countercultural stance of Jesus comes into boldest relief. There is no consensus among scholars on the origin of the distinction between the pure and the impure. The reflections that follow are, admittedly, tentative and exploratory.[31]

The distinction between the pure and the impure has its origin in the world outlook of the 'primitive' man. In most primitive cultures there is the myth of the origin of the world from primordial chaos, the belief that things with name and form (*nama-rupa*) came out of the formless and the chaotic. The formless was also identified with death. On dying, everything - plants, animals, and men — dissolves into the formless stuff of the earth. It was, therefore, natural for the 'primitives' to think of life as emerging out of death and returning to it. They saw the process at work before their own eyes. The sun set and disappeared into the darkness of death to rise up again the following day. Plants dried up and decayed, but only to sprout into a new life. Our forebears found themselves constantly threatened by these forces of death and dissolution operative in the world. And in an age when they had not yet fashioned the tools for controlling the forces that environed them, it was crucial to discern between the life-giving and the death-dealing so that they could foster the one and ward off the other.

It is here we should seek the roots of the distinction between the pure and the impure. The pure is whatever contributes to life; impure whatever is detrimental to it. 'Sages' then appeared on the scene who applied their minds to making a catalogue of things pure and impure, and framed rules of conduct for the common people. Carcass, blood, feces, bodily excretions, hides, and similar things were held unclean because they had to do either with death or with the process of decay. This applied also to whatever was formless, deformed, hybrid, in short, everything that resembled the chaotic. Eventually, the notion of purity was extended to professions, classes, and groups as well. A further extension of the principle took place, thanks to the magical world view which identified the microcosmic with the macrocosmic - the eye with the sun, the breath with the wind, sex with cosmic reproduction, etc. The pure was identified with the Divine and the impure with the demonic. What was originally a magico-mythical conception was thus overlaid with religious meaning. This served to further intensify the contrast between the pure and the impure.

It was now possible to establish a hierarchy of the pure and the impure, of the sacred and the profane. At the fountainhead of life was God, the supremely pure and sacred. Among the Jews, this conception found spatial expression in the belief that the temple, especially the Holy of Holies, was the centre of the sacred universe.[32] The farther removed was any space from the temple the less sacred it was. Society, too, was structured after the pattern of a descending gradation of purity. Priests formed the apex, set apart as they were to mediate life divine and to deal with sacred things like the altar, sacrifice, and worship. Lower came the laity, who, in turn, were classified in terms of descending degrees of purity concerning the origin, profession, food habits, and the like. This suited admirably the interests of the priestly class who, with their knowledge of the pure and the impure and with their control over the means of cultic purification, could henceforth exercise domination over the entire population. As far as the Hebrews were concerned, though the notion of pollution originated in very ancient days, it was the priestly class that elaborated it into a system.[33] At the time of Jesus, the Pharisees and the Scribes were equally zealous in the observance of the laws of purity, while the mass of people cared little about it.

Before I pass on to Jesus' stand in this regard, let me make a few critical observations on the notion of ritual purity in general. The notion represents primitive man's answer to the problem of how to defend himself from the mysterious forces of death which he could neither understand nor bring under control. The answer was sought in magic and myth whereas today we would rely on observation, science, and technology. The notion is essentially *a-moral*, in so far as purity or impurity is conceived as an objective quality inhering in things, actions, and situations, irrespective of the free decision of individuals. It becomes also immoral when human beings, too, are classified as pure and impure. For it leads to the fragmentation of the community and to the domination of some by others. Neither has the notion of purity anything to do with religion, understood as man's relationship to the transcendent ground and goal of all being. The identification of the forces of life with God is magical. It is one thing to say that God is the transcendent ground of the cosmic process; quite another, to identify Him with the latter. Besides, a God whom humans could control through the knowledge of the pure and the impure can only be a projection of their own mind.

Cult probably originated in an attempt to re-enact the primordial cosmic origins, when chaos gave birth to cosmos, the formless to form, death to life. Whenever the community felt threatened by the forces of death, it chose one among them to die for all, so that from his death would burst forth new life in terms of health, prosperity, children, cattle, and vegetation.[34] Later, a product of labour was substituted for man. In this sense, all sacrifice may be said to have arisen from human sacrifice and has to do with cosmic purification and renewal. Hence all religions, dominated by the notion of purity and rites of purification, are not only *a-moral* but also *a-religious*. Admittedly, what I have just described is the system of purity as an ideal-type. In all historical religions, however, the a-moral system of ritual purity coexists or combines with the ethical system of justice and love. This is true also of the Old Testament, where the former is embodied in the priestly tradition of the Leviticus and the latter in the Elohist-Deuteronomic tradition, each, however, with elements assimilated from the other.[35]

Jesus' attitude to the laws of pollution is best illustrated by his controversies with the Scribes and the Pharisees regarding the washing of hands before meals.[36] He defended his disciples when they ate with hands unwashed. Quoting Isaiah, he reminded his opponents, "This people honours me with their lips, but their heart is far from me." No amount of ritual washing can help man bridge the distance between him and God. The rules of purity touch only the periphery of human existence since it is a moment in the cosmic process of life and death, birth, and dissolution. To effect a rupture in the cosmic membrane and achieve a breakthrough into the true realm of freedom, one has to shift one's attention from the periphery to the centre. And that centre is the heart, the deepest core of each person where loving, knowing, willing, and feeling have their common root. The heart is the seat of love and the knowledge born of love. It is that point of irradiation from which humans reach out to communion with God and humankind. It is through the heart that they hear every word God utters. Hence the accusation, "You leave the commandment of God, and hold fast the tradition of men". The God of Jesus is the God of the prophets, who can be encountered only in his commands. And all his commands boil down to the single one of loving one's neighbour.[37]

Contrasted with the command to seek justice and love, the laws of purity are merely traditions of men, which may or may not be observed depending on whether they contribute or not to human well-being.[38] Here too the radicalism of Jesus does not consist in declaring the pure impure and the impure pure according to the prevalent criterion of evaluation but in introducing an entirely new criterion, that of love:

> "There is nothing outside a man which by going into him can defile him,
> but the things which come out of a man are what defile him."[39]

In other words, the sole source of defilement is unlove and injustice.[40]

This brief survey is enough to show that Jesus' teaching and practice were subversive of the value system of his day and that what he initiated was nothing less than a counterculture.

The Birth of a Prophetic Movement

Every counterculture needs a community as its bearer. It was therefore natural for Jesus to have called men and women to be his disciples. These were "to be with him and to be sent out to preach."[41] Being with him meant the disciple was to identify himself with the faith, the hope, the commitment, and the destiny of his Master. It also involved severing all links with the dominant culture. The Gospels tell us that the disciples gave up their means of production,[42] broke all ties with their families,[43] refused to conform to the rules of ritual washing,[44] violated the laws of the Sabbath,[45] and flouted the prevailing taboos governing the relationship between the sexes.[46] No less marked was the countercultural character of the post-Easter community.[47] According to the Acts, the early believers held everything in common, to be distributed to each according to his need.[48] Among them, there were no distinctions based on office or status. Paul's letters were addressed to the community as a whole, whom he called brothers. This shows there was not yet any hierarchical gradation.[49] Until the end of the first century, the community of disciples defined itself in opposition to the world around.[50] This is reflected in the Gospel narratives on the controversies between Jesus and his religious adversaries as well as in the conflict between the Hellenists and the Judaizers.[51]

The counterculture represented by the early believers was essentially prophetic, centred as it was upon the reign of God to come. Being with Jesus was geared to being for the new humanity. The community lived from the future. It did not feel called to settle down around Jesus and find fulfillment in worshipping him. Its destiny was to march forward to the unknown Beyond, with Jesus at their head. Hence it would be more appropriate to call what Jesus inaugurated a movement rather than a community. As has recently been pointed out by an anthropologist, the early Christian communities bear many features that are specific to millenarian movements, such as homogeneity, equality, anonymity, and absence of property.[52]

This does not, however, mean that the early believers maintained in every respect the prophetic-subversive thrust of Jesus or remained true to every detail of his teaching. Forces in the opposite direction began to crop up soon after the Easter event. Nevertheless, it is beyond doubt that the broad features of a prophetic movement could be observed in the Christianity of the first century. But by the end of the third century, Christian communities had come to terms with the world and all but lost their countercultural character.[53] In the section to follow I shall dwell more at length on the developments that led to it as they will throw light on the nature of the Christian churches and on the contemporary role of Jesus' disciples.

3

The Decline of Prophecy

The decline of Christianity as a prophetic movement can be understood only within the framework of the dialectic of consciousness and being. At the level of consciousness, the most decisive factor was the non-fulfillment of the hope in the imminent coming of the Kingdom. The social order was not overthrown and the disprivileged continued their existence much the same way as before. This created among believers a crisis of consciousness, which some have called cognitive dissonance, meaning a "condition of distress and doubt stemming from the disconfirmation of an important belief."[1] That the non-realization of the Kingdom called in question the very reason for the existence of the community may be gauged from the second letter of Peter:

> "First of all, you must understand this, that scoffers will come in the last days with scoffing, following their own passions, and saying, 'Where is the promise of his coming?' For ever since the fathers fell asleep, all things have continued as they were from the beginning of creation."[2]

Under such conditions, the community was impelled to reinterpret its faith to bridge the gap between expectation and fulfillment. One form the new interpretation took was to understand imminence in terms of divine time as distinct from human time. Thus Peter consoles himself and his readers with the words,

> "But do not ignore this one fact, beloved, that with the Lord one day is as a thousand years, and a thousand years as one day"[3]

The more dominant form of reinterpretation consisted in viewing the reign of God as already come in the event of the resurrection of Jesus. The attempt at rationalization eventually led to the identification of Jesus with God himself, though the earliest *kerygma* did not go beyond affirming that "God was with him."[4] Of course, the community still entertained the hope that the Christ would come again to reconcile the world to God. But even that hope receded into the background and the focus of faith shifted to God already come in Jesus. From then onwards, the centre of the community was no more the God ahead but the God within the Church.

From here it was but one step to identifying the Church with the reign of God;[5] understandably so, since salvation was available to human beings *here* and *now* through faith in the risen Lord present within the Church. This had serious consequences for the self-understanding of the community. If the Church is the sphere in which alone salvation is available, people can be saved only if they are converted and join its fold. Thus began the mission in the traditional sense aimed at expanding the boundaries of the Church or transplanting it in other countries. Mission, therefore, is the direct consequence of the decline of prophecy, of the loss of that hope in which Jesus lived and for which he died. No wonder, the withering away of prophecy and the emergence of mission saw the eclipse of the historical Jesus.

The alienation of prophetic into institutional consciousness was hastened by the Church's attempt to adapt itself to the cultural milieu first of Judaism, then of the Greco-Roman world. Christianity took over from Judaism its synagogue structure, its external patterns of worship, its apocryphal, and other writings.

> "Diaspora Judaism provided the blueprint for the adaptation of Christianity to the Greco-Roman world."[6]

Further, as a result of the eclipse of the historical Jesus and the impact of the mystery cults, the table-fellowship of Jesus, which was originally an attempt to translate eschatological hope into historical praxis, was transformed into a cult. Nor was the person of Jesus left untouched.

Made to pass through the Greco-Roman mould of thinking, he was reduced to a set of dry, metaphysical essences. Looked at from this angle, what is usually acclaimed as the conquest of paganism by Christianity is the capitulation of prophecy before the wisdom of the philosophers.

These changes at the level of consciousness must be seen as conditioning and conditioned by the profound transformation that took place in the social base of Christianity. The social constituency of Jesus was the disprivileged classes in Palestine. He addressed himself primarily to the poor, to those who labour and are burdened, to the powerless, to the uneducated, to 'sinners', in short, to the common people despised by the 'respectable' classes. It is from among them that he chose his followers. The situation continued much the same during the first two centuries. Here Engel's evaluation is substantially correct:

> "The history of early Christianity has notable points in common with the modern working-class movement. Like the latter, Christianity was originally a movement of the oppressed people: it first appeared as the religion of slaves and freed men, of poor people deprived of all rights, of peoples subjugated or dispersed by Rome."[7]

The factors which made the new faith attractive to the poorer classes were (a) its religious exclusivism that provided a clear choice in an age of anxiety, (b) its universalism, and (c) its active philanthropy.[8]

But a counter-trend set in from the third century onwards. The loss of eschatological consciousness and the policy of accommodation to classical culture made Christianity acceptable to the upper classes in Roman society. On the other hand, the same classes had become more open to non-Roman cults because of the induction into their ranks of people from the provinces, who brought along with them their own religious beliefs and practices.[9] The result was an influx of intellectuals and rich people into the Church, who eventually came to control her destiny. This, in turn, prompted an attempt to reinterpret the radical social message of Jesus to suit the interests of the well-to-do among the believers. Wealth came to be looked upon as a means to the Church's ministries. Clement of Alexandria, for instance, propounded the view that not money but its misuse stood in the way of salvation.[10] The concept of the Kingdom was spiritualized so that there was no difficulty in conceiving it as coexisting with misery, unlove, and exploitation in the real world. Jesus' radical critique of political power was toned down to make Christianity subserve and legitimize Roman power.[11] The beginning of this trend may be seen in Romans 13, where Paul exhorts everyone to submit to the supreme authorities since all "existing authorities are instituted by him." Such an interpretation was made easier by the objective situation of the Hellenistic Christian communities which, on the whole, lived in harmony with imperial power.[12]

The lesson for us is clear: No project of hope can survive if it is not translated into historical praxis. And it cannot be so translated unless it takes hold of the oppressed classes. Even that is not enough. The oppressed must be in a position to forge their project of hope into a theoretical weapon for political action. Where the conditions for such action are not realized, the resulting political impotence will find an outlet in a religiosity of escape. Faced with the impossible task of changing the conditions of exploitation and domination, the oppressed classes will transfer the same task on to the sole initiative of God. I suggest that this accounts for the strong emphasis on the gift character of the Kingdom and for the spirituality of resignation which was very pronounced in the early Church and continues to hold sway in contemporary Christianity. This whole development is aptly summed up by Engels in his reply to the query, Why socialism did not emerge on the fall of the Roman Empire?:

> "Socialism did in fact, as far as it was possible at the time, exist and even became dominant in Christianity. Only this Christianity, as was bound to be the case in the historic conditions, did not want to accomplish the social transformation in this world, but beyond it, in heaven, in eternal life after death, in the impending *millennium.*"[13]

I would not be doing full justice to historical facts, were I not to mention that at no time in the history of Christianity was prophecy completely dead. In this context, of particular significance are the so-called heresies. They are not to be seen as mere deviations from the right doctrine, but were rather attempts - however, distorted and misguided they might have been - to return to the prophetic radicalism of the message of Jesus.[14] In the latter half of the second century, the Montanists sought to defend charismatic authority against institutional authority. While the official Church relegated women to an inferior position, both Montanus and Marcion tried to assert their equality with men. Subsequently, such charismatic and prophetic tendencies as could not survive in mainstream Christianity found a home in monasticism. The social message and the eschatological hope of Jesus were kept alive on the periphery of the official Church by the dissenting movements of the Middle Ages, represented by the Waldenses, the Albigenses, Thomas Muenzer and Weitling. Unfortunately, for reasons which we cannot go into here, none of these movements developed into a world-historical force.

4

Countercultural Movements in India

The dialectic of culture and prophecy, which formed the historical context and shaped the very texture of Jesus' life, has its parallel in Indian history. But the class character of Indian culture and the contradictions inherent in it have been ignored by most scholars. They tend to view Indian culture as something homogeneous and valid for all castes and classes. Thereby they distort reality. The supposed neutrality and universality of our cultural heritage is a myth created and kept alive by people who want by all means to perpetuate their cultural hegemony. Historically, there always was a tension between the culture of the oppressors and the culture of the oppressed, a tension that developed into a crisis of civilization more than once in the past. The first such crisis saw the emergence of Buddhism around the sixth century B.C. and the second gave rise to the medieval Bhakti movement. In what follows I shall try to provide a rapid overview of the fundamental contradictions that determined our cultural history and of the various attempts to create a counterculture.[1]

Let me begin with the development of Vedic religion which provoked the first crisis of culture. By Vedic religion I mean that stage of religious consciousness represented by the Samhitas, the Brahmanas, and the Upanishads, spanning over 1500 years ending with the rise of Buddhism.

The Vedas are the product of the Aryans who conquered India from the west, destroying in the process the more developed urban civilization of the original inhabitants. Among the gods whom the former worshiped were *Agni* (the fire-goddess), Indra (the warrior-god, also known as the thunder-god), and Varuna (the god of righteousness "who is the third whenever two plot in secret"). Indra is invoked as the "protector of the Aryan colour" and the "destroyer of the dark skin". The reference here, obviously, is to the conquest of the original inhabitants of dark complexion.[2]

This shows that already in very ancient times, the deity functioned as the guardian of the superior race and the legitimizer of violence against the weaker ones. The complicity of the gods in human aggression is also referred to in later scriptures. In the *Bhagavad-gita*, for instance, Krishna, the incarnation of the supreme God, would try to persuade the doubting Arjuna to embark on the extermination of his kinsmen and preceptors on the ground that his duty as a *Kshatriya* required him to do so.[3]

The gods were made to sanction not only war but also oppressive social institutions. According to the *Rig-veda,* the four *varnas* (castes) arose out of the sacrificial dismemberment of the Primal Person (*Purusha*):

> "His mouth became the Brahmana; his two arms were made into the *Kshatriya*; his two thighs the *Vaisyas;* from his two feet the *sudra* was born."[4]

The same idea re-echoes in the *Gita* where Krishna claims to have created the four-caste system.[5] From the earliest times, the dominant religion denied the lower castes even the right to live. In the *Yajur-Veda* collection of rituals, we read,

> "Like the Vaisya… tributary to another, to be eaten up by another, to be oppressed at will …Like a *Sudra* …the servant of another, to be slain at will."[6]

Another trait of Vedic religion was sacrificial ritualism. Its significance must be understood in the light of my earlier reflections on ritual purity and cult. From the beginning, the Divine was identified with the cosmic order (*Rita*), conceived as the cyclic process of life and death. Vedic ritualism arose out of the fusion of this belief with the notion that one could influence the macrocosmic cycle of life and death by reenacting it at the microcosmic level through verbal and actional symbols.

Since the gods were looked upon either as the ground or as the guardian of the macrocosm, sacrificial rituals came to be invested with the power to compel them to do what the sacrificer wanted.[7] At the same time, there emerged a priestly class who claimed a monopoly of the magico-religious technology. They held the key to the mystery of the universe. On their services depended the availability of food, the growth of cattle wealth, and the health and prosperity of all. Even kings had to seek their help as the performance of sacrifices was indispensable for victory in war.[8] Thus the ritual power of the priests was compounded with political power. Priests stood to gain economically as well, entitled as they were to a share in sacrificial offerings.[9] Religion thus became an instrument of domination and exploitation. In ritual processions, the lower castes were made to march sandwiched between the Brahmanas and the ruler, a practice apparently intended to train them in obedience and submissiveness.[10]

Another trend came to the fore in the later Vedic period, this time towards monism and gnosis. In a sense, the development is inherent in magic. I have already referred to the magical identity between the microcosm and the macrocosm. Further reflection led the early seers to the realization that the identity lies on a deeper level: between the ultimate ground of the empirical ego (*Atman*) and the ultimate ground of the macrocosm (*Brahman*). Consequently, the goal of the religious quest was seen to consist of knowing the identity of the *Atman* and the *Brahman*. The absolute as *Atman-Brahman* is at once being (*sat*), knowledge (*chit*), and bliss (*ananda*). For the seeker, bliss springs from the knowledge of the unity of all, and fear from the illusion of diversity. "Fear arises from the other", says one Upanishad.[11] What then is the ontological status of the world? There are two views on the matter in the Upanishads: According to one, the world is but an illusion and has no ultimate reality; according to the other, the world is real but its reality is not something apart from *Brahman*.[12]

In either interpretation, the source of all human alienation is ignorance (*avidya*). It is ignorance that makes us attribute reality to the everyday experience of multiplicity, and liberation consists of ridding ourselves of ignorance and attaining enlightenment (*jnana*). The class implications of this doctrine are obvious. It points to the birth of an intellectual elite living on the margin of society, far removed from the real sufferings of the people - poverty, exploitation, and oppression. Equipped to pursue the higher way of knowledge, they could claim superiority over the rest of society. Down to our day, the doctrine has proved useful to the ruling classes. For, what is wrong with rape, murder, exploitation, and oppression if the rapist and the raped, the murderer and the murdered, the exploiter and the exploited, the oppressor and the oppressed, are all, in the end, *Atman-Brahman*? To the one who knows, all such inhuman practices are but the play (*lila*) of *Brahman* or a manifestation of its illusion-producing power (*maya*).

The Dissent of the Buddha

Both ritualism and gnosis were bound to be called in question by the common people. The conditions favourable for it arose in the sixth century B. C. with the emergence of new classes on the social horizon: free peasants, farmers, traders, and patriarchal householders.[13] These found the endless sacrifices involving the indiscriminate killing of cattle a heavy burden as well as a drain on the economy. Under the circumstances, popular discontent found expression in dissident sects like Jainism and Buddhism. Of the new teachers, who appeared on the scene, the Buddha was the one whose teachings have had by far the most profound impact on the history of Asia. As recorded in the Buddhist canonical writings, the questions he was called upon to answer were:

> "What covers this world, what keeps it from the light? What can take a man out of the crosscurrents of life? Who is the fully contented man in the world? What constrains sages, kshatriyas, Brahmanas and other people to offer sacrifices to the gods? What is the source of the many sorrows of

the world? Is the real sage he who has philosophic knowledge, or is the master of ritual? What is the nature of that salvation which is gained by whoever frees himself from desires and doubt?"[14]

What was the Buddha's answer? He brushed aside all metaphysical questions as irrelevant. His concern was with the alienated existence of human beings. He saw the sum of human alienation in sorrow (*dukha*), which has its source in craving - the craving for pleasure, for life, for power. Only the elimination of all craving can ensure complete emancipation.[15] The stress is on removing the roots of what we would call today existential alienation. On this point, the new teaching did not represent any departure from current thinking. However, the Buddha's diagnosis of the human predicament implied a different view of the availability of the means of salvation. The road to the elimination of craving was open to all, whereas freedom from ignorance was beyond the reach of the *Sudras* as they were forbidden to read the Vedas, the source of all saving knowledge. The Buddha made it clear that his teaching was meant not for the initiated few but for all:

> "I have taught the truth without making any distinction between exoteric and esoteric doctrines; for... with the *Tathagata* there is no such thing as the closed fist of the teacher who keeps some things back."[16]

The rudiments of a universal humanism may be discerned in the Buddha's understanding of final emancipation. Wary of defining the undefinable, he would describe it in negative rather than positive terms. The ultimate goal (*arahatta*) consists in the absence of acquisitiveness (*alobha*), absence of oppressiveness and hatred (*adosha*), and freedom from illusory knowledge (*amoha*).[17] The inclusion of the first two elements among the characteristics of *nirvana* implies that the goal is a community of men and women bound together by mutual friendliness and love. This, indeed, is a far cry from the fear of the 'other' that haunted Upanishadic seers.

For the Buddha, however, employing the right means was more important than conceptualizing the end of all human striving. And the right means are summed up in the famous eightfold path consisting of right vision, right aims (not seeking wealth or power at the expense of others, not indulging senses, loving others and promoting their happiness), right speech (truthful and friendly), right action (eschewing theft, killing, and adultery), right livelihood (by honest methods, not by selling liquor or dealing in animals for ritual slaughter), right effort, right mindfulness, and right meditation. Significantly, no mention is made of rituals, sacrifices, priests, or gods as helps to liberation. Man is thrown back on his own resources. One of the last instructions of the Buddha to his favourite disciple runs,

> "So, Ananda, you must be your own lamps, your own refuges. Take refuge
> in nothing outside yourselves."[18]

No less striking is the central place given to ethics in the pursuit of *nirvana*. And the morality he inculcated was not one of exclusion founded on family, clan or caste but one of inclusion centred upon all-encompassing love and compassion.

Gautama affirmed the centrality of friendliness (*maitri*) and compassion (*karuna*), which, along with joy and equanimity, go to form the four cardinal virtues of his religion. For him, the eternal law was not the cosmic order (*rita*) but the law of love:

> "Never in this world is hate appeased by hatred; it is only appeased by
> love - this is an eternal law (*sanatana-damma*)."[19]

He extended the horizon of love to cosmic proportions to include all living creatures as may be seen from the following poem on friendliness:

> "May all be happy and safe,
> May all beings gain inner joy.
> All living beings whatever
> Without exception, weak or strong,
> Whether long or high,
> Middling or small, subtle or gross,
> Seen or unseen,
> Dwelling afar or near,

Born or yet unborn -
May all beings gain inner joy.
May no being deceive another,
Nor in any way scorn another,
Nor, in anger or ill-will,
Desire another's sorrow.
As a mother cares for her son,
Her only son, all her days,
So towards all things living
A man's mind should be all-embracing.
Friendliness for the whole world,
All-embracing, he should raise in his mind,
Above, below, and across,
Unhindered, free from hate and ill-will..."[20]

The universal love Gautama advocated is by no means a mere help to attain *nirvana* but is itself *nirvana*. That is why he could say,

> "By charity, goodness, restraint and self-control man and woman alike store up a well-hidden treasure - a treasure which cannot be given to others and which robbers cannot steal. A wise man should do good - that is the treasure that will not leave him."[21]

The Enlightened One also initiated a radical critique of contemporary religion and society. He rejected sacrificial ritualism and the ritual slaughter of animals. For him, the highest form of sacrifice is following the *eight-fold path*.[22] He sought to replace the "worship of the six quarters" with the performance of one's social duties. One worshipped the East by fulfilling one's duties to parents; the South by fulfilling one's duties to teachers; the West by fulfilling one's duties to wife and children; the North by fulfilling one's duties to friends and companions; the Depths by fulfilling one's duties to servants and workers; and the Heights by fulfilling one's duties to religious teachers.[23] The Buddha thus shifted the axis of religiosity from man-nature relationship to interhuman relations. He also instructed the *Bhikkus* to refrain from all magical practices and from votive offerings to gods and goddesses.[24]

He was equally forthright in repudiating the caste system and the notion of ritual purity associated with it. Thus runs a famous saying of his:

"No Brahmana is such by birth,

No outcaste is such by birth.

An outcaste is such by his deeds,

A Brahmana is such by his deeds."[25]

To one Assalayana, an emissary sent by the Brahmanas to refute his teaching on the equality of all castes, the Buddha is supposed to have said,

"Do the Brahmanas really maintain this (their caste superiority), Assalayana, when they are born of women just like anyone else, of Brahmana women who have their periods and conceive, give birth and nurse their children, just like any other women?"[26]

He flouted all canons of ritual purity to the extent of choosing disciples even from the lowest castes and the outcastes. His disciples included a scavenger, a dog-eater, and a lowly barber.[27] What is more, to the dismay of his Brahmana critics, he ate from the hands of the outcastes.[28]

Though the Buddha shared the current belief in the law of *karma* and *samsara*, and laid undue stress on renunciation, his teachings represent a definitive breakthrough in the direction of a humane religiosity. The message of universal love he proclaimed makes him the greatest point of the incandescence of the human spirit in Asia. No wonder, he won a wide following, and his influence spread as far as Japan and China in the east, and Afghanistan and Palestine in the West. Unfortunately, Buddhism all but disappeared from the Indian scene, due, among other things, to the virulent opposition it provoked on the part of Brahmanism, the erosion of its social base through the decline of agriculture and trade in the post-Mauryan period, and the failure of its adherents to live up to the teachings of their master. Still, it has left an indelible mark on the Indian mind. Much of what is humane and tender in the Indian ethos is to be traced back to the influence of Buddhism.

From out of the struggle between Vedic religion and heterodox movements like Jainism and Buddhism was born what is today called Hinduism which reached its golden age in the Gupta period (300-700 A.D.). Many factors contributed to the new development. To begin with, Brahmanism succeeded in integrating within itself popular religions. Popular deities were absorbed into the Vedic pantheon through a process of identification or subordination. Krishna became an incarnation of Vishnu, and Siva was identified with Rudra of the *Rig-veda*. Even the Buddha was given the status of a vishnuite incarnation. Hanuman, the monkey-god, whose cult flourished among the peasants was made a servant of Rama, himself an incarnation of Vishnu. The cobra, once worshipped in his own right, became a bed for Vishnu to sleep on. Yet another deity, *Nandi* (the bull) whose worship goes back to Neolithic times, was demoted to the position of a beast of transportation for Siva. The policy of subjugation through co-option was also extended to the mother goddesses originating in the pre-Aryan matriarchal society. They were made consorts of one or other of the principal gods. Thus Parvati became wife to Siva and Lakshmi to Vishnu.[29] The subordination of popular deities to the Vedic gods no doubt reflected the social dominance of the higher castes. The epics and the Puranas provided ideological underpinning to the cultural annexation of popular religion. This whole process initially met with resistance on the part of the masses, who, with no political backing, had in the end to submit.[30]

The most powerful weapon the priestly class fashioned for the enslavement of the low castes and the outcastes was the sacred law codified by Manu, which shapes the conduct of Hindus even today.[31] According to it, the Brahmana is the very incarnation of the law. He is the lord of all creation; others live from his benevolence. He is not to do any physical work. The king is exhorted to make him gifts of land and money. The Brahmana may appropriate other people's property for sacrificial purposes, but none may take anything that belongs to him. If he kills a Sudra it is but a minor offense, whereas for the latter to kill a member of the priestly class is a capital crime. The Brahmana must avoid all contact with people engaged in professions held impure.

As for the Sudra, he "was created by the self-existent to be a slave of a Brahmana."[32] He may not acquire property, nor study the scriptures. Still lower than the Sudras come the outcastes, "those tribes in the world which are excluded from those born from the mouth, the arms, the thighs, and the feet of *Brahman*."[33] What is worse, the king is enjoined to enforce this system of institutionalized sadism.

Bhakti as Counterculture

The organized cultural aggression perpetrated by the higher castes provoked another movement of dissent in the middle Ages, resembling the earlier one spearheaded by the Buddha. Historical conditions favoured a new offensive from the oppressed. With the recurrence of foreign invasions, centralized state power had weakened, and a looser, feudalistic form of political organization had come into being. On the economic level, taxation weighed heavily on the peasants, whose surplus was expropriated for the construction and upkeep of temples and palaces.[34]

The revolt of the masses found socio-religious expression in the *Bhakti* movement, which originated in Tamil Nadu but soon spread to Karnataka and Maharashtra, and eventually swept through the whole of north India. Like Buddhism, it repudiated Vedic sacrifices and the practice of ritual purity.[35] It was critical of the worship of images as may be seen from the following passage in the *Bhagavata Purana*:

> "I am always present in all beings as their soul and yet, ignoring Me, mortal man conducts the mockery of image-worship."[36]

The *Bhaktas* saw no meaning in devotion to the Lord divorced from neighbourly love and the practice of justice. As Bhasava of the 12th century wrote,

> "Good behaviour is what pleases God...Kindness is the root of all righteousness."[37]

Thus also Kabir (1440-1518):

> "The man who is kind and who practices righteousness, who remains passive amidst the affairs of the world, who considers all creatures on

earth as his own self, he attains the immortal Being, the true God is ever with him."[38]

Not all the leaders of the movement, however, were equally radical in their criticism of traditional religion. Nor could they withstand the Brahmana strategy of subjugation through co-option.

It is undeniable that the *Bhaktas* represented the aspirations of the downtrodden masses as against the interests of the twice-born. As though echoing the Hebrew prophets, the *Bhagavata Purana*, the main scriptural authority of the movement, comes out with the startling idea of a God who is partial to the poor:

> "Hari, fond of those persons destitute of wealth and whose sole wealth is himself, and knowing their affection, does not accept the worship of evil-minded persons who by their conceit about their Vedic learning, wealth, family, and deeds bestow harm on good people who are poor."[39]

Similarly, Krishna tells his wife,

> "We are poor and are always the favourites of poor persons; therefore, rich people generally do not resort to me."[40]

The devotee is reminded that "the pleasing of Vishnu is when all the distressed, the blind, and the pitiable have eaten."[41] Though not forthright in its rejection of caste, the same *Purana* ridicules all claim to superiority based on birth and allows persons even of the lowest castes to resort in times of distress to occupations of the higher castes. As has been pointed out by a recent scholar,

> "Praise of poverty and compassion for the distressed characterize the social teachings of the *Bhagavata*. From these emphases, as from the evidence of conflict, with the wealthy and secure, we can assume that the devotees, in general, were poor. The extension of salvation, through devotion to Sudras and even to the lower unclean castes, indicates a definite attempt to bring members of these groups into *Bhakti* movement, and one would suspect that they made up a large part of its mass support."[42]

The same conclusion may be drawn from the history of the movement in Maharashtra.[43] There the *Manbhav* sect, founded by *Cakradhara* in the 12th century, sought to realize the ideals of tribal egalitarianism.

It denounced the system of caste and practiced communal sharing of wealth. *Jnaneswar*, another important leader of the movement in Maharashtra, had to live under the Brahmana interdict. He was led to commit ritual suicide, while his parents drowned themselves in the Ganges. The Maratha saints who followed him came from all castes. *Namdev* was a tailor; *Gora*, a potter; and *Cokha Mela* an untouchable. *Tukaram*, the greatest of Maratha saints, was a peasant. Famished by hunger and persecuted by the Brahmanas, he finally drowned himself in a river. Of these dissenting saints, the eminent historian Kosambi wrote:

> "These men represent a general movement by no means confined to their province and language. The generally painful tenor of their lives shows that they were in the opposition, and did not care to exercise the meretricious art of pleasing those in power — quite unlike the Brahmanas, who did not scorn to develop the cult of these saints whenever it paid, but always pandered to the rich."[44]

Unfortunately, the *Bhakti* movement could not maintain its initial thrust and was domesticated by Hindu orthodoxy. But the will to resist could not be smothered once and for all.

There was a fresh upsurge of collective dissent during the colonial rule. The factors involved were both economic and cultural. The new rulers changed the traditional pattern of land-ownership by conferring on the landlords absolute right to property. The latter were even allowed to raise their own police force to keep the labouring classes under control. With the spread of the capitalist mode of production, the situation of the poor deteriorated. Indigenous crafts declined and craftsmen were thrown out of their jobs. To make matters worse, caste Hindus set about Hinduizing outcastes and tribals. To meet this challenge, there arose from the beginning of the 18th century several prophetic movements among the marginated sections of the population.[45] In the aim, they were both religious and political. On the religious-cultural plane, their stand was often ambivalent. On the one hand, they wanted to return to the purity of their original tribal beliefs; on the other, they were willing to assimilate aspects of Hinduism. Some of them had come under the influence of Islam or Christianity. Almost all believed in the return of the golden age that would restore the primal condition of happiness. They were led by charismatic leaders whose claim to special illumination was not always genuine. In some cases, they were able to raise their own militia to fight the landlords and the British. But they were no match for the superior military power of the British and were ruthlessly crushed. In any case, these prophetic movements were doomed to fail. They had too many internal weaknesses: inadequate understanding of society, the beclouding of reason by millenarian enthusiasm, reliance on magical-supernatural powers, and the inability to initiate enlightened social praxis. What is significant for us today is the mere fact that such forms of collective protest emerged at all. That they did belies the prevalent notion regarding the passivity of the Indian masses. They also prove that revolutionary movements can draw inspiration from the folk tradition of myths and symbols.

Counterculture Today

The cultural situation today defies all attempts at a clear definition. It is characterized by the interplay of diverse and conflicting factors: the superimposition of bourgeois culture over the traditional, the uneven development of capitalism and of the culture germane to it, the overlapping of caste and class, the rise of ritually inferior castes to economic and political dominance, the ambivalence of socialist ideologies. Beneath this complexity, however, one can discern some major contradictions worth noting.

There is, first, the contradiction between traditional and bourgeois culture. Traditional culture is centred upon the notion of ritual purity, hierarchical organization of society, the importance of kinship relations, the prevalence of group loyalty, respect for authority, and the magico-religious view of the world. In contrast, bourgeois culture stresses rationality, private interest, individualism, competition, consumerism, monetization of human relations, the rule of quantity over quality, and the cult of efficiency. That there is a conflict between the two cultures will be readily granted by all. The crucial question is whether the conflict has reached a point of crisis or is likely to generate one. The answer seems to be in the negative.

True, there is a steady erosion of feudal values. The status of a person today is determined less by birth than by money or power. Loyalty to family and caste is slowly being replaced by loyalty to one's class, at least among the organized working class. The laws of ritual purity are no longer strictly observed. Blind acceptance of authority, whether of parents or religious teachers, is fast giving way to the rational investigation; similarly, the magico-religious interpretation of the world is being eroded by the scientific attitude.

It would, however, be wrong to conclude that traditional values are dying out. Rather, they are being integrated within bourgeois institutions. The masses, attuned to the collectivism of the joint-family and caste, have little difficulty in adapting themselves to the collectivism of capitalist production. They have been conditioned by the hierarchy of caste to accept as natural the hierarchy of status and functions proper to bourgeois society. The personal and group loyalty which the poorer classes formerly showed to feudal landlords is now transferred to capitalists, politicians, and government officials. The psycho-structure created by the caste division of labour harmonizes with the capitalist division of labour, social as well as technical. Traditional ideas and values are thus both negated and preserved. They are transferred to new objects and invested with new meanings. Hence there is no absolute antagonism between the two cultures; in any case, not at the present stage of capitalist development. Another factor that would prevent the development of a crisis is the capacity of the Indian to live in two worlds, in the world of magic and science, of myth and reality, of spiritual quest and social unconcern, of tradition and bourgeois modernity.[46]

The second contradiction is internal to capitalist culture and in its actual working out assumes the form of a widening gulf between expectation and fulfillment. Capitalism is driven by its own inner logic to disseminate its values far and wide to reach every section of the population and permeate every social institution. But the universality of its values is contradicted by the limited possibilities it offers to people of realizing them. Capitalism proclaims the primacy of private interest; but most people have no private interest to promote, deprived as they are of even the minimum means of subsistence. Again, all are taught the value of competition but only a minority have the means, whether raw materials or instruments of production, to compete with. Not even labour is competitive as it is available in plenty, while employment is limited. In consequence, millions in our country are marginated from the game of competition, being either unemployed or underemployed. In like manner, capitalism creates ever new and varied needs in people but it can satisfy the needs only of a minority. The vast majority sink into frustration, resentment, and bitterness, all instinct with violence.

Here lie the roots of the prevailing social unrest. Take, for instance, the proliferation of strikes among industrial workers. What inspires strikes is not so much the longing for a classless society as private, individual, and group interests. Even labour unions are competing with one another, often to the detriment of unorganized workers and the unemployed. Unionism has created a labour aristocracy which has a vested interest in preventing any improvement in the condition of the unorganized poor.

The same culture of private interest also underpins the unrest among students. What they want is not the elimination of exploitation but employment in firms and government offices. No different are the values determining the conduct of politicians and bureaucrats. What we are witnessing today is the working out of private interest in the sphere of public interest. For the average politician or government official, institutions meant for the common good - party, legislature, judiciary, administration - are nothing but so many means towards furthering his own interest in terms of money, power, or both. This being so, the social unrest and political confusion rampant in contemporary India can in no way be taken for symptoms of a socialist upsurge. They are but manifestations of the revolt of the masses against such conditions as deny them a share in the fruits of developing capitalism.

There is yet another contradiction, this time within traditional culture itself. It manifests itself, above all, in the form of a growing conflict between caste Hindus and the outcastes. Though in part generated by capitalism, the conflict has basically to do with the caste system, the cornerstone of traditional culture. It points to the attempts of the Hindu orthodoxy to maintain at any cost their traditional position of caste dominance.

The caste system helped a minority in Indian society to keep a large slave class of *Sudras* and outcastes. Over time, the *Sudras* were able, to a degree, to raise their economic and social position. But in many parts of rural India, the outcastes still form the main source of surplus labour for caste Hindus. However, education, elections based on universal suffrage, and the politicization carried on by leftist parties and activist groups have created a general social awakening among them. They are no longer prepared to submit to the social degradation to which they have been condemned. But, on the other side, the constraints of capital accumulation are forcing the rural bourgeoisie to resort to super-exploitation either using bonded labour or by lowering wages below the value of labour power. It is in the interests of the rural elite to perpetuate, if not reinforce traditional forms of group dependence and maintain the social backwardness of the rural poor. These must be denied their traditional rights without in any way being released from their traditional duties. Thus exploitation is compounded with heightened social oppression. This explains the revolt of the outcastes and the atrocities against them perpetrated by the dominant castes.

The upsurge of the rural poor, however, does not point to a total rejection of caste. Their resistance is directed against the exploitation and discrimination practiced by the higher castes. This is clear from the fact that both the lower castes and the Harijans are still bent on perpetuating casteist distinctions among themselves. The struggles going on in rural India do not derive from a radical critique of caste; nor are they inspired by a socialist alternative.

I do not mean there is no potential for a radical cultural revolution in India. The longing for a free and egalitarian society, which more than once in the past generated movements of protest, has not been smothered once and for all. It has only been driven back into the collective subconscious. Driven back by twofold censorship: by the external censorship of the family, the school, the media, the temple, the bureaucracy, and the police and by the internal censorship exercised by the masses themselves who have long since made their own the taboos and injunctions imposed by the ruling classes. The day the twofold censorship is relaxed in the wake of either an economic crisis or political chaos, the subterranean forces locked up in the collective subconscious are likely to burst all bounds, shaking the very foundations of the existing system. But, for that to happen there is a need for a concerted historical initiative on the part of the intelligentsia and the masses.

Further, even the prosaic struggles carried on today by tradeunions, landless labourers and the outcastes have a culturally radical dimension. Admittedly, the explicit and conscious aim of such struggles is the satisfaction of immediate material wants or the elimination of caste discrimination. But implicit in them is the desire for deep-going social changes. This is due to two important factors: First, schooling, elections, political propaganda, and the media have instilled in people notions such as socialism, equality, human dignity, democracy, and social justice. Though these terms are today understood in the framework of bourgeois democracy, their full meaning can be realized only in a truly socialist society. Second, the consciousness of at least the organized proletariat is charged with memories of the Russian and the Chinese revolution. This is particularly true of states like Kerala, West Bengal, and Andhra Pradesh which are the strongholds of the Communist movement.

Indian communism has made a significant contribution to radicalizing the consciousness of the poorer classes. The cultural action it initiated helped bring about a mutation in the field of vernacular literature. For the first time in the history of India, the life of the masses became a worthy theme for literary and artistic creation. Plays, novels, short stories and essays began to appear, highlighting the misery of the common people, holding up the vision of a classless society, and calling for the overthrow of the existing social order. The cell studies, libraries and reading rooms sponsored by the Communist Party helped disseminate revolutionary ideas among the youth. But, as time passed, the heralds of revolution retraced their steps, made peace with their 'class enemies', and found each for himself a comfortable niche in the Establishment or tailored their radicalism to suit the requirements of power politics. With that, the Marxian concept of a classless society was reduced to an impotent myth. Nonetheless, that it survives even as a myth is something positive. Though relegated to the periphery of consciousness, it might, given suitable conditions, evoke revolutionary commitment and motivate socialist praxis. Another hopeful sign is the willingness on the part of some sections of the communist movement to radically rethink their theory and practice in the Indian context.

From this brief historical survey certain conclusions may be drawn

1. Far from being a monolithic whole, from the beginning Indian culture has been an uneasy combination of two opposing strands: one, priestly, patriarchal and elitist; the other, popular, matriarchal, virtually egalitarian. The first is ascetical and, concerning one's fellowmen, tends to become sadistic; the second is life-affirming, creative, and self-expanding. The former has served as an ideology legitimizing the institutionalized inequality of caste; the latter has always been a source of destruction and creation. Neither of the two strands has existed in its purity; each contains an admixture of the other. But it is the second that has generated the movements of protest in the past. If these movements proved abortive, it is because they were either neutralized or smothered by the guardians of the priestly-elitist tradition. The lesson for the future is clear: The forces that can re-create Indian society can emerge only from the repressed culture of the lower castes, outcastes, and the tribals.

2. What Hindu orthodoxy did to the dissenting movements from the Buddha onwards, capitalism is doing to all critical forces in Indian society today. These are being co-opted in the service of commodity production and formal bourgeois democracy. Not even Indian communism has been able to withstand capitalism's integrating power.

3. The contemporary situation is characterized, on the one hand, by the objective need for a total - and therefore also cultural - revolution, and, on the other, by the absence of a collective agent capable of bringing it about. Hence the challenge to mobilize the forces for change latent in the consciousness and the subconscious of the masses to create a countercultural movement.

5

Jesus and Transculturation

Our investigations thus far go to show that the counterculture Jesus started has much in common with the protest movements of our own past. It is also clear that his natural allies in contemporary India are those social and political forces that seek to supersede both casteist and capitalist culture. I shall now try to define the contribution his life and message can make to the creation of a new liberating culture. But first, let me briefly state why I speak of Jesus and not of Indian Christianity.

The Christian Ambivalence

Indian Christianity has, by and large, retained its imported character. The Christ of theology and popular devotion still bears the marks of his origin in the West. So too the Church that made him. Her dogmas and forms of worship took shape in the context of the Greco-Roman world. No less foreign is the Canon Law regulating her internal life. The spirituality of resignation and worldly prudence she instills in the faithful derives less from the Gospels than from Neo-Platonism and Stoicism. Still worse, ever new spurious theologies and spiritualities continue to pour in from the West. Small wonder that neither the Christ of the Church nor the Church of Christ has made any profound impact on the Indian people.

Christianity has also erred in the opposite direction. It has, in more than one respect, identified itself with the culture of the ruling classes in

India. The ethos prevailing in its religious institutions is, on the whole, one of blind obedience, personal dependence, patronage, and privileges, while its secular institutions (schools, colleges, hospitals) tend to reflect the values of bourgeois society. Even the caste system has found its way into the ranks of Christians. Politically, Indian Christianity has always sided with whoever happened to be at the helm of affairs. Nor could it have done otherwise. Only by allying itself with the powers that be, could it safeguard its economic interests, especially the free inflow of foreign money. Further, the type of religiosity it represents dovetails, in the main, with that of popular Hinduism. Both religions hold fast the distinction between the pure and the impure, cultic priesthood, the veneration of images, and pietistic devotions. The figure of Christ, who had already taken on features of a Hellenistic God, became further assimilated to the gods of Hinduism. He has lost much of his uniqueness and has, consequently, little new to give to India.

The root of this ambivalence lies in Christianity's failure to radically criticize its own self-understanding as well as its understanding of non-Christian religions. To substantiate my point, let me, though briefly, assess the current Catholic position in this regard.

From the Catholic point of view it is asked, How can the Church use the wealth of Indian culture for the fulfillment of her mission? The answer is given in "Gaudium et Spes" as follows:

> "The Church, living in varied circumstances in the course of centuries, has made use of various cultures to spread and explain Christ's message in her preaching to all nations, to examine and understand it more thoroughly, and to express it more aptly in her liturgical celebrations and in the life of the diverse communities of the faithful."[1]

On the surface, the statement is beyond criticism, but, in reality, it is riddled with ambiguities. First, the focus is not on the Kingdom of God and its justice but on the Church. Non-Christian cultures are seen as but a means to explain her message and express her life. Universal history is thus subordinated to the history of the Church. It is also implied there is a hardcore of liturgy and doctrine that is eternal and immutable, valid for all peoples and ages. There is no recognition of the fact that what is usually taken for the hardcore contains much that is the product of western cultural history.

This whole approach is based on the belief in the lordship of Christ. The "Decree on the Missionary Activity of the Church" says:

> "Thus, in imitation of the plan of the Incarnation, the young Churches, rooted in Christ and built upon the foundation of the Apostles, take to themselves in a wonderful exchange all the riches of the nations which were given to Christ as an inheritance."[2]

Now, the lordship of Christ is not a notion that forms part of the self-awareness of the historical Jesus. It is rather the product of early Christianity's search for compensation in the face of the non-advent of the Kingdom. It, in turn, provided theoretical justification for a missiology of conquest. If the wealth of the whole world belongs to Christ by right, what is wrong with the Church, his bride, taking de facto possession of it? How very different was the perspective of Jesus who admitted no lordship other than that of the one God! The message of the reign of God would be welcomed by all men and women. Not so the lordship of Christ, as it implies the superiority of Christians over the rest of mankind. The average Hindu would reckon it an affront and an act of theological aggression were he told that the culture his forebears produced belongs to Jesus Christ, just as any Christian would if he were told one fine morning that all the wealth of the Christian tradition belongs to Siva or Vishnu by right.

No less problematic is the attempt to define the meaning of non-Christian cultures in the light of the so-called theology of incarnation, referred to in the passage cited above. The idea of a pre-existing spiritual Logos who 'eventually' became incarnate is to be traced to the impact of Greek philosophy on early Christian reflection. It has little to do with Jesus' authentic teaching.

For Jesus, as for the prophets before him, God is in a sense eternally incarnate as he is encountered always and only in history. Besides, what does incarnation mean in respect of cultures? If it means that Jesus' message of the new age must assume the idiom and language of the people, none would disagree. If further, it means that the Church herself must become enfleshed in the culture of India, many problems crop up. Is not the Church already incarnate in the alien culture of the West? If so, how can she take on the body of yet another culture? Again, what is that culture in which she is to become incarnate? Is it the culture of the ruling classes or that of the ruled? How can a Church that has already come to terms with the culture of the status quo identify herself with the culture of protest and dissent?

Nor may we overvalue the Church's role of redeeming cultures. Such a role is implicit in the official pronouncements of the Church. One such pronouncement reads,

> "The good tidings of Christ constantly renew the life and culture of fallen man; it combats and eliminates the errors and evils resulting from the ever-threatening allurements of sin."[3]

Again,

> "Particular traditions, together with the individual patrimony of each family of nations, can be illumined by the light of the Gospel and be taken up into Catholic unity."[4]

Of course, nothing is said here directly of the redeeming role of the Church. But in so far as she is the official interpreter and vehicle of the tidings of Christ, she too may be said to be entrusted with the task of purifying and illumining cultures. No doubt the message of Jesus can inspire various peoples to initiate a critique of the respective cultures, as has happened, to a degree, in our own country. But there arises the embarrassing question, How is it that the same message has failed to purge the Church of beliefs and practices that are not in harmony with it?

Might it not be because the purifying, illumining power of the Gospel has been neutralized by the concrete reality of the Church? If that is the case, the more urgent task confronting her today is to engage in an anguishing self-assessment and self-renewal. Else the non-Christian could well retort: Physician, cure thyself.

It follows that to be a subversive-creative force in Indian society, Christianity must, on the one hand, radically revise its traditional self-understanding and repudiate all complicity with the culture of the ruling castes and classes. What this calls for is nothing less than a revolution of consciousness within the Churches. Until that happens, the question as to what contribution Christianity can make to the creation of a truly socialist culture will remain a merely academic one. Hence our option to focus the historical Jesus.

The Indian Presence of Jesus

The historical Jesus did not land on the Indian soil directly from some heaven above. Paradoxically, his life and message were mediated by the same Churches that had thrown a veil over him. Neither dogma nor cult nor institutions could totally smother his message of freedom and love. The light he was, radiated, as it were, through the pores of the organized Church: through her witness of service to the sick, the disabled, and the unwanted, and through teaching the Bible as literature. And with Jesus, a new humanism entered the mainstream of Indian history, a humanism that proclaimed the equality of all men and women irrespective of race, caste, or colour. So also a new religiosity indissolubly bound up with concern for one's fellow human beings.

Unlike the Christ of dogma, the Jesus of history had an impact that reached far beyond the confines of the Christian community. He has left an imprint on the consciousness of large sections of the intelligentsia. Gandhi was deeply influenced by the sermon on the mount.[5] His disciple, Vinoba Bhave, was a devout student of the Gospels. The pilgrimages he made on foot were modeled on Jesus' sending out the disciples on their mission. The Ramakrishna Mission was founded on the Christmas eve of 1886 after its founder, Swami Vivekananda, told his followers the story of Jesus and exhorted them "to become Christs in their turn."[6]

Nehru spoke of Jesus as a "great rebel" against the existing social order.[7] Ram Manohar Lohia wrote:

> "Christ is undoubtedly a figure of love and suffering, than which there has been no other figure in history. Buddha and Socrates are probably greater in wisdom or even in fine feeling, but are they greater in love?"[8]

For M. N. Roy, original Christianity represented the revolt of man against the tyranny of the Jewish God and the despotism of imperial Rome, and the Sermon on the Mount contained the highest moral ideals ever conceived by human imagination.[9] Ambedkar, the author of the Indian constitution, spoke of the Buddha and Jesus as the two personalities that captivated him most.[10] Not even the Indian communists have anything but praise for Jesus of Nazareth. One of their great leaders spoke of him as a prophet whose ideals and values conformed to the needs and desires of millions of men in their time and for centuries afterward.[11] The figure of Jesus has had an irresistible fascination for modern literary writers. Authors of repute have written dramas, poems, and novels on Gospel themes.[12] Symbols, similes, and metaphors of biblical origin have found their way into the language of the people.

The impact of Jesus, however, was too diffuse and vague and, perhaps, too confined to the educated classes to be a significant creative force in India. It could not become collective praxis. How could it, considering the conservative preaching and practice of the Churches? As far as the Catholic Church is concerned, the situation changed for the better with the Second Vatican Council. In its wake, there has been a renewed interest in the Bible and in the historical origins of Christianity. The perception has dawned on many thinking Christians that the Jesus of the Gospels is more relevant for their life than much that official Christianity has to offer, that theology and tradition had served to obscure his visage and soften down his message. The encounter with the historical Jesus has inspired them to join popular struggles for justice. It is in this context that we pose the question, What contribution the Jesus tradition can make to the revolution of consciousness India needs.

What the Jesus Tradition Can Give to India

We should first rid ourselves of the illusion that the Gospels contain the answer to every problem our people are facing. Jesus was no social theorist, no authority on the strategy of social change. But as a prophet whose life changed the very course of history, he can, as will be shown in the pages that follow, help energize the positive forces in Indian society that seek to transcend what is obsolescent in our world-view, religiosity, and ethos and to initiate a humanizing praxis.

From the cyclic to the dialogical view of history

For the average Indian, life follows the pattern of the ever-rotating, wheel. This is because his view of history has been formed based on cosmic processes. In nature, everything follows the rhythm of emergence, decay, and re-emergence. Plants spring up from the earth, grow, and decay, thus returning to where they came from but only to sprout once again in a fresh spurt of life. The seasons too follow a pattern of birth, death, and rebirth. The Indian mind has always thought of man as part of this cosmic process and consequently subject to the law of cyclic return. It sees history as "a perpetual creation, perpetual preservation, and perpetual destruction."[13] The world emanates from *Brahman* into which it is reabsorbed at the end of every world period (*kalpa*) and where it remains in a state of pure potency until it emanates again, thus initiating a new cycle. The world periods and the periods of repose that follow form, consecutively, the days and nights of *Brahman*.[14]

Inherent in this view of time is the principle of inevitable deterioration. Each cosmic eon unfolds itself in a sequence of progressive deterioration. At one end is the age of perfection (*Krita-yuga*) and at the other a period of universal misery, evil, and untruth (*Kali-yuga*). The present human race has been living in *Kali-yuga* for the last 5063 years and will have to live through another 420,000 years before it will see the end of this age of ever-increasing decadence.

The cyclic understanding of time has serious implications for man's attitude to life. It may lead him to either indifference towards the past or glorification of it. To indifference, because the unending creation and destruction of the universe makes the achievements of the past devoid of any real meaning; to the glorification of the past, because the principle of progressive deterioration involves belief in the golden age. It is the latter attitude that has characterized the Indian mind to the present day. There is much truth in the oft-repeated saying that India is a country where nothing is forgotten. The tenacity with which people cling to age-old practices points to a certain nostalgia for the bygone. But an uncritical affirmation of the past is not a properly historical attitude and is characteristic of people who have not come of age. Maturity requires that one opposes oneself to the past to transcend it, without, however, sacrificing the genuine values realized in it.

The cyclic conception of time has also prevented the birth of a vision of the future that does justice to true human aspirations. In a repetitive pattern of world cycles, there is no scope for progress and maturation. The values of the present are not carried over into the future but are doomed to eventual destruction. All that man creates, therefore, is stamped with the sign of death. Nor is the new creation that follows the night of *Brahman* any richer for the achievements of earlier ages. The end being nothing more than a mere return to the beginning, nothing new, nothing original, ever appears in history. Such a perspective is apt to beget a sense of futility and boredom.

The past is no more; the future is yet to be. The present alone is given to man, to redeem the past and father the future.

It is in the present that he is called upon to fulfill the task of self-creation. In the cyclic view of things the now pales into insignificance. It is emptied of its unique, irreplaceable quality as one's present life is but a link in the endless chain of existences. Moreover, since the past is not assumed by the present, and the present will not find a home in the future, man is condemned to live in the oppressive solitude of the now. The *now* contains no other invitation but to flee from it.

To mobilize her potential for self-creation and world-creation, India will have to leave behind the cyclic notion of time. The challenge is not anything unique to her, as though resulting from the very mental constitution of her people. Other nations have had to face the same challenge and have done so successfully. The early Hebrews had a cyclic conception of time. So also the Greeks, even of the time of Plato and Aristotle. But all of them were able to get free of the cosmic wheel and step out into the open space of history. We, on our part, for long got stuck at the cyclic phase. Only in recent centuries were we able to make a breakthrough, thanks to the impact of western civilization and the advance made in science and technology. But the most decisive factor hastening the process has been the day-to-day struggles of the exploited classes, following closely upon the struggle against colonialism. It is, above all, through organized action that the masses are learning that they are not mere cogs in the ever-rotating cosmic wheel but creators of their own future. In reinforcing this trend, the Jesus tradition can play a significant role.

Jesus did not propound any view of history but lived the dialectic of negativity - which is the mainspring of historical growth - to its last consequences. He was born into a tradition charged with the power of a historic negation, the defiant refusal of the Hebrews to slavery under the Pharaoh of Egypt. This negation had for its reverse side an affirmation of freedom crystallized into a project of hope, the hope of settling down in the land of Canaan flowing with milk and honey. The same dialectic of negation and affirmation, of protest and hope, later found powerful expression in the prophets - in their critique of social injustice and political corruption, on the one hand, and in their project of a future of justice and peace, on the other. And Jesus stands out as the one great prophet in whose word, deed, and death the dialectic of negativity worked itself out to the full. His no to injustice, religious bondage, and political domination at once sums up and radicalizes all previous prophetic protest and project. And the Cross becomes the most telling symbol of man's refusal to be enslaved and of his resolve to march forward to a fuller life. The dialectic of negativity governing universal history finds its concrete, concentrated expression in the personal life and death of Jesus of Nazareth. With him, world history enters a new phase.

From where did Moses, the prophets, and Jesus receive this world-transforming power of negating and creating? Undoubtedly from their experience of God. And here we touch upon what is most specific to the Judeo-Christian religious experience. The prophets experienced God, above all, as an unconditional challenge to break loose from all fetters and set out on the road to freedom which He himself is. To encounter God in this fashion was to take into one's own heart the absolute negation that the Divine is, the negation of all that cripples and debases the human. It was like swallowing a flame, which, in turn, consumes the world. So that whoever met God was bound to exclaim,

"Can any of us live with a devouring fire? Can any live in endless burning?"[15]

Such a person became himself a power that creates the world anew. Hence the relevance of Jesus' prophetic experience for the millions in India who long to see the birth of a new social order in which every man will be a brother to his neighbour.

From escape to transcension

Consistent with its cyclic understanding of human existence, the Indian mind conceives liberation (*mukti*) as a release from history itself. The goal of life is to realize freedom from death,[16] mortality,[17] and the womb,[18] from phenomenal existence,[19] and unreality,[20] from sin and the "knots of the heart",[21] from good and evil,[22] from darkness,[23] from material nature,[24] from the bondage of works,[25] from desire,[26] from suffering and pain,[27] and from illness.[28] The object of the human quest, however, is not merely freedom from but also freedom for, freedom for serenity,[29] for peace,[30] for unfailing joy,[31] for seeing one's Self as the self of all,[32] for union with *Brahman*,[33] for participation in the divine being.[34]

This way of looking at human liberation is based on the assumption that what constitutes alienation is not a mode of human existence but the very fact of human existence. One can, therefore, speak only of liberation from history, not of the liberation of history. Nature and the product of labour are excluded from the realm of freedom. Such a view of the end can create an attitude of escape and act as a mental block to refashioning nature and society. There is, however, in the Indian tradition another view that sees the goal of life in the attainment of heaven (*svarga*) where man will enjoy the company of gods.

Here cosmic existence is not left behind. For, even the gods are subject to the law of karma and samsara. Nonetheless, this view also fails to recognize the liberation of what humans create in history. Hence the need for a new concept of liberation that is in tune with the demands of collective action for social change.

Here the Jesuan vision of the ultimate future becomes highly relevant. The reign of God he proclaimed is not a new creation in total discontinuity with the past. Nor is it but the last phase in a unilinear evolution of history. It will be rooted in our earth and in our history. "Blessed are the meek, for they shall inherit the earth." In the humanized universe of the future, man will have land, houses, brothers, sisters, and mothers hundred-fold; those who mourn will have their tears wiped away; the hungry will be satisfied, and all will see right prevail and peace reign supreme. The "new heaven and the new earth" is none other than our heaven and earth suffused with love divine and human. While preserving whatever is good in human creation, it will leave behind everything tainted with sin. Only in this sense of dialectical transcension may we speak, from the Jesuan point of view, of mankind's liberation from nature and history.[35]

From cosmic to ethical religiosity

Orthodox Hindu religiosity tends to lack genuine humanizing power. True, Hinduism enjoins injunctions and taboos regarding individual and social life. But the moral law (*dharma*) is generally assimilated to the cosmic law (*rita*). The performance of the duties inherent in one's caste (*jati-dharma*), clan (*kula-dharma*), and individual avocation (*sva-dharma*) is meant to ensure the harmonious functioning of the cosmos.[36] To be moral in this context means conforming to tradition. Even such conformity is, in the final analysis, no more than a means towards attaining liberation, which lies beyond good and evil.

Moreover, in the cosmic perspective of unending emanations and dissolutions, the individual person is divested of all absolute value. What constitutes personhood, the capacity for self-determination is sacrificed to the determinism of cosmic evolution and involution. And where the abiding value of the person is not recognized, there can be no universal love, no all-embracing solidarity. Instead, one sees one's fellowman either as an element in a predetermined social structure (family, caste) or as an evanescent manifestation of the creative power (*maya*) of the Absolute, not as a being worth loving in his own right. Only as members of family or caste do individuals become subjects of rights and obligations. Within these institutions the average Indian knows how to relate to others; outside them, he is at a loss, with neither norms nor guidelines to go by. That is why in the political sphere of bourgeois democracy which recognizes the equality of all before the law the Indian behaves as though he is above all law. Equipped with the particularistic morality of caste, he is unable to cope with the universal morality of citizenship. Here lies the root of the crisis of morality in contemporary India.

The rudiments, however, for a creative morality of universal love can be found in the Indian tradition itself: in the ethical teaching of the Buddha and the saints of the *Bhakti* movement. They need to be rediscovered and their hidden powers released. Here the Jesus tradition can act as a stimulant. For, the God whom Jesus encountered is one who reveals himself as love and calls upon human beings to love one another.[37] He is an angry God, angry with all those who trample upon their weaker brethren. Of course, the angry God is not unknown to the people of India. Indian art and the Puranas depict Siva, Kali, and even

Vishnu as emitting the fire of wrath and destruction.[38] But theirs is anger directed not against unlove and injustice but against demonic, cosmic forces. It is not instinct with moral indignation but is a manifestation of the primal creative-destructive energy underlying the world process. The same holds of most saints and ascetics of Indian mythology. Their wrath is not born of love; it is only a manifestation of the magical energy accumulated through asceticism. In contrast, the anger of Yahweh is the violence of love seeking to exterminate the love of violence on the part of the mighty. Hence it is that the religious experience of Jesus is charged with the ethical power, to uproot and to plant, to demolish, and to build up. Only by appropriating this religiosity of creative love will India be able to overcome the divisiveness of caste and the inhumanity of existing social conditions.

From individual to communitarian salvation
The idea of collective salvation is foreign to the Indian religious tradition. Each individual is left to work out his liberation on his own. The reasons for this are both socio-historical and ideational.

Historically, what India has succeeded in realizing is some form of organic social unity, not any real community. The nearest she came to a community was in tribal society when the property was owned in common and all important decisions were taken based on consensus among tribal chiefs and elders. But tribal society broke up, giving way to the divisive unity of caste. Within the system of caste, the lower castes were subordinated to the higher ones, and, within each caste, the individual to the collective centre of decision making. Nevertheless, within the caste system and each social group there was at least a semblance of community, some sense of collective responsibility. For, even the servile castes had some rights which their masters could not ignore. Today even this alienated unity is eroded by the disruptive power of capitalist exploitation. And the individual is exposed to the war of all against all. If any genuine sense of community remains, it is only in those tribal societies which have successfully refused to be integrated into caste society and have managed to maintain their autonomy. For the mass of people, the historical experience provided no basis for the notion of communitarian salvation.

On the ideational plane, since history was viewed in cyclic terms, the community of men and women could not emerge as an ultimate value, destined as it is to be reabsorbed into the Absolute. The belief in karma and samsara also led to the devaluation of the community. How could one have a sense of human solidarity if in the life to come one might find oneself demoted to the level of an animal or raised to the status of a god?

The attempt to compensate for the loss of community resulted in the idea of the metaphysical unity of all. The Upanishadic equation, "Thou art That"(*tat tvam asi*) meant that the ultimate ground of the individual self and the ultimate ground of the world are one and the same. Which, in turn, implied that in their most profound being, all men and women are the same *Atman-Brahman*. Such an understanding of the unity of mankind could easily be reconciled with actual social inequality. As Ram Manohar Lohia wrote,

> "Hinduism has given its votaries, the commonest among them, the faith of the metaphysical equality or oneness between man and man, as has never been the lot of man elsewhere. Alongside this faith in metaphysical equality goes the most heinous conduct of social inequality."[39]

For the abstract concept of the oneness of all humans not to become an ideology of legitimation, it must be transposed to historical categories and concretized in social relations. Neo-Hinduism, is, in fact, moving in that direction. Here is how a Marxist theoretician sums up the trend:

> "The self was no more abstracted from life. The self was the social self that could find its fullest being only in social life. Self-realization or the realization of the identity of the individual self with the universal self meant the identification of oneself with the whole community. Man could realize himself only in other men, in the totality of human existence, that of *Brahman*."[40]

The quest for a new societal humanism brings the Indian tradition closer to the Judeo-Christian. The Hebrew idea of the collective destiny of mankind is rooted in the unity of tribal life, the collective experience of slavery in Egypt, and in the organized march into the Promised Land. Jesus is heir to the same idea. The nodal point of his message is not the salvation of the isolated individual but the final reconciliation and reintegration of humanity as a whole. The project of the reign of God involves the emergence of a universal community, which will sacrifice neither the individual to the collectivity nor collectivity to the individual.[41]

From the culture of fear to the culture of freedom
If the West has developed a culture of craving for pleasure, profit, and power, India, on her part, has perfected a culture of fear. Fear seems to pervade every aspect of life. There is the fear of being defiled by things, events, gestures, persons. Eating, drinking, sleeping, touching, mating, working, all become potential sources of pollution. Man fears woman as a threat to ritual purity and moral integrity. Woman, in turn, fears man's sexual violence and social dominance. And all, men and women, are afraid of the spirits good and evil, hovering about and menacing illness, destruction, and death. Under the grip of fear, the human spirit withers away and creativity dies. Neither literature nor art nor the sciences could develop in such a climate of fear. No wonder commodity production and artistic creation could flourish untrammeled only outside the pale of caste society as among the followers of Buddhism and Jainism. The ethos of fear, however, is much less in the lower rungs of caste hierarchy and is all but absent among the tribals.

Of this culture of fear, Jesus' message is the antithesis. He repudiated the distinction between the pure and the impure, a distinction which is at the source of much fear in all religions. True, he believed in the existence of demons, but he showed through word and deed that anyone who surrenders himself to the Divine is master over them. By proclaiming the primacy of man over the Sabbath, he set man free from the fear of guilt arising from the violation of man-made laws, and free for the enjoyment of sex, love, friendship, and beauty. His message, therefore, is an antidote for that spirituality of self-castration - coupled with its own opposite of naked hedonism and debauchery - propagated by the Brahmana tradition.

Learning from the Indian Tradition

Every prophet is a product of his age, conditioned by a specific culture and conjuncture of history. This applies to Jesus as well. Though his life and message do set the pattern of authentic human existence for all times to come and for all peoples, they do not exhaust the plenitude of the Divine. His religious experience has its own wealth and limitations just as similar experiences in other cultural and historical contexts have their own. The Jesus tradition can, therefore, be enriched by dialogue with other religions. I shall now proceed to indicate some aspects of the Indian religious tradition which the disciples of Jesus would do well to assimilate.

The immanence of the absolute Other

Jesus experienced God as in the world and yet *beyond*. But he saw transcendence-immanence more in ethical than ontic terms. That is, God transcends the world as the unconditional negation of injustice and unlove. He is the absolute Other to the evil that man begets. For the same reason, he is also immanent in the world as the One who affirms human fullness and freedom. To believe in divine transcendence, therefore, means translating into praxis the divine no to whatever degrades the human. Of course, ontic transcendence and immanence are not denied; rather, they are presupposed. This essentially prophetic, experience of God is suited to founding and sustaining moral endeavour on the part of man.

For, the believer cannot leave the scene of history. He has to seek the Unconditioned in the conditioned, the Absolute in the relative. The present is thus endowed with an ethical density and finality.

But this way of encountering the Divine has its limitations. It lends itself easily to an all too anthropomorphic conception of God as a person. Personhood evokes the idea of a centre of willing and loving, distinct from, and opposed to, nature and other personal centres. Hence the temptation to view God as standing outside man and nature, as though the universe were something added to the Divine. Moreover, it is difficult to experience a personal God as the all-pervasive presence as the One who is in everything and in whom everything is. So it is important for the Jesus tradition to dialogue with indigenous religiosity which stresses the ontic indwelling of Divine in nature and society. Both in the cosmic religion of the masses and the gnostic religion of the elite, the Divine is one with the world of names and forms. In this perspective God is neither personal nor impersonal but transpersonal; not only being but also becoming reveals himself; not only *in* but also as nature and history. Openness to this tradition will help Jesus' disciples to experience the ethical God of the Bible as the Absolute that becomes what he is in and through the world process.

Discovering the self within

While popular religion sought God in the world without, among the elite there was a search for him in the world within, in the inner recesses of the human spirit. The aim here was the discovery of the Self beneath the self, of the *Atman* that is identical with the *Brahman*. To this end was harnessed the technique of asceticism and integration called *Yoga*. Whether an experience of God can be engineered is a moot question. I personally do not think so. In any case, my concern is to highlight the type of humanism this kind of search for the Divine promotes. The technique of Yoga involved withdrawal from the world of senses, from the world of action and passion, and the activating of the subliminal forces latent in the deeps of the human spirit. It sought, to create the fully integrated man, self-possessed and serene amid the thousand strains and stresses of daily life. Here is how the *Gita* pictures the fully integrated man:

> "That man I love from whom the people do not shrink and who does not shrink from them, who is free from exaltation, fear, impatience, and excitement. I love the man who has no expectation, is pure and skilled, indifferent, who has no worries and gives up all enterprise... I love the

man who hates not nor exults, who mourns not nor desires, who puts away both pleasant and unpleasant things...I love the man who is the same to friend and foe, whether he be respected or despised, the same in heat and cold, in pleasure as in pain, who has put away attachment and remains unmoved by praise or blame, who is taciturn, contented with whatever comes his way, having no home, of steady mind."[42]

Admittedly, the spirituality enshrined here can breed cosmic pessimism, inscapism, and even absolute unconcern for the welfare of one's fellowmen. It has helped the upper castes to reconcile religion with ruthless exploitation. There is also the danger that one may mistake certain heightened experiences induced by yogic concentration for the self-unveiling of the Divine. Nevertheless, the pursuit of the inner self has a positive value in so far as it serves as a means towards freedom from the tyranny of lust, acquisitiveness, hatred, and violence. It can show the way to that mastery of the self so highly-priced by the Buddha, who said,

"If a man should conquer in battle a thousand and a thousand more, and another man should conquer himself, his would be the greater victory, because the greatest of victories is the victory over oneself."[43]

The technique of Yoga can also help create the psychic prerequisites for the humanization of revolutionary praxis. The Jesus tradition must, therefore, incorporate the yogic ideal of detachment in the spirituality of commitment to the Kingdom and its justice.

The motherhood of the earth

Jesus saw nature as the object of divine action as is clear from his saying,

"Consider how the lilies grow in the fields; they do not work, they do not spin; and yet, I tell you, even Solomon in all his splendour was not attired like one of these. But if that is how God clothes the grass in the fields, which is there today, and tomorrow is thrown on the stove, will he not all the more clothe you?"[44]

Familiar with the book of Genesis, he must also have viewed nature as the object of human action in response to the Divine call to fill the earth and subdue it. Yet one has the feeling that something is wanting in this way of looking at nature characteristic of the Hebrew tradition. It is too male, too aggressive and too remote. There is no real sense of kinship with the earth. Possibly because the Jews lived in desert regions inhospitable to man and beast alike.

How different is the traditional Indian attitude to the earth! To the Indian mind, nature is not something to be conquered or manipulated. She is the great mother, the womb of all creation, the source of all fertility. The same life force that courses through her veins also throbs in the human body. The Indian sees nature less from the pragmatic than from the religious, emotive point of view. The sense of kinship with the earth finds poignant expression in the great poetic work, *Sakuntalam*, where the heroine, on leaving the hermitage where she had been brought up, tenderly bids farewell to every plant she had nurtured and the deer she had lovingly fed from her own hands.

It was from nature too that man learned his first lessons in the art of living. So the Buddha could tell his followers,

> "Develop a state of mind like the earth. For on the earth men throw clean and unclean things, dung and urine, spittle, pus, and blood, and the earth is not troubled or repelled or disgusted. And similarly with fire, which burns all things, clean and unclean; and with air, which blows upon them all; and with space, which is nowhere established."[45]

For our forebears, nature was also the self-revelation of the Divine; the sound of *Brahman* could best be heard in the rustling of leaves and the chirping of birds and the music of the sea. So in times past the seekers after truth withdrew into the solitude of the forest to feel the Divine in the heartbeat of Mother Earth. Even for the common people, the things of nature had a symbolic value over and above their mere use-value.

Today, with the development of commodity production, nature is being reduced to a sum of exchange values. Man's umbilical bond with the earth is being severed and human existence impoverished. All the greater, therefore, is the need for us to recapture something of the traditional aesthetic, mystical approach to the earth.

Hindus who happen to read these pages might feel somewhat irked by the pre-eminence I attach to the Jesus tradition. True, I do affirm the unique position of Jesus as one who ushered in a new phase in the planetary evolution of the human spirit. He stands for the supersession of all religions including Christianity and heralds a future when human beings will worship God not in man-made temples but in spirit and truth. That future is also the future of India. But the higher phase he inaugurated had already dawned, however dimly, in the message of the Buddha and later reasserted itself in the *Bhakti* movement. But these gropings towards an ethical, creative religiosity could not come to fruition in the face of opposition from Brahmanaic Hinduism. What I claim, therefore, is not the superiority of Christianity over the Indian religious tradition but the superiority of the humanizing religiosity of the Buddha, the radical *Bhaktas* and Jesus over the magico-ritualistic religiosity of orthodox Hinduism and the depropheticized religiosity of tradition-bound Christianity.

If, on the other hand, Indian religiosity can enrich the Jesus tradition, it is because the former had developed for centuries the immediacy of man's relationship with nature and society and has for that very reason been able to maintain the sense of oneness of the cosmic, the human, and the Divine. Jesuan prophecy must appropriate this sense of oneness and wholeness, while India must make her own the Galilean's dream of the Total Man.

6

Communities for Countercultural Action

For the dialogue between the Jesus tradition and Indian culture to become a historical reality, there is a need for a mediating factor. If the historical Jesus has already become part of the consciousness of at least sections of the intelligentsia, it is due to mediation, not so much of official Christian preaching as of secular education and the teaching of the Bible as literature. What official preaching projected was, in the main, Christ the King out to conquer and convert pagans. Before this militant Christ, the Indian mind shrank back in sheer self-defense. But to the Jesus of the Gospels as depicted in the parables, sermons, and sayings the student of the Bible could warm up. This was particularly true of colonial days when secular education was chiefly in missionary hands. But today, with education becoming ever more technical and subservient to capital accumulation, the role of mediating the Jesus tradition will have to fall on new communities of committed disciples. Here the official Churches will be able to play only a marginal role until such times as they recapture Jesus' prophetic radicalism.

Open Communities

What is envisaged are communities patterned not after the Churches, which tend to be exclusive and sectarian, but after Jesus' table-fellowship with social outcasts, which was inclusive. They will be open to all who look forward to the reign of God and seek to do his will: "Whoever does the will of God is my brother, my sister, my mother." The important thing here is not adherence to dogmas, rituals, and rules but preparedness to work for the emergence of a new and universal community of love. Such communities will draw inspiration from the prophetic religiosity of Jesus and the ethic of assent and dissent inherent in it: assent to the divine project of the Total Man and dissent from the status quo of human alienation. In concrete terms, the dissent will involve a four-fold rupture - rupture in the sense of critical self-distancing - in relation to what is obsolescent in traditional Christianity.

A new baptism of immersion

Prophetic communities must leave behind Ghetto Christianity with its sectarian, exclusivist, narcissistic sub-culture. On the positive side, they must join hands with people of other religions and persuasions in meeting the common task of giving a human face to the earth. In order the better to merge with all socio-cultural forces that uphold freedom and wholeness of life, they must give up all false dichotomies such as between the sacred and the profane, the natural and the supernatural, believers and unbelievers. The spirit that led Jesus to the desert, then to the hamlets and towns of Palestine and finally to the cross will descend on his disciples only if they undergo a baptism of immersion in the life of the masses.

Beyond Churchist Theology

The time has come to leave behind the imported Churchist theology in favour of a theology of the living God. The former tended to invest the Church with monopolistic rights over divine revelation and equate her with the Kingdom of God. For the latter, God is nobody's private property. He is available to men and women of all times and places. The first made conversion a prerequisite for salvation; the second knows no conversion other than conversion to God to which all are called, Christians as well as non-Christians. The one projected a God who appeared on earth two thousand years ago, said all that he had to say once and for all, and then left the scene, leaving it to his vicegerents to interpret his word and will for all generations to come; the other sees God continuously at work in history, revealing his will in ever new ways and challenging human beings to a decision.

Admittedly, what I have just said about Churchist theology needs to be qualified when applied to the contemporary situation. Official theology has on some points toned down its traditional conservative stance. Today, for instance, it admits that salvation is possible outside the Church, without, however, entirely rejecting the premises from which the theory of conversion followed. Still, it is vain to hope that official Christianity will take the lead in radically revising traditional positions as it would go against its own deeply entrenched interests. A universalist theology that respects the equality of all human beings as children of God can come only from open communities of committed disciples. These have no vested interests to protect. Besides, they will be encountering God not in the nebulous world of concepts but in the immediacy of the joys and sorrows and strivings of people. The source, as well as the criterion of validity of the new theology, will not be inherited formulations but the contemplative praxis of self-and-world transformation.

From customary to essential morality

Customary morality consists in the strict observance of rules and practices handed down by tradition. It can easily coexist with much unlove and arrogance and even act as a cover for the pursuit of wealth and power. Essential morality, on the other hand, consists of that purity of heart Jesus enjoined on his disciples when he said, "Blessed are the pure in heart, for they shall see God." What he meant to inculcate is not just avoiding unchaste thoughts but eschewing evil intentions against one's kind. Positively, the call is to develop an attitude of universal compassion and friendliness, to speak in the language of the Buddha. Whatever you do is essentially moral if it flows from genuine concern for the well-being of all. Hence the saying of St. Augustine, "Love and do what you like." A person may be essentially moral and yet flout many an injunction of customary morality, as did the Buddha, as did Jesus.

Parting with dead symbols

Many of the Christian symbols in use today are the end-result of a long process of alienation. They have lost their moorings in the prophetic praxis of Jesus. Take, for instance, the Eucharist. In its origins, it was an attempt on the part of Jesus to anticipate in the form of a meal the reign of God to come. But today it is no more than a routine symbolic repetition of the past. What was a protest against the ritual and social divisions of contemporary Judaism has become a symbol of conformity and resignation. What was open to all has become an instrument of exclusion and division. Similarly, Jesus' practice of restoring to men and women the wholeness of body and soul - itself a foreshadowing of the wholeness of the end-time - has all but degenerated into quasi-magical rites. So the need to return to the sources, recapture the original thrust of the sayings and doings of the Galilean prophet and translate it into the language of today. We should not, however, confine ourselves to reinterpreting the past but remain open to the new symbols of protest and hope arising from the unconscious underworld of the masses as they struggle to create a better society.

Thus far about delinking the link with what is obsolete in the Christian tradition. A similar rupture must be effected also in regard to secular society. One must break loose from all alliance, overt or covert, with casteist and bourgeois culture. Not that the followers of Jesus must shun all contact with the privileged castes and classes. Whatever contact they may have must be such as to provoke the affluent to self-criticism, after the manner of Jesus whose encounter with Zacchaeus made the latter call his own wealth in question.

Cultural Action

The new communities must embody their hope in subversive-creative praxis. Leaving out directly political action, let me focus on the important areas of cultural action. By cultural action, I mean action aimed at subverting the cultural hegemony of the ruling classes and restoring to the common man the right to think his own thoughts and frame his own scale of values. Since economic and political institutions are also the expression of ideas and values, such action will have consequences extending to society as a whole.

Criticism

Christianity has always engaged in a critique of traditional culture. But its criticism was vitiated by its all too exclusive claims to truth and the means of salvation. In Hinduism, it tended to see nothing but magic and superstition. What is needed today is a new critical approach that is non-partisan: one that applies the same standard to all religious traditions. Further, it must be geared to superseding all alienated forms of religion while releasing their creative energies. The main target of criticism will have to be the divorce of religion from social ethics and the divisive culture of caste.

In the long run, however, traditional religion and caste culture are bound to undergo profound changes as their economic base, the pre-capitalist mode of production, is being steadily eroded. The economic foundation of bourgeois culture, on the other hand, is fast expanding from industry to agriculture, from urban to rural areas. The same culture, spearheaded by transnational companies, is invading every nook and corner of the country. Its seductive power over the educated strata is considerable, associated as it is with affluence, technological rationality, and military might, while little is known in our country of the enormous human costs the West had to pay for the development of capitalism.

Jesus' disciples are bound to take a critical stance in regard to bourgeois culture in virtue of their very faith in the reign of God. In collaboration with other progressive forces in society, they must carry on a relentless fight against the many manifestations of that culture: the debasing of language into a means for commodity exchange, the harnessing of science to profit-making and the resulting pollution of the earth, air and water, the quantification of the human sciences and the cult of the statistical individual, the co-opting of art and artists in the service of commodity production, the exploitation of sex and female nudity, the use of religion as a means for legitimizing unjust structures, the morality of individualism and private interest, the glorification of aggression and military might, the regimenting and manipulation of human needs, and so on and so forth. A scientific critique of these evils is also a prerequisite for projecting a new culture of free self-creation.

Aesthetic creation

Critique appeals only to the intellect. But man is more than mere intellect. He also needs to contemplate the meaning of life in sensuous forms. Hence the relevance of creational practice. Creation differs from mere production. Production issues in commodities for use; creation, on the other hand, lets the deepest meaning of life appear in bodily shape. Meaning may body forth in stone (architecture, sculpture), wood (carving), colour (painting), tone (music), bodily movement (dance), or word (literature). These are not mere luxuries but an essential revelation of humanness. They reveal the wealth and poverty, the power and glory of human existence. They tell not merely what the human community is but also what it must become if it is to realize its authentic possibilities. Their appeal reaches down to the subliminal realm of the unconscious. That is why they have the power to galvanize people into transformative action.

From this world of aesthetic creation, Indian Christianity is all but absent. There are among Christians scarcely any novelists, writers, dramatists, or artists worth the name. I suggest that the reason for this cultural barrenness is the kind of ethos that prevails in the Christian community. What I said earlier about the Hindu ethos of fear also applies here. Creativity can flourish only in an atmosphere of freedom - freedom to experience and explore the frontiers of love and hate, hope and despair, ugliness, and beauty. And freedom became a casualty when the Jesus movement congealed into dogmas, rituals, laws, and taboos. The proliferation of laws created a pervading sense of guilt and sin. The stoic rule of "the golden mean" prevented the human spirit from experiencing the abysmal and the vertiginous. Fear held the soul prisoner, wound it round and round with innumerable invisible chords. To make matters worse, Christianity has remained a foreign body on the Indian soil, without an indigenous memory and without roots in tradition.

Once freed from the stranglehold of dogma and customary morality, Jesus' disciples will once again become capable of genuine creation. From among them will rise up writers, poets, and artists who will give word and shape to the muted longings of the people.

Letting Jesus appear in person

Political action, criticism, creation - all are ways of letting Jesus be in the Indian context. But they are no substitute for letting him appear in person. As a unique manifestation of the Divine, he belongs to mankind as a whole and all have a right to know him. He represents a historic mutation in human consciousness which all men and women have to go through in their search for the Divine. As such, he is perennially and universally relevant. We have seen how he can help activate the energies of the new age to come, energies long since repressed by caste Hinduism. So too, he is a source of strength for all who are involved in the struggle for a richer and fuller life.

But this Jesus could not come to his own within official Christianity. Dogma reified him; theology reduced him to a sum of concepts; cult degraded him to a god among the many gods. His visage was further marred and mutilated by Christianity's alliance with the rulers and principalities of this world. This state of affairs continues even today in spite of much radical rhetoric on the part of Church leaders. Until the Christian Churches undergo a radical conversion to God, the task of presenting Jesus in person before the Indian people will devolve primarily upon small communities of committed disciples. These alone can initiate a new exegesis of the Gospels that is unclouded by class interests and dogmatic bias. From them, we may expect a new genre of writing through which Jesus will speak to the people of India in their own idiom and as one among them.

PART - 2
ESSAYS

7

The Prophet of Hope

All human experience is ambivalent. We encounter pain, anxiety, despair, hatred, injustice, and inequality, on the one hand; and love, goodness, peace, and beauty, on the other. By instinct, as it were, we reject the former and welcome the latter. We want to root out whatever cripples our spirit and smothers our creativity. We wish the good and the beautiful we experience to endure forever and attain ever greater fullness. We nurse the silent hope that our longing for the fullness of being, knowing, and having will one day be realized. It is against the horizon of this hope that our life unfolds with its varied decisions and actions. It forms the mainspring of our life and spurs us on to actions despite obstacles and failures. Were hope to die, life would come to a standstill and everything would lapse into meaninglessness.

The more truly human we are, the more our individual horizons of hope tend to coincide with that of society as a whole. The concerns of all become our concern. Every blow dealt to a neighbour is experienced as dealt to us. So, everything that gladdens the hearts of others will find an echo in us. It becomes impossible for us to seek our own happiness unconcerned about the happiness of others. The measure of our humanity, then, is the measure in which we find our well-being in the well-being of the community.

The personal-social horizon of hope in the ultimate fullness of man is not a mere product of creative fancy. It is not so much that we project it as that we are projected by it. We both pursue and are pursued by it. Though rooted in our experience, it also reveals itself as coming into our life from the Beyond and taking hold of us in such a way that we are under its command. No longer are we free not to hearken to it. We cannot deny it without denying ourselves. Thus the human fullness we hope for manifests itself at the same time as divine fullness.

Though this dimension of ultimate hope is found in all communities and cultures and is a part of universal human experience, it finds articulate expression only in some people who feel called specially to bear witness to it. Such men are called prophets. Their mission is to confront their contemporaries with their common hope as revealed in concrete historical events and situations. They point to the present and the promises it bears for the future. They call upon their fellowmen to respond to the challenges which the realization of that future poses. Their message is, therefore, essentially time-bound. Thus, for instance, Amos and Isaiah interpreted the times for the people of Israel at a time when they lived under the shadow of threat from the Assyrian empire; Jeremiah, when the neo-Babylonians were poised to conquer Palestine; Haggai and Zachariah in the context of the political convulsions that overtook Persia. In their respective historical situations they saw the footprints of the Divine and where these led to, namely, the age of human-divine fullness yet to come.

It is in the line of these great prophets that Jesus of Nazareth stands. At a critical period in the history of the Jews when they were groaning under the weight of Roman imperialism, he deciphered for them the ultimate meaning of history. More than any other prophet and in a unique manner he was taken hold of by the horizon of mankind's hope for the fullness of freedom and love. This happened on the day he underwent the baptism for the forgiveness of sins at the hands of John the Baptizer. Then the Spirit (power) of God descended upon him and took command of his destiny (Mk. 1:9-12). It was when he publicly proclaimed his oneness with the condition of all men as sinners - as estranged from nature, other men, themselves, and God - that the challenge of man's absolute future gripped him by the very roots of his being.

On the banks of the Jordan, he received a new mind and heart, a new faith and hope. From then on he began to see things in a new light, in the light of the God who is to come, of his glory yet to be reflected in the faces of all men. From then on his only and ultimate concern was the realization of the fullness of man which be termed, as did his contemporaries, the reign of God. When he told his disciples, "Set your mind on God's Kingdom and his justice before everything else, and all the rest will come to you as well,"(Mt. 6:33) he was but enjoining on them what he himself did. For him too the hoped for reign of justice and love was the pearl of great value, the treasure hidden in the field (Mt. 13:44-46), for the sake of which he was prepared to sacrifice everything else. Compared with this all-absorbing concern, things like what he should eat, how he should clothe himself, and where he should lay his head were but trifles. It is therefore in the light of Jesus' hope in the reign of God that we should understand his teaching, his controversies with adversaries, his practice of working cures and driving out demons, his conflict with the religious and the political establishment, and, above all, his tragic death on the cross. Unfortunately, the all-determining role which the reign of God played in the life and teaching of Jesus was lost sight of from very early times. The stress came to be shifted from the hope in the future to the past of Jesus' death and resurrection or to his presence as experienced by the community of believers. Worse, the community itself began to be looked upon as the reign of God. From then on what mattered was not so much striving towards the future as either conserving the past or legitimizing the present. This trend needs to be reversed. We have to recapture the original thrust of Jesus' hope, which alone can release the creative energies of mankind for the building up of a more humane society. This is particularly true of our age in which science and technology have provided us with the means either to create a better future or to destroy ourselves. Never in the past was mankind faced with such frightening options. In this critical juncture of history, nothing less than an absolute, unconditional hope can save man and his creations from chaos and destruction.

(Anawim, No. 1; *Jesus and Society*, Chap.1)

8

Towards Theandric Fullness

We have seen that Jesus lived in the hope that God will come in power and that his coming will coincide with the *coming-to-be* of the fullness of man. Let us now enquire how Jesus conceived the new humanity. For a complete answer nothing less than a study of his entire life and teaching will suffice. For the present, we shall confine ourselves to highlighting some of the salient features of the age to come on the limited basis of an analysis of the Beatitudes. Here is how Mathew formulates them:

> "Blessed are the poor in spirit, for theirs is the Kingdom of Heaven. Blessed are those who mourn, for they shall be comforted. Blessed are the meek, for they shall inherit the earth. Blessed are those who hunger and thirst for justice, for they shall obtain mercy. Blessed are the pure in heart, for they shall see God. Blessed are the peacemakers, for they shall be called sons of God. Blessed are those, who are persecuted for the cause of justice, for theirs is the Kingdom of Heaven." (5:3-10)

Subversion and Re-creation

In the Beatitudes, as they stand in Mathew, one may distinguish three closely related layers of meaning. First, they specify the proper attitudes men should have — poverty of spirit, meekness, concern for justice, mercifulness, purity of heart, commitment to the cause of peace, and perseverance in the face of persecution — which qualify them for entry into the Kingdom of God. Second, they forecast the definitive subversion of the existing conditions in which man cannot fully be a man. Third, they project a picture, though couched in symbolic language, of the re-created humanity of the future. The first layer of meaning is decidedly secondary; for the Beatitudes as formulated by Luke (6:20-22), which are generally recognized as more faithfully reflecting what Jesus himself must have spoken, make no mention of the attitudes one should have in order to be received into God's Kingdom. However, the moral prerequisites enumerated in Mathew are, if properly understood, quite in harmony with the general tenor of the teaching of Jesus. Be that as it may, the main thrust of the Beatitudes is to be sought in the message of the reign of God as the subversion of the old and the re-creation of the new. The subversive-constructive character of the Kingdom may be viewed from three different angles — man's relationship to the earth, to his fellowmen, and to God.

The Poor Shall Possess the Earth

The reign of God means, first of all, the abolition of man's estrangement from the earth. "Blessed are the meek, for they shall inherit the earth." Here the meek stand for the same class of people referred to as poor in the first Beatitude, both terms being translations of the same Hebrew word anawim. Which meant "those bent under the weight of oppression", those who have none to plead their cause, and therefore look to God alone for liberation (Is. 61:1). What Jesus envisaged, therefore, is the overthrow of all economic systems in which an aggressive few deprive the helpless many of the earth (the means and the fruits of production), and the creation of a new community in which the earth and its abundance will belong to all. He looked forward to the definitive vindication of the poor and the return of the land to the dispossessed so that these will not have "to build for others to inhabit, nor plant for others to eat" (Is. 65:22; see also Ps 37:11). If so, the Kingdom of Heaven is nothing but our earth transformed into "a home of justice" (2 Pt. 3:13). It is the land flowing with milk and honey promised to "those who hunger and thirst for justice."

The New Family of Man

Common possession of the earth and its plenty is at once the result of, and the condition for, the reconciliation of man to man. God's reign will mark the end of all class domination and abolish the rule of private interest and competition. Not the market where commodities are bought and sold but the home where everything assumes the form of a gift is the true symbol of the new humanity. With its coming, things, be they products of labour or not, will become the bond between man and man instead of being instruments for the exploitation of man by man. Similarly, authority and power will give way to service as the true measure of human greatness.

> "You know that in the world the recognized rulers lord it over their subjects, and their great men make them feel the weight of authority. That is not the way with you; among you, whoever wants to be great must be your servant, and whoever wants to be first must be the willing slave of all." (Mk. 10:42-44).

Only the pure in heart, i.e. those who do not harbour evil intentions against their fellowmen (Ps. 24:4), will belong to the new family of man in which all will be brothers to one another and bestow peace on one another. "Blessed are the peacemakers, for they shall be called sons of God."

A Human-Divine Community

For Jesus the ultimate future of human fullness necessarily involves the superseding of all alienation from God. In fact what is most revolutionary in his teaching is the assertion that where men love one another they have already met God. To attain the Divine means being fully human. Negatively, the subversion of whatever dehumanizes man is the self-disclosure of the Divine. In this sense all the Beatitudes have for their theme man's reconciliation with God. The manner of this reconciliation is further specified as one of knowing (they shall see God) and of loving (they shall be called sons of God). These two ways of communion with God are in the last analysis one and the same; for only through love can the Ultimate be known.

"No one knows the Father except the son." (Mt. 11:27)

God can exercise his rule over this mutilated humanity that we are, only by pulling down the old in order to build anew, only by uprooting in order to plant again. Therefore, to have a share in his reign is to participate in the task of subversion and reconstruction. And this will necessarily invite repression from the side of the powers that be. Hence the relevance of the last Beatitude:

> "Blessed are those who are persecuted for the cause of justice, for theirs is the Kingdom of Heaven."

(*Jesus Today*, Chap. 2; *Jesus and Society*, Chap. 2)

9

The Not-yet and the Already

The Gospel according to Mark sums up the central message of Jesus in these words:

> "The Kingdom of God has come upon you: repent, and believe in the Gospel." (Mk. 1:15)

Paraphrased, it would run: The God who will come to lead you to the fullness of being, knowing, and loving is *already* here knocking at your gate. Wake up, then, and go to meet him; the time has come for you to take a decision either for or against him. The tension between the *not-yet* and the *already* that underlies this proclamation needs to be understood in all its implications.

Jesus understood the Kingdom of God as the *ultimate* future of man. To convey this meaning to his listeners he used many and varied symbols. One such symbol was that of a festal meal in which all, irrespective of race or colour, will participate.

> "Many will come from east and west to feast with Abraham, Isaac, and Jacob in the Kingdom of heaven." (Mt. 8:11)

The life-situation in which the saying is rooted could have been none other than his table-fellowship with tax-collectors and sinners, i.e. with the outcasts of Jewish society. The joy and togetherness-in-love experienced in these meals were for him a foretaste of that universal human communion signified by the meal of the end-time. The same looking-forward-to-the-future inspires also the prayer he taught his disciples. They were to pray: "Thy Kingdom come" (Mt. 6:10). Here too, the reign of God, for whose coming one is to pray, is conceived in terms of a joyous meal. This becomes clear when we relate the petition to the subsequent one: "Give us today our daily bread" (Mt. 6:11). The Greek word for daily bread could equally have meant *the bread for the morrow,* i.e. the bread broken at the meal of the end-time. The petition would then mean: "Grant us today an anticipation of that meal-fellowship of the future when all men shall live for one another and share what they have." Since, for Jesus, his meals with the socially unwanted were such an anticipation, it is likely that they formed the social context out of which was born the prayer 'Our Father'.

If Jesus envisioned the reign of God as the ultimate future of man, it is equally true that for him that future did not begin where our history ended, as though nothing in the latter had any abiding value. Rather, he saw the ultimate future as already germinating in the present. This is implied in the texts we have just commented on. Besides, we may cite those sayings of Jesus in which he compares the reign of God to the seed that falls on good soil and yields a hundredfold (Mk. 4:8), to the mustard seed that springs up and grows taller than any other plant and forms branches so large that birds can settle in its shade (Mk. 4:32), and, finally, to the little yeast that leavens a huge mass of dough (Mt. 13:33). Underlying all these metaphors is the idea that the power of God at work in the present will burst into a flower as the new humanity of the future.

Furthermore, Jesus saw in the cures he worked for the sick and the possessed, the revelation of the same creative, liberating power of God.

> "If it is by the finger (= power) of God that I drive out the devils, then be sure the Kingdom of God has already come upon you." (Lk. 11:20)

That the inbreak of the reign of God can be discerned here and now in the life of the human community is further shown by the saying:

> "You cannot tell by observation when the Kingdom of God comes. There will be no saying 'Look, here it is!' or 'there it is!'; for in fact the Kingdom of God is among you." (Lk. 17:20)

As against the Pharisees who held that the coming of the Kingdom can be ascertained by observing the extraordinary cosmic convulsions and historical upheavals preceding it, Jesus taught that it is to be encountered in the ordinary world of human striving and social relationships. But, where among men may we encounter the presence of God's reign? Jesus saw in the freedom he brought from illness and possession the irruption into the world of the Kingdom. Where man reaches out in love to his fellowmen to shatter their fetters of ignorance, sin, illness, and injustice, where, in consequence, "the blind recover their sight, the lame walk, the lepers made clean, the deaf hear, the dead are raised to life, the poor are hearing the good news." (Lk. 7:22-23; 4:14-21).

There we witness the emergence in history of a new age of human-divine fullness. To promote the integral freedom of man is, to work with God for the realization of his ultimate purpose in history. This task is addressed to all men. Hence Jesus' words to his disciples:

> "And you, like the lamp, must shed light among your fellows, so that when they see the good you do, they may give praise to your Father in heaven." (Mt. 15:16)

The good done to one's fellows is, then, what announces and makes present God's reign in the world. In other words, only a community governed by self-giving love can radiate the glory of God.

We have thus far explained how the reign of God is at once future and present, or, more precisely, how it is a future that is already breaking in upon the present. This tension between *the not-yet* and *the already* must be maintained at any cost. And this for two reasons: First, all authentic human existence is marked by the tension between faith in the present and hope for the future. How empty, for instance, would be our experience, here and now, of love and fellowship, if it did not at the same time project a horizon of fullness! How half-hearted our commitment to any cause, if it is not at the same time commitment to an absolute cause! How far, indeed, shall we be from realizing the possible if we did not risk striving for the impossible! What does all this show but that man is an animal condemned to live from the future? Conversely, all our hopes for a better future have for their matrix the lived *present* of our joys and sorrows. No future, not even in the ultimate future, can command our loyalty if it has not somehow already met us in the world of our present concerns. Viewed from this angle, Jesus' message of the Kingdom not only is in accord with what man is in his nakedness as well as glory but also is the guarantee that his hopes will one day be fulfilled.

There is yet another reason why we should hold fast to the tension between *the not-yet* and *the already* that characterizes the reign of God. Were we to forget the not-yet, we shall run the risk of making idols of our past as well as present achievements, and refusing to march forward to the God who beckons us from the beyond. We shall then rest content with preserving the past instead of creating the future. Such an attitude is but a disguised form of atheism, which has in the past assumed three main forms: dogmatism, cultism, and institutionalism. Dogmatism sought to imprison the living God in dead concepts and formulae derived from fossilized systems of thought. Cultism substituted for the God of history, for the God of Abraham, Isaac, and Jacob, a static God presiding over the ever-rotating wheel of rituals and rubrics, and gloating over the smell of incense and the mumbling of supplications. Institutionalism, on its part, reduced God to the status of a cosmic policeman whose duty it is to enforce the strict observance of laws, customs, and norms, which the privileged classes created to exploit the ignorant and servile masses. All these forms of atheism have one thing in common: the worship *of the God of the dead.*

Equally disastrous will it be, if we were to swing to the other extreme and stress exclusively the future character of the reign of God. That will render us indifferent to the real challenges of the present and incapable of any historical initiative to change existing conditions, however oppressive they may be. Faith in the Kingdom will then act as a narcotic that kills our feelings of social guilt and breeds dreams and illusions into which we can conveniently escape from the frightening prospect of having to confront the living God of *the here* and *the now*.

To steer clear of these deviations the disciples of Jesus must learn to respond to the call of the future as it makes itself heard in the realities of the present.

(*Jesus Today*, Chap. 3; *Jesus and Society*, Chap. 3)

10

The Future:
A Gift and a Task

"Blessed are those who hunger and thirst for righteousness, for they shall be satisfied."(Mt. 5:6)

Those here characterized as hungering and thirsting for righteousness are the same class of people who are elsewhere in the Beatitudes referred to as the poor, the sorrowful, and the gentle in spirit. Denied all rights, they long to witness the overthrow of the social conditions which hold them captive. This hope, Jesus announced, will be fulfilled.

What is that righteousness which the coming of God will usher in? In the Bible the word has a much broader meaning than justice as commonly understood. It means not merely giving each his due but also, and above all, human behaviour and social conditions in harmony with the will of God as expressed chiefly in the ten commandments. Here is how Ezekiel describes the righteous individual:

"He oppresses no man, he returns the debtor's pledge. He never robs. He gives bread to the hungry and clothes to those who have none. He never lends either at discount or at interest. He shuns injustice and deals fairly between man and man. He conforms to my statutes and loyally observes my laws. Such a man is righteous: he shall live, says the Lord."(Ezek. 18:7-9).

Righteousness is attributed not only to the individual but also to the community as a whole. Isaiah spoke of the new people, God's coming will bring into being as a garden planted with trees of righteousness (Is. 61:3), as a home in which justice dwells (Is. 1:21; 32:6). In that new society there will no more be violence and aggression (Is 11:3-5; 16:4-5; 29:18-21; 49:8-10, 25-26, 60: 17-18; 61: 1-2; Ps 37; 147:6)

The righteousness Jesus required of his hearers as a condition for entry into the Kingdom of God is substantially the same as what the Prophets had proclaimed, with this difference, however, that he universalized its demands. He taught that justice and love should be shown also to one's enemies (Mt. 5:44). In contrast to the Pharisees who had reduced righteousness to mere external observance of the written and the oral law, he radicalized its meaning by extending its demands to the very heart of man, to that inmost centre where he is alone with himself and stands naked before his Maker (Mt. 5:21-22,27-28, 33-37; 6:1-4,16-18). More, he wanted justice to inspire the structures and institutions of society as is clear from his criticism of the wealthy and of those who exercise political power (Mk. 10:23-25, 42-45).

What was the basis of Jesus' certain hope that man's hunger and thirst for justice would be satisfied? It was none other than the belief he shared with the prophets of Old Testament that God is one who not only acts justly (Gn. 18:25; Dt 32:4; Ho. 2:18-22; Is. 41:1-5; 56:1-2) but is himself justice.

"The Lord is a God of justice" (Is. 30:18).

He is one who keeps faith and fulfills his promises. Besides, he is not a neutral God who judges impartially between the wronged and the wrongdoer, or confers his blessings equally on the exploiter and the exploited, according to the established norms of an unjust society. The God of Jesus is partial to the poor and the oppressed (Am. 2:6-8; 4:1-3; 5:7-17; Is 1:17, 21; 61:1-3; Ps 37) because he knows that justice is on their side. He is the absolute, unconditional no to evil in every form, He owes it to himself to repel injustice, as light owes it to itself to dispel darkness. Therefore, he cannot but oppose those who grind the heads of the poor in the dust of the earth. It is just in this total rejection of evil that his holiness consists.

> "The Lord of Hosts sits high in judgement, and by righteousness the holy
> God shows himself holy." (Is 5:16).

Naturally, when such a God irrupts into history, there is a war against the oppressors, himself fighting on the side of the oppressed. The justice of God thus becomes a history of struggles for justice among men. It is in this sense that we should understand the biblical accounts of the wars and victories of God (Mi. 6:5; Is 41:2-10; 56:1-2). Any man who is taken hold of by such a God becomes in his turn a wielder of the sword in defense of the downtrodden. Such indeed was Jesus:

> "I have not come to bring peace but the sword" (Mt. 10:34).

Viewed from this angle, hungering and thirsting for righteousness means much more than a pious, even intense, longing. It, rather, expresses the attitude of one whose soul has been so invaded by the God of righteousness that he cannot but join in the social and political struggles for justice. For such a one, to worship God is "to loosen the fetters of injustice, to untie the knots of the yoke, and to set free those who have been crushed." (Is. 58:6). In the eyes of Jesus only such people will have a share in the blessings of the age to come.

> "Not everyone who calls me Lord, Lord, will enter the kingdom of Heaven,
> but only those who do the will of my heavenly Father." (Mt. 7:21).

From our reflections thus far, it follows that the definitive reign of justice is at once a divine gift and a human task. Because it is a gift Jesus asked his disciples to pray for it. The Beatitude we have been studying corresponds to the third petition of the Our Father:

> "Thy will be done, on earth as in heaven" (Mt. 6:10).

However, that the fullness of justice is the result of the free initiative of God does not make it any less the goal of human striving. God comes into the life of man in the form of a call to which the latter has to respond unconditionally. The divine challenge seeks to be enfleshed in human practice, individual as well as collective. Hence Jesus' repeated call for action on the part of his hearers, especially of his disciples: Act upon my words (Mt. 7:24), do good (Mt. 5:16), be reconciled with your brother (Mt. 5:23-24), practise radical honesty (Mt. 5:37), give when asked to give (Mt. 5:41-42), forgive those who wrong you (Mt. 6:14), love your enemies (Mt. 5: 44), treat others as you would like them to treat you (Mt. 7:12), sell what you have and give to the poor (Mk. 10:21), preach the good news (Mt. 10:28), take up your cross and come with me (Mt. 16:24), seek first the Kingdom of God and its justice (Mt. 6:33). We are thus confronted with a paradox: God's war on the forces of unrighteousness will come to a successful issue only if man joins in the fight. A telling formulation of the same paradox we have in the words of Jahweh spoken through the prophet Isaiah:

> "Maintain justice, do the right,... and my righteousness will show itself victorious." (Is 56:1)

If this interpretation of the Beatitude is correct, the question will naturally arise: How is it that Jesus never explicitly called upon the oppressed classes of his day to overthrow the prevailing social system? The answer is to be sought in the fact that his teaching has aspects that are historically conditioned. Live as he did in an age in which productive forces had not yet developed, in which the conditions necessary for the emergence of an organized proletariat had not yet matured, he could not possibly have envisaged any social macro-revolution. This does not mean that his disciples ought, under whatever historical conditions they live, to eschew the path of revolution understood as a planned and radical transformation of the social system. On the contrary, fidelity to the main thrust of his teaching and practice requires that they commit themselves to the subversion of all unjust social systems.

(Anawim No. 2; *Jesus Today*, Chap. 4; *Jesus and Society*, Chap. 4)

11

A Manifesto of Freedom

In the preceding pages, the main theme has been Jesus' teaching on the Kingdom of God. We shall now consider how Jesus himself responded to the challenge of the Kingdom. Of particular relevance in this context is the account of his first visit to Nazareth as recorded in the Gospel according to Luke.

Armed with the power of the Spirit, Jesus came to his hometown and, as was his wont, went up to the synagogue. He stood up to read the lesson, which happened to be from Isaiah:

> "The Spirit of the Lord is upon me because he has anointed me; he has sent me to announce good news to the poor, to proclaim release for prisoners and recovery of sight for the blind; to let the broken victims go free, to proclaim the year of the Lord's favour" (Is 61:1-2; Lk 4:18-19).

Good News for the Poor

The content of Jesus' message to the people of his hometown is substantially the same as that of the Sermon on the Mount. There the stress was on God's intervention in history to set men free; here it is on Jesus' commitment to the liberation of man in response to the divine call. In either case, the message is beamed to the poor, to the oppressed classes weighed down under the yoke of exploitation, with none to defend their cause. The divine bias in favour of social underdogs is as much in evidence here as in the Sermon on the Mount.

That the freedom promised is total is clear from the text itself. It has to do not only with the inwardness of each person but also with his body whereby he is one with nature and his kind. For the body too needs to be freed from the shackles of illness, decay, and death. Hence the promise of recovery of sight to the blind, which is to be understood as representative of the many and varied cures Jesus was to work in the course of his journeys up and down the country. The power of God was with him, and it would go out of him and heal all (Lk. 5:17; Mk. 5:30).

Man is rendered truly whole only when he rejoins his external body, that is nature and the product of his labour. And this is what the year of the Lord's favour was meant to achieve. In the Old Testament, Jahweh had ordained that every fiftieth year was to be a year of liberation for all the inhabitants of the land. In this year of Jubilee, whoever had sold his land and was not able to redeem it was entitled once again to take possession of it. Likewise, whoever, in dire poverty, was forced to sell himself to another as the bonded labourer was free to leave his master and go back to his family and ancestral property (Lev. 25:8-41). Seen in this light, what Jesus announced was nothing less than the end of man's alienation from land and its produce. Equally, it was a charter of freedom for the poor who lived in bondage to the privileged classes.

Jesus' mission extended also to securing release for prisoners. Prisoners are the means of the state, itself an instrument of oppression in the hands of the exploiting classes, which they employ to break the spirit of man. At the time of Jesus too, there were probably many languishing in prisons. Jesus would let these broken victims go free and usher in a new age in which there would be neither State nor prison, in which service would replace power and violence (Mk. 10:42-44).

Why Only the Words of Grace?

How did the people respond to this message of total liberation? Positively, it would seem. For we read:

> "There was a general stir of admiration; they were surprised that words of such grace should fall from his lips" (Lk. 4:22).

In that case it is difficult to understand how the same people turned violent and even tried to kill him, as the sequel shows. Luke may have telescoped into one account different visits Jesus made to his hometown. Another, more probable, solution has been suggested by Joachim Jeremias. According to him the Greek original of verse 22 could equally have meant: "The people were incensed and shocked at the fact that only the words of grace fell from his lips." In other words, in quoting Isaiah 61:1-2, Jesus had deliberately left out mentioning the day of the vengeance of God on the enemies of Israel and thereby repudiated the exclusive claims of his audience to divine favour. More, in support of his view, he cited the example of God sending his prophet Elijah to succour an alien widow while his own people were facing a severe famine; and Elisha to heal a Syrian leper while lepers were plenty in Israel. His listeners could not tolerate the fact that he rejected the God they had fashioned in their own image, attributing to him their own itch for blood and vengeance.

Is Not This Joseph's Son?

This query shows that there was probably another reason why the people reacted adversely to his message. In all societies in which there is a social division of labour into intellectual and manual, invariably a class comes into existence which monopolizes all ritual production, the production of ideas, beliefs, and myths. Members of this class become the accredited teachers and the sole depositories of wisdom. Such, for instance, were the Scribes in the time of Jesus. Only they were authorized to discourse on God and things divine, which meant that God himself had to go through the proper channels if he wished to secure a hearing with his people. No wonder, people asked themselves: How could this country bumpkin of a carpenter, untrained in Scribal lore, make the stupendous claim to speak in the name of God? If he still wants us to believe in him, let him first establish his credibility by working signs and wonders. By thus demanding miracles they proved their want of faith. And where there is no faith, even the Spirit of God is powerless.

Mark tells us bluntly: "He could work no miracles there" (6:6). All of which drew from Jesus the remark tinged with sadness:

"I tell you this: no prophet is recognized in his own country." (Lk. 4:24)

The lesson for us, disciples of Jesus, is clear: Jesus lives. But he can change the world, our world, only if we accept him as he is, without cutting him to our size, domesticating him to suit our purposes, and reducing his universal message to an ideology geared to legitimize our individual or class interests. He can change the world only if we believe in him, i.e. let his Spirit invade our souls and bodies and become enfleshed in our historical practice.

(Anawim No.13; *Jesus and Society*, Chap. 6)

12

Freedom for the Body

The liberation of the body is an essential aspect of the prophetic practice of Jesus. To grasp its full significance, it is necessary, in reading the Gospels, to keep in mind the Hebrew mode of thinking which Jesus shared.

The Hebrew View of the Body

We are wont to think of body and soul as parts of man that are essentially opposed to each other, as though the body were a prison housing an alien soul. This view is derived from the Greek way of thinking. The same is found with variations also in some of the traditional systems of Indian thought. The Hebrews thought differently. They did not even have a word for what we name body. The nearest equivalent for it is 'basar' which is better translated flesh rather than body. Basar (flesh) is not just a part of man but the whole man considered in his weakness and corruptibility, physical and moral. It is in this sense that I use the term body in what follows. Similarly, the Hebrews had no idea of a soul that is immortal and capable of existence apart from the body. The Hebrew equivalent of soul, 'nepes', referred, once again, to the whole man but seen as the conscious subject of action and passion, as a self distinct from other selves. It is clear from this that body and soul each stood for the person as a whole, although seen from different points of view. The body (basar) is the outwardness of the soul, and soul is the inwardness of the body. It is this inwardness, this within that Jesus had in mind when he spoke of "the things which come out of a man (from within him, from his heart) that defile him" (Mk. 7:15; 20-23). Closely related to the concept of the soul (nepes) is that of 'ruah', spirit, which is the principle of life, courage, and activity, viewed not as a permanent attribute of man but as given by God, to be taken back when he wills. It is the power of God become the power of man in the measure in which the latter is open to the call of the Divine. Spirit as power is contrasted with flesh as powerlessness.

Furthermore, the Hebrews did not contrast, as we do, the whole of the body with its parts. In their view even parts of the body like heart, loins, and kidney could represent the whole man; this shows they had a profound sense for totality which we, sadly, have lost. In another respect too their mode of thinking differed from ours. We tend to consider the body as the basis for our existence as individuals, distinct and separate from other bodies, whether animate or inanimate. This is all the more true of capitalist society in which the body is reduced to an item of private property, into an instrument of competition and aggression. In contrast, the Hebrews saw in the body the principle of solidarity of all men in the one family of man. The body is also one with the earth and with all the living things in it.

It is in the light of this Hebrew conception of the body - which, incidentally, reflects more faithfully the reality of man than current notions in the matter - that we should understand Jesus' social practice aimed at the humanization of the body.

Body in Alienation
The alienation of the body from which Jesus sought to liberate man has many dimensions, depending on whether we consider the body in itself or in relation to the world of things, to other men, and to God.

The most obvious form of bodily alienation is illness involving loss of physical wholeness. The Gospels provide many instances of Jesus coming face to face with diseases of various kinds: possession, leprosy, fever, paralysis, hemorrhage, blindness, dumbness, lameness, epilepsy, dropsy, deformation and many others. All these maladies carried with them the diminution, if not the loss, of the capacity for acting upon, and reacting to, the world around, whether it be through seeing, hearing, touching, tasting, or working. Besides, they deprived the body of its beauty of form, and rhythm. Finely attuned as he was to the beautiful - to the lilies of the field, the birds of the air, and the innocence of children - Jesus could not but have perceived the ugliness brought by illness.

The body becomes alienated also when it is denied communion with the world of things. How can the body be truly human when the feet have nowhere to tread on, when the eyes are denied the vision of the beautiful and the noble, when the ears remain closed to the world of music and laughter, in short, when the senses have no access to the wealth and measure of things around! Where there is rupture of the bond that unites the body with the earth and its fruits, whether, in consequence of illness or of social conditions of exploitation, the body withers away and finally succumbs to premature death. This was the case of the innumerable sick that were brought to Jesus as also of the poorer classes in Palestine. No better is the condition of the poor and the sick in our own country. The splendour and glory of the human body will be revealed only in a society in which man will have mastered the forces of death and aggression.

To be fully human, to unfold all the wealth of its meaning, the body needs to draw nourishment from its vital milieu, which is other bodies: the presence, look, touch, and odour of other people. We know too well how a look of love can set aglow a face emaciated by illness or grief, how it penetrates into the marrow of another's bones healing him from within. And how, on the other hand, a hostile look can tear one to pieces and bring ruin to the health of mind and body. And it is the human, humanizing milieu of other bodies, which the sick who approached Jesus had been deprived of. Their very presence was a curse in a society that believed illness to be the result of sin and the work of demons. Particularly to be avoided was any physical contact with lepers. Besides, the prevalent notions regarding ritual purity had condemned many to the position of social outcasts like publicans, shepherds, barbers, tailors, and tanners. So too, many of the then existing sexual norms, customs, and taboos functioned as instruments in the hands of man for the domination of women and erected so many invisible walls between human bodies. What God had put together, man indeed had set asunder. Besides, the desire for one's neighbour's wife, for his house, his slave, his cattle, and whatever else belonged to him necessarily begot aggression destroying his body.

At a still deeper level, the body can become estranged from God, which in the Bible is expressed in terms of the conflict between the flesh and the spirit. The spirit here is understood, as explained earlier, as the power of God communicated to man. Man himself may be called spirit in the measure in which he responds positively to the challenge of God revealed in the concrete situations of life. The body as fragile, corruptible flesh can swerve man from his commitment to the unconditional demands of God and make him fall from authentic existence. That is why Jesus warned that if any member of the body - hands, eyes, or feet - causes a person to sin, it is better for him to cut it off rather than go to hell with that member intact (Mk. 9:43-48). This injunction contains a profound paradox: The loss of physical wholeness can co-exist with, and is even conducive to, human wholeness provided such loss is incurred for the sake of the reign of God. Bodily functions have meaning only inasmuch as they are drawn into the orbit of man's dialogue with God. History has written down this truth in letters of blood, in the blood of all prophets, protesters, and rebels, who courted imprisonment, torture, and even death for the sake of a future without injustice and exploitation. The same truth has found its supreme verification in the destiny of Jesus himself. He too experienced the conflict between the weakness of the flesh and the demands of the spirit in the very centre of his being. The words, "The spirit indeed is willing, but the flesh is weak", point as much to the situation of the disciples as to his own.

(Mk. 14:38) He, however, came out of the struggle victorious, as one who chose to enter life maimed and broken rather than - in the language of myth - go to hell with all the members of the body intact.

If the body can occasion man's estrangement from God, so can estrangement from God rob the body and the senses of their authentic function. We find a reference to this in what Jesus told the disciples who failed to understand the deeper significance of the miraculous feeding of the multitude in the desert.

> "Why do you discuss the fact that you have no bread? Do you not perceive or understand? Are your hearts hardened? Having eyes do you not see, and having ears do you not hear?" (Mk. 8:17-18)

Here the hardening of the heart is presented as the cause of the eye not seeing and the ear not hearing. To understand the meaning of the text, two things must be borne in mind. First, in the Bible the heart is almost a synonym for the soul (nepes), the within of man. The heart becomes hardened when it, seduced by the prevalent ideology, ceases to be open to the Spirit of God that confronts man with demands, judgement, and promises. Second, the Bible does not recognize any dichotomy between senses and understanding, just as it does not presuppose any opposition between body and soul. Unless clouded by other factors, the senses perceive not only the surface of things and events but also their meaning. In the case of the disciples, their hearts (souls) were so hardened (by the ideology of the Zealots?) that having ears they did not hear, having eyes they did not see. This shows that the darkness of the soul can overflow into the body and the senses. Similarly, the evil lodged in the heart finds expression in the deeds of the body.

> "What comes out of man is what defiles a man. For from within, out of the man, come fornication, theft, murder, adultery..." (Mk. 7:20-22).

The Humanization of the Body

Let us now see how Jesus responded in word and deed to the problem of alienation of the body. To do justice to this theme, it is necessary to carefully analyze the entire message and work of Jesus, which is not possible here. We shall, therefore, confine ourselves to a consideration of Jesus' work of healing as recorded in the Gospel according to Mark.

The visible result of the healings was the restoration of wholeness to the sick, who thereby recovered also the capacity to relate themselves to the world of things. The leper recovered his sense of touch; the paralytic immediately took up the pallet and went out before them all; the man with the withered hand was able to stretch out his hand and thus was rendered capable of working; Jairus' daughter was able to eat; the dumb man had his ears opened and his tongue released so that he could speak clearly; the blind man of Bethsaida began to see everything well. In all these instances. what is brought about is not merely the wholeness of the body but the wholeness of man's relationship with the world. It is also to be noted that the Greek verb employed to denote the act of healing has also the meaning to save, which goes to show that for Jesus salvation is achieved in the body in its relatedness to the environment.

The work of healing had for its effect also the reintegration of the body of the sick with the bodies of other persons. Rid of fever, Peter's mother-in-law could serve her guests; the demoniac of Gerasenes who lived in tombs outside the pale of human society could now go home to his friends; the paralytic could return to his people and be a working member of the family. The healed were also freed of the odium of being under the sway of demonic powers and could henceforth conduct themselves as equal among equals in the company of men, like the leper who from being untouchable became touchable and approachable. In all these instances liberation from the powers of death released the powers of life, particularly, of life together.

The reintegration of the body and its integration with the community is achieved within the framework of man's reconciliation with God. This comes out clearly in the words,

"Your faith has made you well". (Mk. 5:34)

What we have here is a circumlocution aimed at avoiding the mention of the name of God. The meaning intended is: God has responded to your faith and made you well. The agent of healing is the power of God which revealed itself through the body (touch, gesture, words, looks) of Jesus and communicated itself to the body of the sick. Significantly, Jesus himself does not claim to be the agent of healing. He does not say: I have healed you. He is no more than that privileged point where the Divine erupts and radiates to renew the within and the without of man. Does this mean that all that was expected of man was to remain passive? No. The faith attributed to the sick is more than a passive acceptance of and surrender to the healing power of God. It is also action, striving, to come within the orbit of His creative, renewing activity. Did not Jesus himself recognize as faith the effort of the paralytic and his friends to gain access to him and of the woman with the flow of blood who defied the crowd and the censuring disciples so that she might but touch the hem of his garment? Faith, therefore, is also praxis, struggle, which is at once a response to the power of God and a condition for being drawn into the sphere of its creative action. Once the power of God has taken hold of the heart of man, it overflows into his body conferring on it wholeness, unity, and harmony. In this sense Jesus' work of healing is at the same time the reconciliation of man with God and the resolution of the conflict between the flesh and the spirit.

Thanks to the healing touch of Jesus, the sick and the infirm regained the power to commune with nature, with men, and with God. Such communion is in fact the measure of one's humanity. That is why I have characterized the practice of Jesus as one of humanization.

(Anawim No. 13; *Jesus Today*, Chap. 7; *Jesus and Society*, Chap. 6)

13

Salvation as Wholeness

Jesus' response to the call of the reign of God took the form of commitment to the freedom of man. The shackles he set out to break were many and varied. First there was man's subjection to the blind forces of nature, to illness, decay, death, cyclone, floods, drought, pestilence, and plague. There were also other forms of bondage that owed their origin to man's lust for pleasure, profit, and power, such as economic exploitation and political domination. In this chapter I shall deal with Jesus' response to the problem of illness, as illustrated in the healing of the leper, by commenting on the text as it runs:

"Once he was approached by a leper, who knelt before him begging his help. 'If only you will', said the man, 'you can cleanse me.' In warm indignation Jesus stretched out his hand, touched him, and said, "Indeed I will; be clean again." Leprosy left him immediately, and he was clean. Then he dismissed him with this stern warning, "Be sure you say nothing to anybody. Go and show yourself to the priest, and make the offering laid down by Moses for your cleansing; that will certify the cure." But the man went out and made the whole story public; he spread it far and wide, until Jesus could no longer show himself in any town, but stayed outside in the open country (Mk. 1:40-45).

He was approached by a leper

The very fact that the leper approached Jesus is itself significant. By law he was excluded from the community of men. Thus Leviticus:

> "One who suffers from a malignant skin disease shall wear his clothes torn, leave his hair disheveled, conceal his upper lip, and cry, 'unclean, unclean.' So long as the sore persists, he shall be considered ritually unclean. The man is unclean: he shall live apart and must stay outside the settlement" (13:45-46).

In approaching Jesus, therefore, the leper was doing nothing less than defying the existing traditions and rules of conduct. His was not a mere repetitive gesture but a subversive one. This means that his spirit was free, though his body was still a captive of disease and death. His defiance of social taboos was in itself faith in action. Without such faith, not even Jesus could have done anything for him. However, probably it was the very presence of Jesus, something in his bearing, in his manner of speaking and acting that gave him the courage to flout the accepted canons of society.

If only you will, you can cleanse me

These words tell us how the leper understood himself as well as Jesus. First about his self-understanding. It is noteworthy that he did not ask to be healed but to be cleansed. What weighed on him was not so much the physical fact of his illness but the condition of his being socially and ritually unclean. He was an outcast, deemed unworthy of the company of his kind. Nor could he take part in worship, as though he was also unwanted and unloved by his Maker.

The leper's plea also shows that he took Jesus for one endowed with divine power capable of rendering him whole and clean. He knew that the Law could do nothing for him. It could only protect the community from him. Nor were the rabbis any help; for in their view the cure of a leper was as difficult as the raising of the dead. Contrasted with them, the young prophet from Galilee radiated power, and the leper surrendered himself to that power. Liberation comes only to those who stretch their hands to grasp the Divine that reveals itself in the creative words and deeds of their fellowmen.

Jesus stretched out his hand and touched him
This simple gesture gives us an insight into the soul of Jesus. He knew well enough that in touching a leper he would be defiling himself in the eyes of the people. Still if he touched him it was because he did not subscribe to the notion embodied in the Law itself that purity or impurity is a quality that inhered in things or persons. In his view it was the heart of man that rendered things pure or impure. His gesture, then, was subversive of the status quo of the ideology and practice of his community. Thus the rebel in the leper met the rebel in Jesus. (Is it not when the revolt of the many fuses into one that we have a revolution?) There is also another dimension to the gesture, namely, that of Jesus' compassion (in the sense of suffering with) for the unfortunate man. Through it the humanity of the one communed with the humanity of the other, the stronger giving life to the weaker. For man lives not by bread alone but also by every gesture made, every word uttered, by his fellowmen. When the fellowman in question is one grounded and rooted in God, his touch, his word, quickens life and confers wholeness. Such indeed was Jesus. "I will, be clean", he told the leper, and "leprosy left him immediately and he was clean."

Then he dismissed him
The Greek word (ekseballen) translated 'dismissed' is the same word used elsewhere in the gospels in connection with the driving out of demons. We are also told that the dismissal is accompanied with a stern warning, a weak rendering of the original Greek, which meant to be angry, to express violent displeasure, to groan, or even to growl at. Similarly, we read that it was "in warm indignation" that Jesus stretched out his hand and touched the leper. How could such an expression of anger and indignation be reconciled with the tenderness and human warmth that marked his response to the leper? Of the many solutions offered, the most satisfactory seems to be that Jesus' anger was directed

towards the demon of leprosy, whereas for the unfortunate victim himself he had nothing but the utmost tenderness. The narrative as it stands in Mark is probably a conflation of two accounts, one focusing on the sick man, the other on the demon that had taken hold of him. This would explain why in the text Jesus' strong reaction came to be applied to the leper rather than to the demon.

The reference to the anger of Jesus shows that he shared the belief of his contemporaries that demons were responsible for illness and other natural calamities. In this respect, as in many others, he was very much a product of his age. In an age in which science and technology had not developed, it was but natural that people attributed to personal, supernatural powers that which they could neither understand nor control. To such mythical consciousness must be traced Jesus' conception of his role as one sent to overthrow the rule of Satan.

Be sure you say nothing to anybody

Anything that an individual does is interpreted by the community following its dominant ideology. This creates no problem so long as the deed in question is repetitive and in keeping with the prevalent social expectations. But where the deed is non-repetitive, subversive, popular interpretation may go wrong. People may give it a meaning it does not have, or expect the doer fulfill a role that he does not want. Now, the Galileans, very much under the spell of Zealot aspirations, were like sheep without a shepherd, looking for a political Messiah who would help them throw the Romans out and restore the old kingdom of David. Any premature publicity given to the wonders Jesus did would have made them pin their political hopes on him. Such a role Jesus had once and for all opted against. Hence the injunction to secrecy aimed not at concealing the truth but at preventing its misinterpretation.

Go and show yourself to the priest

This second injunction seems to contradict the earlier one to secrecy, a discrepancy which too may be attributed to the conflate character of the account. Be that as it may, the demand made on the leper to show himself to the priest throws light on an essential dimension of the liberating praxis of Jesus. It should not be interpreted as an instance of Jesus' concern for the Law. Rather, what was at stake was his concern for man. Leprosy had brought on its victim segregation from the community. For him to be welcomed back into the community it was necessary to be legally recognized as clean, which only the priests could do. True, in the new age, Jesus looked forward to, there will be no basis for the distinction between the clean and the unclean. But, in the meanwhile, the social outcast must be restored to the position of an equal among equals. Physically whole, he must also regain social wholeness. What is in evidence here is once again the compassion of Jesus.

(*Jesus Today*, Chap. 8; *Jesus and Society*, Chap. 7)

14

Man, Woman and the Human

The average person can be understood from his social background. His behaviour, reactions, and reflexes conform to the pattern set by society. This, however, is not entirely true of Jesus of Nazareth. For he was by no means an average person. He was essentially an outsider to the society in which he lived, a dissenter who chose to die dissenting. A clear instance of his radical dissent is his attitude towards women.

Jesus was born into what was a man's world. The patriarchal system that prevailed was marked by an extreme hostility to women.[1] The 'pure' and the 'self-righteous' males used to offer thanks to the Almighty for, among other things, not having created them women. And they had every reason to do so, considering the power and privileges they enjoyed. The birth of a female was a cause of sadness to parents. "Woe to female children", the saying went. In every way, a woman was subjected to man. She was expected to wash his feet, even when she had slaves under her. An inferior sort of human being she was deemed to be. Her proneness to evil was taken for granted. "The voice of a woman is something lewd." Were she to attend a party, she would, it was believed, start seducing men by the third cup of wine, and, by the fourth, offer herself to any ass that might pass by. The ass, however, remains above reproach. Women were considered a constant source of defilement. Much more so were sexual relations with her, despite Jahweh's blessing that Israel would multiply and be numberless like the sands of the sea and the stars of the heavens.

Morally too, women were devalued. They were thought to be gluttonous, lazy, jealous, undependable, given to lying, and eavesdropping. In official proceedings, their witness was void and null. Men were advised to avoid them on the streets and to refrain from speaking to them. They were not to be greeted by anyone, except by their own husbands. Not even with one's daughter might a man stay overnight in a lodge. Women were considered enchantresses by nature, a permanent invitation to sin and debauchery. They were told to look upon their frivolity and audacity as their greatest enemies.

No better was their position in religious matters in which they were equated with slaves and children. All of them have this in common that they have to be so engrossed in service of their earthly masters as to have no time left to serve their heavenly master, so it was argued. Nobody, therefore, considered it his duty to instruct his daughters in religion. Worse still, according to the more fanatical among the teachers of the Law, "it were better for the Tora to be burned than to fall into the hands of women."

Against this state of affairs, Jesus protested in word and deed. Among his contemporaries, he was the first to have seen that man and woman are equal partners in the search for fuller humanity. His new vision was born of both remembrance and hope: remembrance of the divine act of creation 'in the beginning' and hope in the reign of God to come. Asked to comment on the Mosaic law of divorce, he appeals to the first account of creation in the Book of Genesis which reads:

> "God created man in His own image; in the image of God he created him: male and female he created them" (1:27-28).

Here man and woman are said to originate in one single creative act. Further, it is implied that the image of God resides neither in man nor in woman taken in isolation but in man and woman as attuned to and completing each other. Conjointly they are called to be fruitful and to increase, to fill the earth, and subdue it. They are equal without ceasing to be different and that both in flesh and spirit: in flesh in so far as they complete each other as sexual persons; in spirit in so far as they are called, each in his/her own way, to be hearers and doers of the words divine. This equality-in-difference, inscribed in the primordial act of creation, will blossom into fullness only with God's re-creative act of the end-time when he will usher in the new heaven and the new earth and reconstitute the family of man. Between that future hoped for and the past remembered, lies the fateful present, the here and now. It is in the present that human beings have to work out their destiny. Here too, man and woman stand on equal footing. This is the burden of the saying,

> "Whoever does the will of God is my brother, my sister, my mother"
> (Mk. 3:35).

Not gender but love is the measure of a person's worth. And where loving is concerned, the male has no advantage over the female. Woman, no less than man, has the power to shape her future in response to the call of God. (Significantly, Jesus ignores the second account of creation in Genesis 2:5-25, where the stress is on the inferiority of woman as one made out of man's rib to be an antidote to his loneliness and as named by him. For the Hebrews, to name something is to have control over it.)

What Jesus taught he practiced. His work of preaching and healing was directed to both sexes: Women too came to listen to his saving word. Power went out of him to heal men and women alike (Mk. 1:31; 5:25ff.). Unlike his contemporaries, he did not treat what women said or did as of little consequence. We find him arguing with a gentile woman and even complimenting her on her clever retort:

> "For this saying, you may go home content" (Mk. 7:29).

He reacted sharply whenever the disciples gave vent to their male snobbery. Indignant he was when they rebuked the women who brought children for him to touch (Mk. 10:13). Similarly when they reproached the woman for anointing his head with costly ointment instead of selling it and giving the money to the poor (Mk. 14:3-9). This last incident has deeper implications. His words, "She has done a beautiful thing to me", shows he saw in the extravagance of the woman a truer sense of values than in the parsimony of the male. For which is greater, to attend to the immediate needs of the poor or to welcome the prophet who came to announce the once for all routing of the rulers and the rich? Partial to the oppressed, Jesus was trenchant in his criticism of the lawyers who ate up the property of widows (Mk. 12:40), that is, who demanded from widows such exorbitant charges for the legal protection rendered that these were constrained to cede to the former whatever property they had.

Revealing in this context is his attitude to the woman taken in adultery, as recorded in the Gospel according to John (8:1-11). To her accusers, he said, "Whoever among you has not sinned, let him cast the first stone". The woman had sinned, true enough. She was "caught in the act". But why was not also the man, the necessary accomplice in the act, brought before Jesus? Because society used a double standard when it came to punishing offenses. It was severe on women and lenient to men. This itself was a sin against womanhood in general. Besides, who among the accusers could claim he had never coveted his neighbor's wife? The sequel showed that none could. For they quietly left the scene one by one, beginning with the elders. Jesus thus tore the mask off the face of his self-righteous adversaries and exposed them for what they were: whited sepulchres. More, he demolished at one stroke the current system of punishment rooted in the arrogance of men who arrogate to themselves the right to sit in judgement over others, a right that should belong to God alone, the Sinless, the Holy. With that system, Jesus would have nothing to do. Hence his parting words, "Nor do I condemn thee. Go in peace and sin no more." True, the story of the woman taken in adultery found its way into the New Testament very late and that too only in the Gospel according to John. But this is no reason to doubt its authenticity. The message it seeks to convey dovetails with the teachings of Jesus. Besides, the story could not have originated in contemporary Judaism with its male-centered sexual morality. Nor could it have come from the early Christian community, which had already assumed the power to bind and to lose, to save or to damn. Hence it must have a historical nucleus going back to the life of Jesus.

The radicalism of Jesus comes into fuller relief in the supreme freedom with which he flouted the customary taboos governing the relation between sexes, taboos which served to confine womenfolk within the four walls of their homes. He related to women spontaneously, uninhibited by the fear of what people might say. He found nothing wrong in conversing, even on matters regarding her sex life, with the Samaritan woman who had come to fetch water. His conduct on the occasion astonished even the disciples, accustomed though they were to the deviant behaviour of their master (Jn 4:8-30). He went further, and associated women in the carrying out of his mission. Luke speaks of the women who had accompanied him from Galilee (23:55) and provided for him out of their means (8:1-3). So also Mark:

> "Several women were also present, watching from a distance. Among them were Mary of Magdala, Mary the mother of James the younger and of Joseph, and Salome, who had all followed him and waited on him when he was in Galilee, and several others had come up to Jerusalem with him" (15:40-41).

Clearly then, the disciples formed a mixed group. This is further borne out by the witness of the two disciples on the road to Emmaus who refer to the female followers of Jesus as of our company (Lk 24:22). The spectacle of a young man going around the towns and villages of Palestine accompanied by a coterie of ladies was not something that would have pleased the Jewish orthodoxy. All the more so since his relationship with women was not always chemically pure of all human warmth and sentiment. With some of them, he was emotionally involved, as with Martha and Mary. John tells us in so many words that he loved them (11:5).

Seen against the male-made society of his day, Jesus' words and deeds are nothing less than the proclamation of a new sexual humanism. Unfortunately, no sooner was that liberating message heard than it was all but stifled. The patriarchal bias reasserted itself with vengeance and produced a theology in keeping with it. The one New Testament writer who contributed most to this development was Paul. There is in his thinking an underlying sexual pessimism. In his view, "it is a good thing for a man to have nothing to do with women" (1 Cor 7:1), and marriage is but a concession to human frailty. Possibly, this attitude is the result of his belief in the imminence of the Kingdom. But this is no real excuse. For he goes on to develop a theology justifying the subordination of woman to man. In support of his injunction that women should veil their hair while at prayer, he argues:

> "A man does not need to cover his head, because man is the image of God and the mirror of his glory, whereas woman reflects the glory of man" (Ibid. 11:7).

This means woman is only the image of the image of God. To buttress his reasoning, Paul has recourse to Christology:

> "But I wish you to understand that, while every man has Christ for his head, woman's head is man" (Ibid. 11:3).

But did not Paul affirm the equality of man and woman when he wrote to the Galatians,

> "There is no such thing as Jew and Greek, slave and freeman, male and female; for you are all one person in Christ Jesus" (3:28)

Indeed he did. But what he had in mind was equality in Christ Jesus, which, far from excluding, presupposed inequality in society. That is why he could in the same breath proclaim the equality of slave and freeman and advise slaves to be obedient to their masters. This indeed is a far cry from Jesus whose concern was the equality of man and woman in real life.

The downgrading of woman received further impetus from the Fathers of the Church. Tertullian held woman responsible for mankind's fall from original grace. Satan knew that his sinister scheme would not succeed with Adam. So he approached Eve, who in right womanly fashion gleefully succumbed. Since it is a woman who brought misery upon humankind and made it necessary for Jesus to die on the Cross, Tertullian exhorted all women to wear sackcloth and ashes and do penance to the end of their days. For Jerome and Chrysostom, woman is the devil's entry-point, a source of danger and a curse for man. But the one Father of the Church who had the most disastrous influence on the subsequent development of the Christian ethos was Augustine of Hippo. His conversion to God was coupled with a neurotic aversion to woman and marriage. In reaction to his early debauchery, he came to view sexual intercourse as something beastly, contrary to the deeper purposes of the Almighty. In thus devaluing sex, he devalued womanhood itself, since woman was seen as the source and object of lust. All this shows that for a humane and humanizing conception of woman we must return not so much to tradition as to the message and praxis of Jesus.

(Anawim No. 30; *Jesus and Society*, Chap. 8)

15

Either God or Money

In chapter 12, Volume IV, I have commented on the story of the rich young man who failed to respond to the call of the Kingdom because he was not prepared to give up riches, power, and the God of the establishment. Commenting on his conduct, Jesus said,

> "How hard it will be for those who have riches to enter the Kingdom of God! It is easier for a camel to go through the eye of a needle than for a rich man to enter the Kingdom of God." (Mk. 10:23-25)

The radical incompatibility of 'entering the Kingdom' and 'possessing riches' comes out still more clearly in the saying reported in Mathew:

> "No one can serve two masters; for either he will hate the one and love the other, or he will be devoted to the one and despise the other, you cannot serve God and mammon." (Mt. 6:24)

The uncompromising either-or presented here so astonished the disciples that they asked, "Then who can be saved?" The saying has been a stumbling block to believers from the earliest days to our own. Not surprisingly, Mathew tones down the demand by making it conditional and thereby reducing it to a counsel of perfection addressed to the generous few. History has witnessed many such attempts to tame Jesus and make him acceptable to the exploiters and the oppressors of mankind. This makes it all the more necessary for us to recapture the original radicalism of his critique of mammon.

The derivation of the word 'mammon' is uncertain. It may mean either money or property in general. Since money can be converted into both means of production and means of consumption, it is an apt symbol to represent wealth as such. It can also be used to sum up the evils of private property. For, money is the universal equivalent of all commodities, and only private property can be exchanged as commodity. Hence, in what follows, I shall use money as a comprehensive term to signify all wealth privately owned. Now, why is it that Jesus rejects the pursuit of money as incompatible with membership in the New Humanity?

First, every accumulation of money is the fruit of aggression aimed at the appropriation of either individual or common property, entailing often much shedding of blood and use of brute force. Aggression is no less necessary to maintain the riches already amassed. For the private interest of one will invariably come into violent conflict with the private interest of others. Besides, where competition is the law, not to acquire more wealth is to lose what one already has; and one cannot acquire more without resorting to either personal or institutionalized violence. Violence, therefore, is endemic to the system of private property. And how can one committed to aggression in any form enter the Kingdom of God whose law is love and concern for one another?

Second, whoever seeks to accumulate money will eventually set it up as an end in itself. He will reduce every other value - whether it is art, culture, knowledge, friendship or sociality - to a mere means for the acquisition of wealth. The same attitude will govern also his relationship with others. The neighbour will be experienced by him either as a possible source of money or as a threat to his material possessions. Worse still, the seeker after wealth will sink in his own estimation. For it is not he who possesses money but money that possesses him. He becomes an attribute of his wealth, a property of his property. Thus capital owns the capitalist; land, the landlord. This reversal of means and ends will also colour one's attitude to God. God too, will be reduced to a means for the accumulation of wealth. It is thus that theologies which legitimize exploitation come into being. A case in point is the belief among the Jews that wealth is a sign of divine favour; and poverty, of divine wrath. Thanks to this belief, the rich could nurse the comfortable feeling that they were the favoured ones of God, and thus derive from religion private consolation for their public sins. A similar function is fulfilled by the notion still held by many that God is concerned only with the soul of man and not with his body, only with his inner core and not with the structures and institutions of society into which he is inserted. This means banishing God from the entire domain of social relations so that an open space is cleared up where the rich can, in good conscience, play their cruel game of exploiting the poor. There are other cruder ways of using God to further economic ends, such as attending religious services and contacts. Whatever be the device employed, every attempt to make use of God as a tool is a way of denying him.

Third, the God who exists to serve the interests of the rich is but a product of the mind. He owes his illusory existence to such priests, religious teachers, theologians and philosophers who provide ideological support to the affluent classes. As a product of labour - of mental labour in the present case - God easily becomes a commodity. It is this commoditized God whom I shall henceforth call the deity. He can, like any other commodity, be bought or sold against payment in money. Thus money, the universal equivalent of all commodities, becomes the equivalent of the deity as well. The rich can from now on buy the grace (favour) of the deity. They can accumulate religious merit by making donations to religious institutions and by having religious services held for the salvation of their souls. Not compelled to work to make a living, they have plenty of leisure to visit shrines and go on pilgrimages. They can indulge both in conspicuous consumption and in spiritual consumption. Thus the economically privileged become also the spiritually privileged. But all exchange is mutual. If money can be converted into grace, so can the latter into the former. Those who claim to be mediators of grace can issue passports to heaven and charge the recipients heavily for it. Consequently, higher the position one occupies in the religious hierarchy greater is his command over money and the world of commodities. All this at once presupposes and begets a form of false consciousness which consists in divinizing money and monetizing the deity. In other words, one develops a religious attitude to money and a monetary attitude to religion. This reciprocal assimilation and fusion of money and the deity finds material expression in the images of the latter wrought in precious metals, the earliest and the commonest form of money. It may also be discerned, at the level of social relations, in the marriage of convenience between the priest and the rich, between the business of religion and the religion of business.

Finally, money as a rule carries with it power, meaning the chances a person has to impose his options - his goals and means - on other people. This is verified in each production unit as well as at all levels of decision making. Those who own the means of production are in a position to determine the options of the working class as to what they should eat, how they should be clad and housed. For it is they who fix the wages and define the goals and conditions of production. Similarly, they usually succeed in controlling the structures of decision making from the lowest to the highest level. Now, whoever wields power in this sense has already parted company with the living God. For He is encountered primarily as a call to total freedom. So, too, the right response to that call is to set free the victims of oppression. The renunciation of power and commitment to integral freedom are, therefore, an essential prerequisite for encountering the true God.

Besides, power too denatures God into a tool for its own self-aggrandizement. To be secure and sure of itself, power needs to be reinforced by divine sanction. No wonder that the powerful seek the support of religious leaders and men of God. This is particularly true of all dictators who are unsure of their own future. The lust for absolute power is what gives birth to theologies legitimizing the domination of man by man, as borne out by the earlier belief in the divine right of kings. In consequence, the powerful are deified, while, on the other hand, the deity is kingified i.e. set-up as an absolute master who lords it over men. Power and the deity become like unto, and support, each other.

On the level of social classes this is attested to, by the collusion between political masters and religious leaders in oppressing the common man.

I have shown how money has power as its concomitant and how money and power remake God each in its own image. Where this happens, man falls into a threefold servitude: to money, power, and the deity. Their combined force is what holds together all systems of exploitation. If so, the seeker after the Kingdom has no other option but to commit himself to their liquidation.

(Anawim No. 18, *Jesus and Society*, Chap. 10)

16

The Temptations
of a Radical

Any person taken hold of by an ultimate concern has to translate the same into action. His faith must become power and deed. Which involves taking decisions regarding goals and means and the strategy of action. But decisions cannot be taken in a vacuum, without taking into account the concrete historical situation, the various social and political forces at work; for, adopting a line of action might require either aligning oneself with current thinking and practice or dissociating oneself from them. In the latter case, the experience can be truly anguishing, a true ordeal, and testing of the spirit.

Some such experience seems to underlie the so-called temptation of Jesus in the desert. On the banks of Jordan, he was taken hold of by the Spirit (power) of God. But the gift of the Spirit has always a social purpose. The inspirited one has to use it for the good of the people. What did the good of the people require? To most of his contemporaries, the answer was unambiguous. They wanted to throw out the hated Romans and restore the pristine glory of Israel as a kingdom. Their longings had found political expression in the movement of the Zealots. The young prophet from Nazareth must surely have known many from among the youth of Galilee who had already made their option in favour of Zealotism. Should he not join hands with them to fight Roman imperialism and, if need be, install himself as king over all Israel? Were not the masses like sheep without a shepherd to lead them to the greener pastures of economic and political freedom? This, indeed, was the core of the temptations in the desert. For we read:

> "Again, the devil took him to a very high mountain, and showed him all the kingdoms of the world and the glory of them; and he said to him: All these I will give you if you will fall down and worship me." (Mt. 4:8-9)

The project held up before Jesus was that of an Israel ruling over the gentile kingdoms of the world and of himself enthroned king over both. Jesus' reply to the tempter was forthright:

> "Begone, Satan! for it is written, You shall worship the Lord your God and him only shall you serve." (Mt. 4:10)

Jesus saw the service of God and the worship of Satan as mutually incompatible. But is that all there is to it? Were it so, it would mean that Jesus' objection was only to the condition laid down by the devil ('if you will fall down and worship me') and not to the demonic project itself of political messianism. But the words, "and him only shall you serve", imply equally the rejection of service to kings. For all kingship reduces people to the position of slaves, on the one hand, and brings about the demonization of the rulers, on the other. Significantly, the text itself suggests that Satan is in effective control of all the kingdoms of the earth. If so, in refusing to worship Satan, Jesus repudiated as well all forms of kingly rule. That this was his mind is clear from his subsequent teaching. For the Spirit he received was one that sets free the oppressed, pulls down prison walls, puts down the mighty from their thrones, and exalts those of low degree (Lk 4:18; 1:52). How could the same Spirit enthrone him as king that he might lord it over his subjects? What use freeing the people from Roman domination if in the end, they are to be subjected to another form of domination? Pursuing the path of power and glory would, therefore, amount to betraying his own true destiny.

> "For what does it profit a man, to gain the whole world and forfeit his life?" (Mk. 8:36)

Jesus thus made a definitive option in the desert against assuming the role of a political Messiah, and Satan departed from him, but, as Luke adds significantly, "until an opportune time." The temptation to political messianism was to dog him throughout his life. The next time Satan confronted him with the same temptation was at Caesarea Philippi when he asked his disciples what they thought him to be. Peter then replied, "You are the Messiah." (Mk. 8:29) He had judged correctly when he recognized in his master the Inspirited One. But, when the latter went on to say that in obedience to the Spirit he must proceed to Jerusalem to confront the religious and political powers that were, and meet with death at their hands, the disciple could not stomach it. He took Jesus by the arm and began to reprimand him, which elicited from the latter the stunning rebuke: "Away with you, Satan, you think as men think, not as God thinks." (Mk. 8:33)

The intense and almost violent emotion this reply betrays is clear proof that Peter was calling in question something which Jesus considered fundamental to his mission. The disciple could not reconcile himself with the prospect of his master meeting with an ignominious death. For he, along with the other disciples, had expected him to set himself up as king over the whole world after freeing the country from Roman imperialism. The Gospels present them as discussing among themselves as to who should occupy positions of importance in the new political dispensation they hoped he would inaugurate (Mk. 10:38; 9:34). This shows they were entertaining the thoughts of men i.e. the nationalist ideology of domination fostered by the Zealots and not the thoughts of God, not the divine purpose in history. In other words, what they held up before Jesus was the same project Satan had confronted him within the desert. That Jesus understood it, as such, may be surmised from the way he addressed Peter, "Away with you, Satan." Thus, at Caesarea Philippi, he once again repudiated political messianism and reaffirmed his commitment to being the servant of Jahweh. He remained true to his original option even against mounting pressure from the people. In the Gospel according to John, we read that, "when the people saw the sign Jesus had performed, the word went round: Surely this must be the prophet that was to come into the world. Jesus, aware that they meant to come and seize him to proclaim him king, withdrew again to the hills by himself." (Jn. 6:14-15)

But the disciples' sympathy lay with the masses as may be inferred from the remark in the Gospel according to Mark that on that occasion Jesus had to compel the former to leave the place.

Yet on another occasion, did the same temptation assail him. And that was in the Mount of Olives, where he retired to pray on the eve of his death. There he began to be greatly distressed and troubled and told his disciples, "My soul is very sorrowful even to death." These words have an emotional content so different from that which characterized his response to the earlier temptations. There his attitude was marked by anger and indignation; here it is one of distress, anguish, and helplessness. There he spoke from a position of strength as one securely anchored in the Will of God; here he speaks from a position of weakness, fragility, and vulnerability. Why this difference? The answer is contained in his subsequent prayer,

> "Abba, Father, all things are possible to thee; remove this cup from me;
> yet not what I will, but what thou wilt."(Mk. 14:36)

On the former occasions, the conflict was between him and Satan/ disciples, himself standing firmly on the side of God. Now it is between him and God, between what he willed and what God willed. And what was it that he willed? That the cup - the prospect of death on the cross - might be removed from him. Does this mean that what made him sweat blood was just the fear of physical torture and death? There is, however, no mention of fear in any of the Gospel accounts. Besides, fear arises in the presence of an unavoidable danger. Here death could have been avoided. Jesus had only to join the Zealots who had come down from Galilee and were camping in the city. If even at that late hour, he had offered to be their leader and king, they would have defended him from the authorities. But that would have meant going back on his original option against political messianism and thereby betraying the call from God. Hence the sadness, the distress, the shame, and the confusion that gripped his soul. The cup he prayed to be removed from him was, therefore, nothing but the 'sadness unto death' resulting from the rupture of his soul into two, one part seeking his own will, the other that of God. This interpretation looks all the more plausible when we consider the structural similarity between Jesus' prayer to the Father and his reply to Peter. The opposition between what I will and what thou wilt seems to convey the same idea as that between as men think and as God thinks. In the garden, then, Jesus was tempted to think the thoughts of men i.e. to align himself with the Zealots and thus save himself from death.

Jesus came out of the ordeal strengthened in Spirit, with his will in tune with that of God. But what of the disciples? There was a real danger that they might go the Zealot way. For they had never fully understood or accepted the mission of their master as the servant of Jahweh. Therefore the warning: "Watch and pray that you may not enter into temptation; the spirit indeed is willing, but the flesh is weak."

A man responsive to the spirit of God is strong, endowed with force to renew the face of the earth, whereas, left to himself, he is fragile, weak, and vulnerable, and has to resort to arms and armies to achieve his goals. The disciples must, therefore, pray that they may follow not the messianism of the flesh represented by the Zealots, but the messianism of the Spirit. Like the In-spirited One, they too must overcome the temptation to take up arms to defend either themselves or their master. We know from the sequel that despite this last appeal, when the decisive moment of his arrest came, one of the disciples drew his sword and struck the slave of the high priest.

Why did Jesus refuse to join hands with the Zealots? Because neither their goal nor their strategy was conducive to genuine freedom. They wanted to restore the old theocratic state, and were for that reason reformists, whereas Jesus looked forward to the abolition of the state itself. The former nursed the nationalist hope of Israel ruling over the rest of the world; the latter, on the contrary, was universalist in his vision in so far as the new humanity he envisaged was to be based on the equality of all. The former hoped to achieve their goal through the violence of hate; the latter saw in the violence of love the force that would change the world.

Unfortunately, the history of Christianity since Constantine has been one of the betrayals of the consistent stand Jesus took against political messianism. In course of time, the Cross entered into an unholy alliance with the Sword. The religious authority sought to control political power. Church and State came to reinforce each other. In modern times, however, with the secularization of society, Christianity has been forced to give up the pursuit of state power. But, in most countries, the Christian Establishment continues to stand solidly behind the powers that be, even where they blatantly violate basic human rights and pursue dictatorial policies. Besides, as though to compensate for the loss of political power, it has erected its own internal structures of power, all the more enslaving for being buttressed with religious sanctions. Such being the case, it is not possible to be a true disciple of Jesus without repudiating the current political practice of the official Churches.

This applies to the Indian situation as well. Here the disciple has also to effect a rupture with the theory and practice of the political parties all of which have this in common that their main concern is the capture of power. Power is sought not only as a means to wealth but also as an end itself. The privileged classes, who for centuries used the caste system to enslave the minds and hearts of the ignorant masses, are employing political structures and processes - the panchayat, the assembly, the parliament, the bureaucracy, and the elections - to perpetuate their domination. A Christian has, therefore, no other option but to part company with the present brood of politicians. Nor can he, without reservation, identify himself with the masses. For these have, on the whole, internalized the values of the dominant castes and classes. Their felt-need may be one thing; their real need quite another. Under these circumstances, a certain political self-margination becomes morally imperative.

But would this not amount to mere negativism and political escapism? Not in the least. The no to the prevalent politics of power must have for its positive side commitment to a new style of political involvement that has for its aim, not the capture but the liquidation of all structures of domination. The goal should be the creation of a new social order in which people will themselves take decisions and implement them without these functions becoming vested in structures independent of, and opposed to them. But to embark on this venture in opposition to the Christian Establishment and to the policies of the political parties and without adequate support from the masses is to invite repression from the State. Hence the insecurity and vulnerability of radicals, Christians or not. Hence also the ever present temptation to give up the politics of liberation to follow the politics of domination, the temptation to save one's life (flesh) at the cost of losing one's true life (spirit).

The temptations of Jesus, therefore, are a warning to his disciples and to all social activists who seek to usher in a society of freedom to break with all politics of power, violence, and expediency and to act as catalysts for a new politics of service, moral integrity, non-violence, and resolute opposition to all structures of oppression.

("The Ordeal and the Option", Anawim No. 22, *Jesus and Society*, Ch. 11)

17

The Abolition of Power

To grasp the full significance of Jesus' criticism and repudiation of power, it is necessary to keep in mind the relations of power that obtained in his time. For, like the prophets of Old Testament, he too read the purposes of God from the horizon of history. And the juncture of history which saw him in action was one of national humiliation, with the Romans holding sway over the whole of Palestine. Judea was directly under imperial rule, while in the north, king Herod was but a puppet in the hands of Rome. What is more, people had to reckon with the evils of a social system which favoured the domination of many by the few.

The Relations of Power

The structures of domination in Jesus' day formed a more or less closely-knit system. The lowest centre of authority was the head of the family, whose word was law. Each village was governed by a council of elders, which, however, met only when communal problems had to be settled. The council consisted of the heads of important families as well as of a priest entrusted with the discernment of the pure and the impure. Similar councils functioned also in towns, but with this difference that the elders came from the lay nobility, themselves large property owners. In these councils sat also the scribes, specialists in matters concerning the observance of civil and religious law. Of all such councils, the most important was the council at Jerusalem called the Sanhedrin, the supreme court of justice. In the first century of our era, it was the priestly class of the Sadducees that controlled the affairs of the Sanhedrin, though among its seventy-two members there were also scribes and representatives of the lay nobility. The Sanhedrin was the seat not only of religious authority but also of political power. It was not always in session but met only as and when the situation demanded it. The permanent seat of political power was the body of chief priests presided over by the high-priest, who in the time of Jesus was appointed by the Romans. However, the Jewish state enjoyed a certain autonomy in matters of internal government. Finally, dominating all the lower centres of power, there was Roman imperialism, which kept the people and the local rulers under control with the help of its army.

As far as the internal government was concerned, power was in the hands of the rich landowners and the priestly aristocracy who made the state apparatus serve their own ends. But what the people hated most was the loss of national freedom and the presence of foreign rule on the soil over which none but Jahweh was to rule. Political power also imposed heavy economic burdens on the common man. He had to pay twenty-five percent of his annual produce by way of taxes to Rome. He was subjected to extortion by the tax-collectors, whom the Romans chose from among the wealthier classes. Also, twenty-three percent of all produce was to be paid to the temple, not to mention a third levy supposedly meant to help the poor. Such were the relations of power when the young prophet from Nazareth appeared on the scene. How did he react to them?

A Sign of Contradiction

We know little of his early youth. Admittedly, the infancy narratives in Mathew and Luke are more like legends than of history. However, they do tell us what the early community of believers thought of him. The hymn of thanksgiving which tradition puts in the mouth of Mary, his mother, shows that they associated him with the subversive presence of God in history.

> "He (the Lord) has scattered the proud in the imagination of their hearts,
> he has put down the mighty from their thrones, and exalted those of low
> degree; he has filled the hungry with good things, and the rich he has
> sent empty away."(Lk 1:51-53)

Jesus is here presented as one sent to overthrow the existing relations of wealth and power, to be the herald of a social and political revolution. The same expectation is voiced by Simeon on seeing the child Jesus,

> "Behold, this child is set for the fall and rising of many in Israel, and for
> a sign that is spoken against." (Lk. 2:34)

It is the destiny of a prophet to be spoken against, to be a sign of contradiction. Why? Because his mission is to contradict (negate) the prevalent state of affairs. As a result, he will himself be contradicted by the accredited guardians of the status quo. In this struggle of opposites, the seats of power will fall to the ground, and those who were till then made to grovel and slave will rise to a new humanity. In painting such a picture the early disciples were only being true to the self-understanding of Jesus himself, as is clear from the claim he made at his first appearance in Nazareth that he had been equipped with the Spirit of God and sent to proclaim release to captives and to set at liberty those who are oppressed (Lk 4: 18-19). How could one set the captives free without overthrowing the rulers who maintain armies and prisons? If so, we cannot escape the conclusion that Jesus viewed liberation from political power as an integral part of his total mission. Besides, this interpretation is the only one that coheres with the basic tenor and thrust of his teaching as a whole.

The First Will Be The Last

Like the prophets before him, Jesus too gave his people a future and a hope. The God, whose coming he announced, was not a neutral God, who administers his blessings evenly to the oppressor and the oppressed but one who is partial to the exploited and powerless - an idea which is central to the Hebrew religion (Is 2:1-10; Jb 5:8-27; 12:13-25; 36:6ff; Ps 107:33-41; 113:7-9; 147:6; Sir 10:14). It is against this background that we must interpret the saying,

"But many that are first will be last, and the last first" (Mk. 10:31).

God will come to vindicate the last, the dominated classes, by toppling those who are first in the hierarchy of power. This should not, however, be taken to mean that there will be only a mere reversal of social positions, the ruled of today becoming the rulers of tomorrow. That would not be doing away with the dichotomy between the rulers and the ruled. The future will by no means be a mere reproduction of the class society of the past. For, the real interest of the last consists not in themselves becoming rulers but in eliminating all conditions of domination. Were they themselves to seek to capture positions of power, God will have no part with them. This means that being first or last in the new age will be determined on the basis, not of power, but love and concern for all. The last of today will then be the first, first in respect of love as being-for-others. Contrasted with them, the first of today, who continue to cling to the lust for power and the itch for domination, will then represent man's fall from authentic existence, and in that sense will be deemed the last. That is why Jesus told his disciples,

> "For everyone who exalts himself will be humbled, and he who humbles himself will be exalted" (Lk 14:11)

Beyond Mastery and Slavery

In this context, of crucial significance is the saying of Jesus:

> "You know that those who are supposed to rule over the Gentiles, lord it over them, and their great men exercise authority over them. But it shall not be so among you, but whoever would be great among you must be your servant, and whoever would be first among you must be the slave of all. For the Son of man also came not to be served but to serve, and to give his life as a ransom for many."(Mk. 10: 42-44)

According to Mark, the life-situation which elicited this saying was the quest of the sons of Zebedee that they are allowed to sit one on his right and one on his left when he came in glory. The request was probably based on their hope that their master would soon lead a successful revolt against the Romans and establish himself king over all Israel and the whole world, a hope which the latter had repudiated more than once, both in word and deed. Quite different was the hope which Jesus himself nursed. What he envisioned was a future when there will be neither rulers nor ruled but only sons of God and, therefore, brothers to one another (Mt. 5:9).

Seen against this hope, the saying is nothing less than a total repudiation of power understood as the possibility some have to impose their options, ends, and means on others. Jesus will have nothing to do with an order of things in which the rulers lord it over their subjects and make them feel the weight of their authority. Hence his call should not be interpreted away as mere advice to use power as a means to service or service as a means to power but to radically and unconditionally renounce all exercise of power. Those who aspire to be great (that is, to have slaves under them) must retrace their steps and seek to be slaves to others. Those who aspire to be first in wealth, influence and prestige, must seek a social order in which all are slaves to one another, none is master over others. Or rather, each man will be master and slave, because he recognizes every member of the community as an absolute value and not a mere means to an end; master, because he, in turn, is recognized by all as an absolute future community of service is the dialectical supersession of mastery and slavery, a supersession which preserves and realizes on a higher level the truth of both, namely *being-for-oneself* (mastery) and *being-for-others* (slavery).

Supersession of the Law

Jesus too takes up the prophetic message (Je 31:33-34; Ezk 36:24-28) that the law as a form of mediation between man and God will have to be left behind. In his view, the Sabbath was made for man, not man for the Sabbath (Mk. 2:27). Where the law goes counter to the good of man, it ceases to have any validity. What never loses value is the human. More, the law will become irrelevant and superfluous where man stands in the right relationship to his fellowmen and thereby also to God. This will become possible only if two conditions are fulfilled: the re-creation of the world (structures and institutions of society) and the re-creation of the world-within (structures of knowing, loving, and being, pertaining to the very inwardness of man) - a twofold re-creation that can be accomplished only in dialogue with God. The same idea is contained in the Beatitude:

> "Blessed are the pure in heart, for they shall see God." (Mt. 5:8).

The pure in heart (i.e. those who do not harbour evil intentions against their neighbour) shall see God and, in seeing God, definitively transcend all law. They will then become a law unto themselves and to others. In other words, they will emerge as original creators of value. This is further attested by the saying,

> "Hear me, all of you, and understand: There is nothing outside a man which by going into him can defile him, but the things which come out of him are what defile him." (Mk. 7:14-16).

Here the prophetic forecast concerning the law being written in the heart of man is reaffirmed with all its revolutionary implications. But what marks Jesus out from the earlier prophets is the stupendous pronouncement that this future without the law is already within the grasp of man if only he would go forward to meet the God who comes.

It is indeed tragic that Christians have forgotten this vision of a new order of things in which there will no more be class, law or State, and have settled down to a manner of permanent compromise with structures of domination. They can become politically relevant only if they, like Jesus, accept to be a sign of contradiction spear-heading the revolt of the least against the mighty.

(Anawim No. 16; *Jesus and Society*, Chap. 12)

18

The Pure and the Impure

The distinction between the pure and the impure has its origin in the world outlook of the primitive man. In most primitive cultures there is the myth of the origin of the world from primordial chaos. It is from the confused and the formless that things with name and form (*nama-rupa*) come into being. Now, the formless is also the symbol of death. On dying, everything - plants, animals, and men - dissolves into the formless stuff of the earth. It was, therefore, easy for the primitives to think of life as emerging out of death and returning to it. They could observe the process at work at the level of the microcosm. The sun set and disappeared into darkness (the nameless and the formless) to rise up again the following day. Plants died and decayed, but only to sprout again to new life. More, man found himself constantly threatened by the forces of death operative in the world. And in an age when he had not yet fashioned the tools necessary for controlling the forces that environed him, it was crucial to discern between the forces of life and the forces of death so that he could protect himself from the latter.

It is here we should seek the roots of distinction between the pure and the impure. The pure is whatever contributes to life; the impure, whatever is detrimental to it. Sages then appeared on the scene and applied their mind to make a catalogue of impure things and actions, and framed rules of conduct which became normative for the common man. Carcasses, blood, feces, bodily excretions, hides, and similar things were held unclean because they had to do either with death or with the process of decaying; so also whatever is formless, deformed, hybrid, in short, all that resembled professions, classes and groups as well. It was probably the chaotic. Eventually, the notion of purity was extended to professions, classes, groups as well. It was probably thus that tribes and classes became castes. Over time, the pure was identified with the divine and in some cultures, the impure with demonic powers. With this what was originally a magico-mythical conception was overlaid with religious meaning. This served to further intensify the contrast and the incompatibility between the pure and the impure.

Thus, it was possible to establish a hierarchy of the pure and the impure, of the sacred and the profane. As the fountainhead of life, God was considered supremely pure and sacred. Among the Jews, this conception found spatial expression in the belief that the temple, especially the Holy of Holies, was the centre of the sacred cosmos. The farther removed was any space from the temple, the less sacred it was. Society, too, was structured after the pattern of a descending gradation of purity. Priests formed the apex, set apart as they were to mediate life divine and to deal with sacred things like the altar, sacrifice, and worship. Lower came the laity, who in turn were classified in terms of descending degrees of purity in respect of origin, profession, food habits, and the like. This suited admirably the interests of the priestly class who, with their knowledge of the pure and the impure and with their control over the means of cultic purification, could exercise domination over the entire population. As far as the Hebrews were concerned, though the notion of pollution originated in very ancient days, it was the priestly class, close to the royal court, that elaborated it into a system. At the time of Jesus, the Pharisees and Scribes also were zealous in the observance of the laws of purity, while the mass of people cared little for it.

Before I pass on to Jesus' stand in this regard let me make a few critical observations on the notion of ritual purity. 1. The notion represents primitive man's answer to the problem of how to defend himself from the mysterious forces of death which he could neither understand nor bring under control. His answer was based on magic and myth whereas today we rely on observation, science, and technology. 2. The notion is essentially *a-moral*, insofar as purity or impurity is conceived as an objective quality inhering in things, actions, and situations, irrespective of the free decision of individuals. 3. It becomes also immoral when human beings, too, are classified as pure or impure. For it leads to the fragmentation of the community and the domination of some by others. 4. Considered in itself, purity or impurity has nothing to do with religion understood as man's relationship to the transcendent ground and goal of his existence and history. The identification of the forces of life with God is magical. It is one thing to say that God is the transcendent ground of the cosmic process; quite another thing to identify Him with the latter.

A God whom man can control through the knowledge of the pure and the impure is but the projection of his mind. What I said about the a-religious character of the notion of purity applies to cults as well. Cults probably originated in an attempt to re-enact the cosmic origins, when chaos gave birth to cosmos, the formless to form, death to life. In times when the community felt that it was under the grip of the forces of death (famine, illness, decay, death) it chose one among them to die for all so that there would be a new outburst of life in terms of health, prosperity, children, cattle, and vegetation. Later, a product of labour was substituted for man. In this sense, all sacrifice may be said to have originated in human sacrifice and has to do with cosmic purification and renewal. Hence, all religions dominated by the notion of purity and rites of purification are *a-moral*, if not also immoral. Admittedly, what I have just described is the system of purity as an ideal-type. In all historical religions, the *a-moral* system of the priestly tradition, particularly in the Leviticus, and the latter in the Elohiste-Deuteronomic tradition, each, however, with elements assimilated from the other.

Jesus' attitude to the laws of pollution is best illustrated by his controversies with the Scribes and Pharisees regarding the washing of hands before meals. He defended his disciples when they ate with hands unwashed. Quoting Isaiah he reminded his opponents: "This people honour me with their lips but their heart is far from me."

No amount of ritual washing can help man bridge the distance between him and God. The rules of purity touch only the periphery of man, only his existence as a moment in the cosmic process of life and death, birth, and dissolution. To effect a rupture in the cosmic membrane and achieve a breakthrough he has to shift his attention from the periphery (the cosmic) to the centre. And that centre is 'the heart', by which is meant the deepest core of man where knowing, loving, willing, and feeling have their common root. It is that point of irradiation from which man reaches out to communion with God and men. It is through the heart that he hears every word of command God utters. That is why Jesus went on to say:

> "You leave the commandment of God, and hold fast the tradition of men." (Mk. 7:13)

The God of Jesus is the God of the prophets, who can be encountered only in his commands. And his commands are all reducible to the single one of loving one's neighbour. Contrasted with the divine command to seek justice and love, the laws of purity are mere traditions by men, which may or may not be observed depending on whether they contribute or not to human well-being. Here also the radicalism of Jesus does not consist in declaring the pure impure, and the impure pure according to the prevalent criterion of evaluation but in introducing an entirely new criterion, namely, rectitude of the heart measured in terms of brotherly love:

> "There is nothing outside a man which by going into him can defile him, but the things which come out of a man are what defile him." (Mk. 7:15)

(Anawim No. 20; *Jesus and Society*, Chap. 13)

19

Mercy, not Sacrifice

Encountering God

We meet God in our glory and our nakedness. In our glory, when he comes to us as a self-giving fullness that fills our emptiness within. This is the case whenever we have an intense experience of beauty, love or human togetherness. In such privileged moments, we feel we have been invaded by an absolute Other whose presence pervades our whole being, endowing it with a new light and a new warmth, with a sense of being well and being whole. Quite different is the encounter with God in the experience of our nakedness i.e. in the experience of frailty, sin, guilt, meaninglessness, of our *being-unto-death*, of exploitation and domination. Here the Divine is perceived not so much as a presence but as an absence that beckons us from the Beyond, as an unconditional challenge addressed to us to break loose from all shackles and march forward to the horizon of human-divine fullness. Where we meet the Divine in our glory, our response naturally takes the form of reverence and thankfulness; where we encounter him in our alienation it is, it should be, one of striving for fuller being, knowing and loving.

These two types of religious experiences are not mutually exclusive. Rather, each implies and merges with the other. The God who presents himself to us in the experience of the beautiful, the true and the good is also absent in the sense that no experience, however profound, can capture his fullness. On the other hand, the absent God who beckons us from the beyond is also experienced as present in the power that enables us to transcend all alienation. A similar reciprocal inclusiveness may be observed also at the level of our response to God. Reverence before his self-giving fullness has implied in it the challenge to preserve the beauty of that experience from everything that may mar or mutilate it as as to share it with others. Conversely, any creative response : the divine call to overcome all alienation will include reverence towards the same call and towards the ultimate destiny we are called to.

Whether we meet God in our glory or our nakedness, the only valid criterion of its genuineness is praxis in the twofold form of preserving what is valuable and true and eliminating whatever dehumanizes us. Any claim to have encountered God is spurious unless it is accompanied by constructive-subversive action aimed at creating a new heaven and a new earth.

Religion Alienated

The encounter with God takes place at the level of concrete life, whether individual or collective. In itself, it is unfathomable and unspeakable. But man is man only because he cannot but try to speak the unspeakable, to express the inexpressible. This he does through symbols, which may take the form of actions (prostrations, dances, offerings, prayers), language (scriptures, myths, legends, epics, hymns, poems) or things (painting, sculpture, architecture). These fulfil a double function: First, they act as an aid to memory. They help man to make his past encounter with God present and thus draw nourishment from it for facing the concrete challenges of life. Second, they keep alive the hope in his future, for the Divine that revealed itself in the past is at the same time the ultimate goal of history. All living symbols are, therefore, woven into the very texture of man's historical existence. They have meaning only in the measure in which they inspire him to create the future out of the possibilities offered by the past. They become alienated and alienating when they are detached from the original God-encounter which gave birth to them, and are set up as autonomous values. I shall now indicate three ways in which religious symbolism, especially that of worship, becomes estranged from its original meaning.

Magical Alienation

In concrete religious practice we find symbolic actions like offerings and prayers which do not spring from any genuine dialogue with God in history. Instead, they derive from a unilateral attempt on the part of man to influence God in his favour. In the process they are invested with quasi-automatic efficacy. But a God who can thus be moved or manipulated from outside cannot be a living God. He is but a product of the human mind. He owes his existence to the magical view of the world. Magic is based on the belief that it is the same force that works in the microcosm and the macrocosm (sexual power = cosmic reproductive force; breath = wind; eye = sun), and that it is possible to influence the latter by manipulating the former. There is no doubt that much of the worship going on in churches and temples today is due to the assimilation of religion to magic. This is particularly true of prayers and offerings whose efficacy is measured in terms of strict adherence to set formulae and stereotype patterns.

Cyclic Alienation

Here a few reflections on time as such may be found useful. One may distinguish three kinds of time. The first is mythical time, meaning that primordial time which was before the origin of the world, which saw the unfolding of the story of gods and goddesses. It is what myths and legends refer to as "once upon a time", "long long ago", "in those days" etc. St. John had in mind the same when he began his Gospel with the words, in the beginning was. The second kind of time is the cyclic. It is the time proper to the working of nature, organic and inorganic. It follows the rhythm of the ever recurring processes of nature, like the rising and setting of the sun, the coming and going of seasons, and the ebb and flow of animal sexuality. In it nothing new emerges; only the old repeats itself. The third is historical time which is rooted in man's consciousness and freedom whereby he creates himself and the world anew. History never repeats itself. There is no mere going back to the origins; there is only going forward to the unknown beyond. However, it must be kept in mind that, though man is essentially a historical being, in so far as he shares vegetative and animal life, he too is subject to the law of cyclic time.

The dialogue between man and God takes place on the plane of historical time. Moreover, it is this very dialogue that constitutes history. Wherever man consciously or subconsciously lets himself fall from historical to cyclic time - and this is what happens when social life becomes routinized and institutionalized - religious symbolism also is assimilated to the rhythm of the ever returning cosmic processes. This is how liturgical cycles with their recurring feasts, devotions, and ceremonies come into being. As a result, God is reduced to a moment in the cyclic process, and his challenge to create a new humanity of beauty and love goes unheeded. Consequently, also, religion becomes divorced from morality.

Mythical Alienation

The cult that follows the pattern of cyclic time presupposes the belief that its object - god or goddess - lived in the primordial mythical time. In many cultures there exists still the belief that the origin of their cultic practices is to be traced back to the gods themselves. In this context, cult represents an attempt on the part of man to re-enact his mythical origins, and recapture the conditions of the golden age of yore when he was, supposedly, in direct contact with the deity. This is true even when a historical person is made the object of cult. He is first mythicized and only then worshipped. Thus, it was not until Jesus of Nazareth was made into the Logos that was in the beginning that a cult developed around him. The same process has been at work in other religions too. Wherever saints, seers and prophets were assimilated to mythical gods,, the concrete example of their lives ceased to be normative for day-to-day life. From then on what mattered was not so much realizing the values they lived for as having ritual-symbolic communion with them, a mode of communion which could easily co-exist with the exploitation of one's fellowmen. Significantly, the proliferation of cult in any religion is in direct proportion to the refusal of man to respond to God's call for justice and love. It is when religion decays that cultic practices of all sorts spring up like mushrooms.

Anti-cultism of the Prophets

The threefold alienation of religion described above amounts to a denial of the true God. That is why it was vehemently attacked by the prophets of the Old Testament. Their concern was to confront their contemporaries with the living God and his unconditional demand for justice for the poor and the oppressed. How incisive was their criticism of cult may be seen from the following words Amos puts in the mouth of Yahweh:

> "I hate, I despise your feasts, and I take no delight in your solemn assemblies. Even though you offer me your burnt offerings and cereal offerings, I will not accept them, and the peace offerings of your fatted beasts I will not look upon. But let justice roll down like waters, and righteousness like an ever flowing stream." (5:21-24)

The same theme is taken up by Isaiah and reaffirmed in equally, if not more, powerful terms:

> "Your countless sacrifices, what are they to me? says the Lord. I am sated with whole-offerings of rams and the fat of buffaloes... When you lift your hands outspread in prayer, I will hide my eyes from you. Though you offer countless prayers, I will not listen. There is blood on your hands; wash yourselves and be clean... Cease to do evil and learn to do right, pursue justice and champion the oppressed; give the orphan his rights, plead the widow's cause." (1:11-17)

It is clear from these passages that the prophets repudiated the magical conception of a God who can be manipulated by man with the help of sacrifices and prayers ("The offer of your gifts is useless"). Similarly, they would have nothing to do with a God who is bound by the cyclic processes of nature ("New moons,...sacred seasons and ceremonies, I cannot endure"). Their criticism also implies an attack on the mythicization of religion, because the festivals and sacrifices they rejected had their basis in Canaanite mythology. Positively, their central concern was to bring home to their contemporaries the all important truth that God can be encountered only in the cry of the poor and the needy (See also Ho 4:1-12; 6: 4-16; Je 22:13-16).

Jesus' Criticism of Cult

Like the prophets before him Jesus knew only of one way of meeting God, namely, through loving one's neighbour. He did not recognize cult as a parallel way to God. That was why he was able to summarize the Law and the prophets in the single injunction:

> "Always treat others as you would like them to treat you." (Mt. 7:12)

An explicit rejection of traditional cult is contained in his reply to the Pharisees who censured him for eating with publicans and sinners:

> "It is not the healthy that need a doctor, but the sick. Go and learn what that text means, I require mercy, not sacrifice." (Mt. 2:12-13)

Showing mercy (compassion = suffering with) to social outcasts (publicans and sinners) is what God wants, and not sacrifices. But did not Jesus presuppose the validity of cult when he said:

> "If, when you are bringing your gift to the altar, you suddenly remember that your brother has a grievance against you, leave your gift where it is before the altar. First go and make your peace with your brother, and only then come back and offer your gift." (Mt. 5:23-24)

This objection may be countered with two comments. First, if the injunction is taken in all seriousness - and there is no reason why it should not - then no worship is possible under the present dispensation where injustice and oppression reign supreme. For, no worshipper can claim that no one in the community has any grievance against him: not the rich, who fatten themselves on the toil of the poor; nor those among the exploited, who refuse to join hands with their kind to fight exploitation. Second, the phrase, "then come back and offer your gift" probably reflects the practice of the early Jewish Christian community at a time when the prophetic movement Jesus initiated had already become a cultic religion.

Jesus directed his criticism also against traditional forms of prayer. He rejected all prayer that is divorced from doing the will of God which for him meant loving one's neighbour (Mt. 7:21). He repudiated the magical belief that God can be moved by the accumulation of epithets:

> "In your prayers do not go babbling on like the heathen, who imagine that the more they say the more they are likely to be heard." (Mt. 6:7)

Only that prayer is genuine which at once presupposes and promotes reconciliation among members of the community.

> "And when you stand praying, if you have a grievance against anyone, forgive him, so that your Father in heaven may forgive you the wrongs you have done." (Mk. 11:25)

This saying, too, proves that it is useless to seek union with God outside of communion with one's fellowmen.

In the cleansing of the temple, we have a powerful expression of Jesus' attitude to cult. It has been argued that his concern in driving out the vendors and the buyers was to vindicate the sanctity of the temple. But it is difficult to believe that he considered the temple itself holy. In his view purity or impurity is not a quality sticking on to objects or persons but something that derives from the within (= heart) of man (Mk.7:15-20). It is his total obedience to God that renders things and actions holy. Neither does the view sound convincing that his purpose in clearing the court of the gentiles of all those engaged in commercial transactions was to restore the character of the temple as 'house of prayer for all nations' probably meant the festal gathering of the end-time, when "many will come from east and west to feast with Abraham, Isaac and Jacob in the Kingdom of Heaven." (Mt. 8:11). It could not have meant the temple which assigned an inferior place to the gentiles. Nor could Jesus have been motivated by moral indignation against any exploitation that went on within the temple precincts. If that were the case, how to explain the fact that not only vendors but also buyers were driven out! I suggest that the real reason that provoked the cleansing was the alienation of religion involved in the selling and buying of offerings. Money was exchanged for offerings, and offerings in their turn were exchanged for the favour (grace) of God. What is this if not reducing God to money, and money to something divine? If so, he who reigned in the temple was not the living God but mammon. The temple had therefore no right to exist; it must be overthrown. Jesus did predict the destruction of the temple (Mk. 13:2). It would incur the same fate that befell the fig-tree, which, because it failed to yield fruits, was cursed into withering. In its place would rise another temple, a renewed humanity, in which true worshippers "will worship the Father in Spirit and truth" (Jn 4:23).

The temple embodied the threefold alienation of religion discussed earlier. Beneath the monetization of the Divine lay the magical attitude in so far as the worshipper could use money to secure command over God. Likewise, the liturgical cycle sought to assimilate God to cosmic forces. Finally, as the centre of the symbolic universe of the Jews, the temple was that privileged point from where the worshipper could take to vertical flight to the mythical God-above and thereby escape from the inexorable demands of the God-ahead. The cleansing of the temple, therefore, is both a prophetic protest against all alienated expressions of religions and a prophetic call for a new kind of religious symbolism geared to the creation of a world of beauty, truth, and love, in response to the challenge of the living God of history.

(Anawim No. 19; *Jesus and Society*, Chap. 14)

20

Faith versus Ideology

Faith was for Jesus a vision and a passion: a vision opening the future of total freedom, fullness, and joy for every member of the family of man; and a passion for realizing the envisioned, a commitment to it unto death. From the day faith took hold of him, he was a changed man. He began to see things differently from the rest of his kind. He started questioning the truth of commonly held ideas and beliefs. He saw in them so many fetters that held people's consciousness in bondage, clouding, and distorting their vision of reality. The prevailing ideas, however, did not form any coherent system. Some were common to all Jews; others peculiar to certain social strata like the priesthood in Jerusalem, the Pharisees, the doctors of the law, and the Zealots who aspired to political power. On the whole, they emanated from the privileged sections of society and were suited to furthering their interests. They could be subsumed under the notion of ideology, meaning a partial vision of reality projected as a total vision, or the views of particular classes held up as valid for all classes. The following reflections are meant to throw some light on the confrontation between faith and ideology in the life of Jesus as recorded in the Gospel according to Mark.

Ideology is to faith what old wine-skins are to new wine. The use of wine-skins is to contain, in the root meaning of keeping within limits. The new wine of faith knows no limits, is by nature expansive, even explosive. It must create new organs and new structures to be fully effective in the world. Any attempt to domesticate it within traditional structures is doomed to failure.

> "No one puts new wine into old wine-skins; if he does, the wine will burst the skins and then wine and skins are both lost. Fresh skins for new wine!" (2:22)

Ideology seeps down to the inmost psychic structure of persons, affecting their thoughts, decisions, feelings, reflexes, and reactions. It makes wax grow in the ears, and scales over the eyes; it causes minds to close in upon themselves. All the more so, when the challenge of faith makes demands that are counter to one's cherished interests. In consequence, one does not see because one does not want to see.

> "Do you still not understand? Are your minds closed? You have eyes: can you not see? You have ears: can you not hear?" (8:17-18)

Or it happens that, under the spell of ideology, one sees in the message of faith nothing but a riddle.

> "To you, the secret of the Kingdom of God has been given; but to those who are outside everything comes by way of riddles so that they may look and look, but see nothing; they may hear and hear, but understand nothing, unless they turn to God and are forgiven." (4:11-12)

To convey the same idea Jesus elsewhere resorts to the parable of the soil and the seed. Ideologies tend to congeal and petrify. Minds encrusted with them are rendered impervious to the call, revealed in the history of total freedom. They are no favorable soil for God's word to strike roots in. Or, if it does, the young shoot withers away in the first heat of the sun (4:3-20).

Whereas ideology closes minds and hearts, faith dis-closes. It opens up new horizons and attunes human consciousness to the faintest whisperings of the Divine. It makes man dream new dreams and dare the impossible. It releases the hidden energies of the soul for the creation of new forms of life together. Neither dogmas nor institutions can dam up its creative upsurge. Its goal is the plentiful harvest of life and love in humanity refashioned.

Ideology does not produce anything new; it only conserves. It paralyzes the spirit, kills the urge to revolt, and tames man into submission. What is worse, it makes him love his own fetters. For, the ideas of the rulers end up being internalized by the ruled so that these come to see them as their own ideas. The result is a situation where people fear their own freedom and look upon it as an insupportable burden. And there is an end to all creativity. Faith, on the contrary, is force, creative power; like the force of the new wine that bursts old wine-skins, of the seed that breaks open the hard crust of the earth to put forth its first blade. Man under the grip of ideology is mere flesh, powerlessness; faith is spirit, that is, the power of the transcendent become immanent (14:38; Is 31:3). It uproots to plant anew, pulls down to build afresh. It is capable of moving mountains (11:23) and raising cities in their place.

"Everything is possible to one who has faith" (9:22).

Ideology begets the false self: the self shaped by existing values, beliefs, and aspirations, the self that judges and is judged by the standards in vogue. It is this self we generally mean when we deem someone good or bad, pure or impure, high or low. The same standards we employ in measuring our own success or failure in life. Man's true self, on the other hand, is born of faith. It judges itself and others not by ossified norms but by openness to the transcendent Beyond. Its centre of gravity is what man ought to become, not what he has been made to be. In every person, this true self is struggling to be born by freeing itself from the shackles of the old. Hence Jesus's demand:

> "If anyone wishes to be a follower of mine he must leave (the false) self behind; he must take up his cross and come with me. Whoever cares for his own safety is lost; but if a man will let himself be lost for my sake and the Gospel, that man is safe. What does a man gain by winning the whole world at the cost of his true self?" (8:34-36)

Ideologies are fashioned by men who are merely men. And a man who is merely man is the inauthentic man. The authentic human being is man as responsiveness to the Divine, man as transcendence. The mere man is reducible to the sum of social and historical conditions at any given time. His ideas are determined by the society in which he lives. They might be of some relevance for the age that produced them. But, set up as absolutes, valid for all ages, they represent the tyranny of the past over the present, of the dead over the living. Unlike such human traditions, faith is divine, being essentially a response to the call of God. It involves seeking, treading unbeaten tracks, launching out into the unknown - hoping against hope. It neither secretes dogmas nor imprisons the Absolute in relative concepts. The conflict between tradition and faith takes place in the heart of every man, of every society. In contemporary Judaism, human traditions had all but stifled genuine faith. This provoked the saying of Jesus:

> "You leave the commandment of God, and hold fast the tradition of men." (7:9)

The same accusation is leveled at Peter, who in Zealot fashion hoped Jesus would proclaim himself a political Messiah: "You think as men think, not as God thinks." (8:33)

Ideology, too, will seek to legitimate itself by appealing to the Word of God; but to the Word of God as reinterpreted to suit the interests of the holders of property and power, as fossilized into dogmas and legal prescriptions. Legitimation is institutionalized when the duty of safeguarding and further interpreting tradition is entrusted exclusively to a privileged caste. With that, even God is made superfluous. Better for the guardians of orthodoxy if he never more opened his mouth! Quite different is the authority of faith. Faith is legitimated by direct encounter with the living God who speaks to man here and now. Whoever believes, therefore, speaks in the name of the God whom he has seen, touched, and listened to. Such, indeed, was Jesus. "For unlike the doctors of the law, he taught with a note of authority." (1:22)

Asked by his adversaries to legitimate his driving out buyers and sellers from the temple, he reminded them of John the Baptizer whom people had acclaimed a prophet directly called by God; thereby implying that his authority too came straight from God. This explains the supreme freedom with which he reinterpreted, modified, and annulled provisions of the law, and the courage he showed in defying accepted norms and accredited teachers.

Our reflections thus far should not be taken to mean that there is an invincible barrier between faith and ideology. As though, once under the sway of false consciousness, a person is doomed to always remain so. Jesus did not believe in any social determinism. His entire teaching praxis was aimed at helping people pass from ideology to faith. Hence the call:

> "The time has come; the kingdom of God is upon you; repent, and believe in the Gospel." (1:15)

A method he employed to this end consisted of unraveling the kernel of truth, of which ideology is a distorted expression, in other words, in revealing the original core of meaning before it became reified. Thus in his controversies with adversaries, he would show that *man-for-the-sabbath* is a distortion of the-sabbath-for-man (2:27); so too the controversy over ritual purity (7:1-23) and the Mosaic law of divorce (10:1-9).

If a man can slough off ideology and attain faith, so can he fall from faith to ideology. The clearest instance in Mark is Peter's repudiation of Jesus:

> "I do not know this man you speak of." (14:71)

The incident proved to be symbolic of what was to happen in course of time when the faith-movement that Jesus set in motion degenerated into an institutionalized religion and ended up as a provider of legitimation for the ruling classes.

(Anawim No. 25; *Jesus and Society*, Ch. 15)

21

Attuning Oneself to the Divine

L ife is a dialogue with the world. In this dialogue what the world speaks to us, the meaning it conveys, depends very much on whether we are inwardly attuned to it. What we are determines, to a large extent, the image of the world that emerges in our consciousness. If this is true of our perception of the world in general, it is much more so where there is a question of our perceiving the depth-dimension of life, namely, the aesthetic, the moral, and the religious. That is why not everyone hears the call of the Kingdom of God as it makes itself heard in historical events and situations. To be able to hear that call, we need to be attuned in a special way to the wavelength of the Divine. The following reflections seek to elucidate the nature of the self-attuning which Jesus demanded of his hearers.

Be Open like Children

Of particular significance here is Jesus' remark to the disciples when they rebuked children for seeking to come near to him:

> "Let the children come to me; do not try to stop them, for the Kingdom of God belongs to such as these. I tell you, whoever does not accept the Kingdom of God as a child will never enter it." (Mk. 10:14-15)

What Jesus praises in children is not their humility or submissiveness but their openness to the future. They are open because their thinking is not, as is generally the case with adults, determined by the prevalent ideas and values which serve to maintain the status quo. The Gospels provide us with many an example of such hardening of hearts due to ideological conditioning. It was because the Pharisees tenaciously clung on to the traditions of men that they could not see the true import of the commandments of God (Mk. 7:8) or appreciate the new freedom from the law that Jesus proclaimed (Mk. 2:28). Similarly, if the Scribes had nothing new to offer and went on repeating the old, it was because they were not prepared to go to school once again and become learners in the Kingdom of God (Mt. 13:52). Again, if the disciples failed to see the true mission of Jesus it was for the reason that their thinking was under the grip of the ideology of the Zealots who looked forward to a political Messiah wielding power over the nation. This, in fact, is what Jesus had in mind when he told Peter:

"You think as men think, not as God thinks." (Mk. 16:23)

The relevance of all this for discipleship today is clear. In order that we may hear the call of the Kingdom as revealed in the history of the oppressed masses of India, we should first free ourselves from the ideas and values of decaying feudalism as well as from those of emerging capitalism disseminated through the mass media and the educational system. We should go a step further and institute a radical criticism of the current religious ideas as well, many of which serve no other purpose than that of legitimizing the exploitation of man by man.

Turn Away from Your Sins

Jesus' proclamation of the Kingdom involved a call to repentance. To repent means to turn away from the path of sin and take the road that leads to God. The sin in question is threefold: First, there is cosmic sin i.e. sin as an objective, quasi-autonomous force which holds man captive, cripples his body and soul, and tarnishes the divine image in him. It is, in all probability, sin in this sense which Jesus had in mind when he told the paralytic. "My son, your sins are forgiven" (Mk 2:5). Here illness is equated with sin; and healing, with forgiveness. There is also structural sin i.e. sin embodied in the laws and institutions of society in so far as these dehumanize man. As examples, we may cite from the Gospels the rules regarding the observance of the Sabbath and ritual purity, the manner in which the affairs of the temple were run, and Roman rule in Palestine. Finally, there is personal sin, sin consisting of the free decision of individuals against the known will of God. Though Jesus did not attribute every illness to personal sin (Lk 13:1-5), it is likely that he saw these three modes of sin as interrelated. Be that as it may, what is important for us is to remember that he demanded from his hearers that they turn away from sin in every form and thus dispose themselves to enter the Kingdom of God.

Translated into the idiom of the contemporary man, the call to repentance means that we should be prepared to wage war against all objective, cosmic forces that mutilate the image of God in man, to pull down all unjust and inhuman structures of society, and to fight the forces of unlove, hatred, and aggression lodged in the depths of our own hearts. In brief, the call is nothing less than a preparedness to restructure personal and social life.

Believe in the Good News

The call to repentance goes hand in hand with the call to believe in the Good News. But Jesus does not give us any definition of what it means to believe. We can, however, derive an idea of it from the different situations in which he uses the term. Where there is mention of faith in the Gospels, the stress is definitely not on seeing or knowing truths, but on recognizing the power of God at work in the world, especially in the word and deed of Jesus. This comes out clearly in almost all the miracle stories. Men and women flocked to the young prophet from Galilee because they believed that the power of God was with him (Lk 5:17). To have faith is, however, more than recognizing God's action in the world. It is at the same time a confident striving to come within the sphere of the re-creating, saving power of God. For instance, Jesus saw in the desperate attempt of the paralytic and his friends to gain access to him (Mk 2:3-5) and in the efforts of the woman with hemorrhages to touch the hem of his garment (Mk 5:27) - so many manifestations of faith. In his eyes, such confident striving was already instinct with the power of God. That is why he could say,

"Everything is possible to one who has faith" (Mk. 9:23).

Significantly also, he had no hesitation in saying, "Your faith has cured you", where we would have expected him to say, God has cured you (Mk. 5:34; 10:52). What does this mean but that in him who has faith the power of God has become the power of man!

That Jesus viewed faith as power becomes clear still when we note that he contrasts it not so much with lack of understanding as with fear. We hear him say again and again, "Do not be afraid; only have faith" (Mk. 5:36; 4:40; 5:14, 35; 6:50). If faith is power, fear is powerlessness; if faith is courage, fear is cowardice; if faith is the order of the spirit, i.e. of man as attuned to the Divine, fear belongs to the realm of the flesh, i.e. of man as subject to weakness and mortality. (Mk. 14:38; Is 31:3) Naturally, he who fears is incapable of meeting the challenge of the Kingdom. For, accepting the challenge will necessarily expose him to the violence of those who maintain structures of evil. In fact, those who chose to become disciples of Jesus had constantly to face the temptation of succumbing to the fear of the Jewish authorities, of Herod, and of the Romans. We know too that in the final moment of crisis they were overcome by fear, and they fled.

What this means for today's disciples of Jesus needs no explaining. They need faith both to read the signs of the times and to accept the challenges of God's reign over the Indian masses. Were they to lack faith, they will invariably turn supporters of the existing regime. Out of fear of those who can kill the body they will sin against the Spirit of God. What is worse, they will project their betrayal itself as authentic discipleship. And in the bargain, they will have sent Jesus of Nazareth once again to the Cross.

(Anawim No. 6, *Jesus and Society*, Chap. 16)

22

Discipleship as Contestation

What is it that marks out a disciple of Jesus from the followers of other religious teachers? Not piety: Jesus warned against the inane, endless muttering of prayers; not the practice of cult, which he subordinated to the works of mercy; not the observance of religious laws, which he often flouted; not even love for one's fellowmen. The injunction to love one's kind is found also in the teachings of other religious seers and saints. What then is the distinguishing feature of discipleship under Jesus?

Fortunately, Jesus himself has answered. The occasion was his momentous journey to Jerusalem. He had just told his disciples that it was his destiny to suffer many things, to be rejected by the elders, the chief priests, and the scribes, and be killed. Then he added:

> "If any man would come after me, let him deny himself and take up his cross and follow me. For whoever would save his life will lose it; and whoever loses his life for my sake and the Gospel's will save it." (Mk. 8:34-35)

Jesus here lays down two conditions for discipleship: denying oneself and taking up one's cross. Denying oneself means disowning one's life, not clinging to it as something to be safeguarded at any cost. It involves supreme detachment from one's vital interests. But why should the disciple disown his life? Because he must follow his master and fall in line with the latter's strategy. And that strategy was one of resolute opposition to everything that deprived humans of the right to live in peace and freedom, one of a radical disowning of the existing relations of wealth, power, and ideas. It required repudiating the entire religio-political system presided over by the imperial power of Rome. How could the disciple assume the same stance and reject the prevailing social order if he jealously clung on to his self anchored in the same society?

If anyone dares to deny the world, the world, in turn, will deny him: refuse him the right to live. That precisely was to be his fate, Jesus knew for sure. He knew that the imperial power, in collusion with the lesser powers, would send him to the Cross as it had many a rebel before him.

> "Would Jesus, who believed himself to be the last of the prophets sent by God, have expected a better fate for himself?" (Joachim Jeremias).

Equally, he could have foreseen that his disciples too would have to meet the same destiny at the hands of those who operated the machinery of repression. Hence the poignant call to them to take up the cross and follow him. There is no compelling reason to believe that the phrase, carrying the cross originated later in the early Christian community. The reference could have come from Jesus himself since crucifixion was a familiar sight in the Palestine of his days. (Vincent Taylor, Edward Schweizer, and others)

But why did Jesus have to contest with the powers that were? The text as it stands is misleading and the answer has to be read between the lines. The would-be disciple is told that he should be prepared to lose his life 'for my sake and the Gospel's.' According to many scholars, this last phrase could not have come from the lips of Jesus, for the Gospel's being a Marcan interpretative addition and for my sake a product of tradition (E. Schweizer, Taylor, Jeremias). In its present form, the text reflects the situation of a Christian community under persecution. The conclusion of the original saying would have read: "and whoever loses his life for the sake of the Kingdom will save it" (Lk 18:29; Mk 10:29). It was, then, commitment to the reign of God that put Jesus at variance with the religious and political power structure. With his eyes planted on the new humanity founded on love, justice, and the community of being and having, he could not have reconciled himself with the ruling classes. Pertinent is T.W. Manson's comment on the saying: "The words imply that Jesus is aware of an irreconcilable hostility between the Kingdom for which he stands and the empire represented by Pontius Pilate." As with the master so with his disciples.

One might object: Is it not possible to believe in a future free from all alienation without having to oppose the world as it is? Yes. But only if one thinks God to be the father of all social evils or if man's aggression against man is seen as the manifestation of God's power (*maya*), as moments of his cosmic play (*lila*). For those who hold such a belief, repudiating the status quo would amount to repudiating God. They can only conform to the given and leave the ushering in of freedom to God. This is the attitude bred by the traditional way of knowledge (*jnana*) and even by certain forms of devotional religion (*bhakti*). In the course of history, Christianity too degenerated to a religion of passive acquiescence in a divine providence that condoned the rich battening themselves on the poor and the mighty lording it over the weak.

Quite differently did Jesus view the world. He did not predicate the wrongs of society on God. If the world is a mess, it is man's doing. He alone is responsible for the corruption within him and the corruption without. He must, therefore, plead guilty and disown his corrupt self ('Repent and believe'). He must accept God's unconditional challenge to remould him and the world anew. Jesus thus deprived the world of all divine legitimacy and sanction. Henceforth man can reject the status quo without being accused of overthrowing God.

Jesus, however, did not go to the other extreme of postulating a total discontinuity between the present world and the Kingdom to come. The ultimate future is not to be created out of nothing. Else, nothing that humans fashion now will be preserved for the future, and all revolutionary praxis would be devoid of meaning. For Jesus, the world is not a mere scaffolding to be dismantled and discarded once the new and definitive world-order has emerged. However decayed and decaying, it is this world of ours that has to be transformed into the reign of God. What is more, he saw the new as already germinating in the old, like the seed buried in the earth, like the leaven hidden in the dough.

Since the new humanity can come into being only as a result of human praxis aimed at transforming the prevailing conditions, the disciple of Jesus has no other option but to oppose the secular and religious powers holding humans in thraldom. He is thus rendered vulnerable to the forces of violence and death, permanently exposed to political reprisal. Here is the ultimate reason for Jesus' call to deny oneself. Only by giving up all security, all safe moorings in the world, can one maintain the integrity of one's discipleship. But that demands courage; and where courage is wanting, one will easily succumb to the temptation of insuring one's life against every possible risk either by marrying money-power or by befriending the keepers of the Establishment or by accepting the tutelage of political parties. But in the bargain, the disciple will have bartered away his fundamental right and duty to dissent. Further, he will have fathered a monstrous form of discipleship without the cross, just as believers have created religions without God, and Christians have brought into being a Christianity without Jesus. This is how one loses one's life in trying to save it.

Will not consistent prophetic dissent render the disciple incapable of any constructive action and condemn him to revolutionary impotence? True, if he were to look for social forces and groups whose goals and strategies are adequate from every point of view, he is likely to be disillusioned. All human reality is ambivalent, a mixture of good and bad, of true and false. Hence the only way open to him is that of critical collaboration with all progressive forces i.e. with forces that stand for a fuller and richer life for all. Where such forces do not exist, they have to be created, just as Jesus himself ushered in a new community through his table-fellowship with social outcasts.

(Anawim No. 28, *Jesus and Society*, Chap. 18)

23

The Spirit Brooding Over A Wasteland

John was preaching the baptism of repentance for the forgiveness of sins. People were flocking to Jordan by the hundreds. The news reached the carpenter's home in Nazareth. Jesus too felt the urge to heed the call from the wilderness. Come to the scene of baptism, he stepped into the cool waters and dipped himself. As he came up, he saw the Spirit coming down upon him in the shape of a dove and heard a voice speak from heaven,

"Thou art my son, my beloved; on thee my favour rests." (Mk. 1:11)

The Spirit that descended on Jesus was the power of God which brooded over primal waters before time was, the power that fashioned cosmos out of chaos, form out of the formless, name out of the nameless void. The descent of the Spirit is not just an event of the past. The Son of Man is We, the sons and daughters of men. What happened to Jesus happens to all men and women of every age and culture. If so, the Spirit must be at work in our history as well. But where in our midst do we find the insufflation, of the Spirit?

Let us go into the cities, towns, and villages and tarry among the toiling masses. What do we see there? No dove divine brooding over the human continuum but vultures perched in high places itching to swoop down on the defenseless, man feeding on the flesh of man, the rich sucking marrow from the bones of the poor, mothers cursing their womb for the young they cannot feed, fathers selling the shame of their daughters at crossroads, children vying with dogs for the refuse of food in wayside dumps while the scholar looks on impassively taking down notes for his dissertation, and a paunchy priest passes by muttering imprecations!

Could it be that the Spirit not finding a foothold in the masses has withdrawn to the more congenial sequestered islands of modernity? In fact, in the more posh areas a different picture awaits us, a picture seemingly more like the handiwork of the Spirit of God: chubby little children, each a blithe poem wrought in flesh and blood, flitting about in well laid-out lawns and gardens; teen-aged cuties tiptoeing in high-heeled shoes as though wary of the defiling touch of the earth; muscular boys and girls nursing dreams of spiraling up from conspicuous to more conspicuous consumption; sleek, presentable, antiseptic ladies and gentlemen exuding seductive perfumes and sweet reasonableness; palatial residences resounding with laughter and rejoicing to the accompaniment of exotic music and dance. Dazzled by so much wealth and well-being, we might exclaim: here indeed is the land flowing with milk and honey, here are the bearers of the Spirit, the creators of the New Humanity. But on a closer look, the vision vanishes, the hope collapses. What looked like the Spirit of God proves to be but scavengers of demon-dung, money. The hilarity and the merry-making show for what they really are: so many devices to drown uneasy consciences and anguished groanings. In this world of make-believe, love is at best a sentiment confined to one's kin or class, at worst a commodity bought in the marketplace; and religion, a convenient means to bridge the gulf between profit and loss.

Disenchanted, we wend our way to the world of religion, the acknowledged domicile of the Divine. Here, in temples, mosques, and Churches, the routine of prayers and offerings and incantations and libations go on without a hitch. But what these confer on the devotees is no more than a private consolation for public sins. They leave the world untouched, as mutilated and fragmented as ever before. Religion even feeds the irrational forces of death and violence as happens in every communal riot. As for the accredited mediators of the Spirit-priests, pastors, and god-men - they can only trot out impotent words, mere vacuous shells from which the Spirit has long since fled. What is worse, they speak at cross purposes. Some say that the Spirit is the spirit of science, technology, and progress; others that the Spirit is the spirit of flight from the world of time and space; others that the Spirit is concentrated in the navel within the navel; still others that the Spirit is brewed in the genitals! But all of them have one thing in common: they know the magical art of condensing the Spirit into gold and silver and real estate. Few know of the Spirit that uproots and plants, demolishes and builds up, of the Spirit that roams about roaring like a lion to avenge the blood of the innocent.

Does this mean the Spirit has deserted the world for good, leaving broken humanity to shift for itself? Is man fated to spend his days licking his wounds in eternal loneliness? No! That cannot be. The very fact that we now pose these questions is proof enough that the Spirit of God lives and is at large. For, our questioning is at the same time a quest born of concern for mankind's ultimate future and, as such, instinct with compassion. More, it is a quest straining to become the saving deed. And what is such questing but the Spirit stirring within us? What is concern and compassion but the Spirit unfolding? What is striving for a new creation if not the Spirit empowering the powerless?

Now to come back to the question we set out from, where do we find today the Spirit of God brooding over the waters of human existence? In all those men and women - young or old, rich or poor, learned or unlearned - who dare question the inhumanity of the world we live in, who are ready to translate their questioning into contesting, who have made their own the cause of the deprived and the unwanted, who long for a new world in which all men will weep when one man weeps. The Spirit reveals itself in our workaday world in many and varied fashions whether as nostalgia for lost oneness and wholeness or as prurience of the inner self which can find relief only in a total giving or as a new light in which truth stands raw and naked or as an invading presence that ennobles and fulfills. It makes its presence felt now as a healing touch, now as a defiant no to the rules of the game framed by the haves for the have-nots, now as concerted action to right the wrongs done to the dispossessed. In every case the Spirit is a spirit of transcension, urging men and women to reach out to the other shore of freedom whole and entire.

Seen in this light, the picture I drew a moment ago of the wasteland of a Spirit-less world represent only a part of the truth. All is not gloom and darkness. There are also points of light flashing out wherever the just exchange their messages. And the just who exchange messages are to be found not only among the poor but also among the rich. Not all the rich have mortgaged their souls to satan. Nor are all men of religion pedlars of divinity. From the subterranean roots of decaying religions, fresh shoots are sprouting. We are on the threshold of a new religiosity of the Spirit which will make dead bones prophesy, muted tongues wax eloquent, and hope blossom in the midst of despair. The earth will be riven in two, releasing new waters for the coming baptism of the Son of Man.

(*Jesus and Society*, Chap. 20)

24

A Quest That Never Ended

Exceptional individuals tend to acquire, often in their own lifetime, a mythical self over and above the existential self. The latter represents the sphere of freedom, striving, sin, guilt, and hope. It is the terrain where the individual grapples with the problem of his *being-unto-death* and life's ultimate meaning, where he experiences the tension between sin and repentance, despair and hope, illusion, and reality. On this level, life is not only forging ahead but also a going astray and retracing of one's steps. In short, the existential self reveals itself as fragile and vulnerable, never fully transparent to itself, never fully sure of its own footing. It is in virtue of this deeper self that individual life is woven into the wider fabric of the human community and becomes a moment in the flux of universal history.

Quite different is the status of the mythical self which is largely a product of the community. But the community does not produce it out of nothing. It uses as raw material the outstanding qualities or achievements of the person concerned. Thus a great leader, sportsman, filmstar, or a saintly person becomes almost inevitably the object of myth-making. Society, so to speak, segregates the person from among them, sets him up in an *other* world outside the flux of ordinary time as though mankind must disown those it admires most! In course of time, the mythical self submerges the existential. The element of tension and contradiction and doubt in the individual thus mythicized is either slurred over or eliminated. His foibles are transmuted into virtues, his opinions into eternal verities.

Now, it is beyond doubt that what the Gospels and the Epistles project is largely the image of the mythicized Jesus: the Son of God, the Son of Man, the Word Incarnate, the Messiah, the Redeemer, and so on. He presents himself to us as one come from above, not as one sprung up from below, from our earth as are plants, animals, and the rest of the humankind. Clothed in power and glory, he stands before us as an alien, as though his humanity were but a garment he put on and then laid aside for reasons of expediency.

This mythical image of Jesus is not all untruth. For myth builds on reality. At the same time, it distorts reality, transforming it into an ideal superstructure over and above the real world. This is because mythical discourse is conditioned by the needs of the collective unconscious and by the economic, political, and cultural factors prevailing at any given juncture in the history of people. The distortion is reinforced by theology, which has its starting point in myth. Hence the need to radically criticize the mythical and theological image of Jesus. This means laying bare the ultimate matrix of myth and theology, namely Jesus' existential self. It is this self that stands in plasmic continuity with the human community. More importantly, it is the privileged place where Jesus encountered - and we encounter - the Divine. Such an encounter with Jesus' deeper self and, through it, with the Divine is possible. For, myth has not succeeded in entirely erasing history. As one goes through the Gospels one can see the true visage of Jesus shining through in places where myth has not hardened into an opaque veil.

All human existence is a quest after wisdom, power, and love. And Jesus is no exception. In what follows, some tentative reflections are offered on his search for saving wisdom.

Mythical discourse delights in making the relative absolute. Thus Luke identifies Jesus with the wisdom of God (11:49). So does Paul in his first letter to the Corinthians (1:24). In this perspective, Jesus has nothing in common with us ordinary mortals who become wise, if at all, through much seeking and doubting and learning and unlearning. Luckily for us, Luke has another passage that lets us see Jesus as he really is. It reads:

> "As Jesus grew up he advanced in wisdom and in favour with God and man." (2:52)

This shows that the young prophet did not suddenly appear on the scene in the fullness of a wisdom infused from some heaven above. Nor did his life unfold according to some pre-determined plan he had foreknown right from the beginning. Not even the descent of the Spirit on the day of his baptism provided him with a blueprint for action. What it gave him was the awareness that he was called to effect a new exodus of his people, of all people, away from servitude to the horizon of absolute freedom. But how to carry out that mission? He had to read the answer from the signs of the times, from the logic of the succession of events over which he had no control.

Thus it was the arrest of John the Baptist that signaled to him that the time was ripe to launch his ministry of preaching and healing (Mk 1:14). The course of that ministry held many surprises for him, pleasant and unpleasant. He went to Nazareth, his hometown, hoping to make disciples there but only to be amazed at their unbelief. He returned wiser, with the sobering conviction:

> "A prophet will always be held in honour except in his hometown, and among his kinsmen and his family." (Mk 6:6)

From then on he would direct his steps to the wider world, Jewish and Gentile. We find him, again and again, redefining his course of action in response to the unexpected turn of events. When, after the multiplication of the loaves, the crowd wanted to make him king, he hurriedly dismissed them along with the disciples, and himself retired to a mountain to pray, that is, to redefine his strategy in the light of what had happened (Mk 6:45; Jn 6:15). Again, when it became plain that Herod and the Jewish authorities planned to get him out of their way, he departed for the pagan territory of Tyre, lest his mission should be prematurely cut short (Mk 8:10). Surely, this is a far cry from the Jesus of mythical discourse who foreknew every detail of what the future had in store for him!

Just as mythical discourse absolutizes the relative, it transforms the contingent into the necessary. It would have us believe that Jesus knew for certain that his life stood under the law of the divine must. He is made to say as early as his sojourn in Caesarea Philippi:

> "The Son of Man must suffer many things, and be rejected by the elders and the chief priests and the scribes, and be killed, and after three days rise again." (Mk. 8:31)

The makers of myth come on the scene after the event. So it is easy for them to make what happened into something that had to happen. The event is transferred from the realm of chance to that of the pre-determined. In the bargain, the existential awareness of Jesus is eclipsed. That awareness included also doubt and uncertainty. To be sure, he knew well enough that going to Jerusalem and confronting the authorities there would amount to risking his life. If Jesus knew his death was a divine must, why did he seek clandestinity during his visit to Jerusalem? After each visit to the temple, he withdrew to Bethany or to the Mount of Olives in order to be in the secure company of his trusted friends. On that fateful night when he wrestled with the God of his destiny, he had his closest disciples act as body-guards. So much so that the Jewish rulers had to suborn Judas to lead them to where his Master was. Again, why the agony in the garden, why the sadness unto death if Jesus had known beforehand that God had willed his death on the Cross? Besides, there are reasons to think that he had planned to lead his disciples, after his prophetic repudiation of the temple, to Galilee and beyond, to the pagan world. In all probability, his death was an open issue until the moment of his arrest. This in no way detracts from his greatness as the prophet of the new age to come. On the contrary, it only adds to his stature if, in fact, he had wished to live longer and continue his mission and in the end freely surrendered to the divine will that had overtaken him.

So far about Jesus' ignorance of his own personal future. But the logic of it applies equally to his message concerning the ultimate future of humanity. He did not know how his work would fructify into the Kingdom of God. Significant in this context is the following parabolic saying:

> "The Kingdom of God is like this: A man scatters seed on the land; he goes to bed at night and gets up in the morning; and the seed sprouts and grows - how he does not know." (Mk. 4:26, 27)

The sower is Jesus; the seed, the message of the reign of God. How the tiny seed will grow into the envisioned cosmic tree of life divine and human, he did not know. Nor did he know of the time when the new age will dawn upon the world: "but of that day or that hour no one knows, not even the angels in heaven nor the Son but only the Father." (Mk. 13:32)

His ignorance seems also to extend to the why of his personal destiny in relation to the ultimate future he believed in. For he died a criminal with the anguished cry ringing from the Cross: My God, my God, why has thou forsaken me? (Mt. 27:46).

(*Jesus and Society*, Chap. 21)

25

Power in Powerlessness

Human existence is instinct with the urge to pass from the formless to the formed, from darkness to light, from death to life. The fullness of light and life and love which is the goal of all human striving is what we call the Divine. To let oneself be taken hold of by the Divine is to have one's instincts, drives, sensuousness, knowing, and willing brought to a point of concentration where one becomes capable of changing one's environment of persons and things. On the other hand, whoever blocks the invasion of the Divine suffers decentration and dissolution, and in the end, succumbs to the forces of death. In the process, he or she becomes a matrix of violence and aggression. Such violence takes a threefold form depending on whether it is directed against the body (economic), the will (political) or the mind (ideological). Contrastively, those who are divinely empowered promote life, freedom, and creativity.

If ever there was a man taken hold of by the Divine and empowered to transform things animate and inanimate, that was Jesus. In his presence the chaotic reverted to form, death ebbed away to make room for the influx of life. At his command the tempest subsided, the raging sea resumed its calm, withered bodies turned whole, the leper was cleansed, the blind regained sight, the mute spoke and the deaf heard. His glance pierced the inmost recesses of the human spirit diffusing light and love. Power went out of him to heal not only individuals but also a sick society and a decaying religion. But the manifestation of power through any human being finds its limit in the inevitability of death and the resistance of other human wills. As, with the onset of old age, one's mind dims, drives slacken, and will is enfeebled, one loses one's grip on the world and lets death have the final word. Jesus did not experience in natural death the limit of his power; for his was not a natural death; he was murdered in the prime of youth. But he did find an outer limit to his power in the resistance of the unbelieving many.

Such resistance on the part of people was due to the hardening of their hearts under the influence of the prevailing ideology. It came from the defenders of the status quo which the same ideology sought to legitimize: from the Pharisees, priests, scribes, and secular rulers. Similarly from ordinary men and women deeply entrenched in tradition as is clear from Jesus' failure to work any miracles in his own hometown. Not even the disciples were free from the stultifying influence of ideology. In their case, it was the ideology of the Zealots, which would have Jesus proclaim himself a political Messiah. An instance is Peter's outburst at Caesarea Philippi when Jesus announced his strategy of confrontation unto death with the powers that were. It elicited from the Master the stunning rebuke:

> "Get from behind me Satan, for your thoughts are not those of God but those of men." (Mk. 8:33)

These words lead us to the heart of the personal destiny of Jesus as well. He thought the thoughts of God which promote life and love; Peter, on the other hand, entertained the thoughts of men (the Zealots) who believed in violence leading to hate and death. No less death-dealing were the thoughts of the religious and secular authorities. These wished to put him to death so that they may continue to reign over their own kingdom of the dead (over money, which is dead labour, over the repressive apparatus of the state that imprisons and kills, and over ossified dogmas). The conflict here is between Jesus and the power of God he mediated, on the one hand, and his adversaries who courted the power(lessness) of death, on the other. The lines are clearly drawn. Jesus stands on the side of freedom, invulnerably anchored in his hope in the reign of God. On the other side are arrayed the ruling classes and the extremist Zealots, the former committed to the status quo and the latter to restoring the Davidic line.

But the scenario changes as Jesus faces the immediate prospect of death. Death is like an ocean. The ocean may fascinate the man sunning on the beach but not him who is drowning. As the violent termination of his life stared in his face, the citadels of his being shook. He began to be afraid and be sad to the point of dying. Understandably. For he loved life, enjoyed drinking from the fruit of the vine, found delight in the lilies of the field and the birds of the air, cherished the company of his friends male and female. He might also have wished to carry his saving message to the gentile world after denouncing the goings-on in the temple. There remained now only one way to save his life, and that was to meet the forces of death on their own terms, i.e. by taking up arms. The way was easy as there were many Zealots from Galilee who had come down for the paschal feast and were camping in the city. They would surely have welcomed him into their ranks and even made him their leader. There is some evidence in the Gospels that Jesus toyed with the idea of armed resistance. An instance is the conversation between him and the disciples recounted in Luke:

> "When I sent you out with no purse or bag or sandals, did you lack anything? They said, Nothing. He said to them, but now, let him who has a purse take it, likewise a bag. And let him who has no sword sell his mantle and buy one. And they said, Look, Lord, here are two swords. And he said to them, it is enough." (22:35, 36)

Dogmatic bias has prevented biblical scholars from taking these words at their face value. Instead, we were told that the injunction to sell one's mantle and buy a sword reflects the practice in the early Church of missionaries equipping themselves with the means to defend themselves from wayside brigands, or that the word sword is to be understood metaphorically to mean the courage necessary for carrying out the mission of preaching the Good News. This, indeed, is doing violence to the text. It is much more likely that Jesus literally meant what he said. If so, the thoughts of men, the strategy of the Zealots, had found an accomplice in Jesus himself. It is as though his soul had split in twain, one part thinking with God and the other with men. The conflict now is no longer only between Jesus and the adversaries. It is internalized and manifests itself as a fission within himself.

This interpretation is reinforced by the account of the agony in the garden. The setting is itself ominous. The dark of night is a symbol of death; so too the sleep that overcame the disciples. The naked body of the young man who escaped into darkness leaving his only clothing behind is again a pointer to the working out of death which divests the body of all raiment and reduces it to utter nakedness. Thus, as the waves of death close in upon him and seek an entrance into the inner sanctuary of his soul, Jesus withdraws himself from his favourite disciples, lies prostrate on the earth and prays to his God, the other pole of his being, the giver of life and love. And what does his prayer consist in?

> "Abba Father, all things are possible to thee, remove this cup from me;
> yet not what I will, but what thou wilt." (Mk. 15:34)

The cup Jesus wished to escape from drinking is none other than of death. This is stated in so many words in the Letter to the Hebrews (probably an echo of Peter's reminiscence of that tragic night):

> "In the days of his earthly life, he offered up prayers and petitions, with
> loud cries and tears, to God who was able to deliver him from death." (5:7)

Humanly there was no way of avoiding death except through recourse to arms, themselves tools of death. But that would have meant adopting the strategy of the Zealots which, precisely, is what Jesus was tempted to do, 'what I will', in contravention of the strategy of God, 'what thou wilt'. Utterly powerless to reconcile his desire to hold on to life with the resolve to do the will of God, he cries in anguish to God: to whom all things are possible.

But, paradoxically, the nadir of his powerlessness is at the same time the supreme revelation of power. This is the meaning of the 'not my will'. The no to his own *self-as-flesh* has for its obverse side the yes to his true *self-as-spirit*. The flesh is weak and needs to lean on the strength of arms; the spirit is a power inherent in the human, so long as it is in harmony with the Divine. The repudiation of his own will on the part of Jesus is at the same time the repudiation of all violence, not only the violence of the Zealots but also the violence of the religious and political rulers of his day. As such, it is the most intense affirmation of life and freedom. That he was killed in no way detracts from Jesus' power. On the contrary, it is in his commitment to the reign of God to the point of death that the full extent of his power is made manifest. Thus he comes out of the temptation, made whole and entire, his inner breach healed, and his self restored to integrity. That is why, dead, he lives.

(*Jesus and Society*, Chap. 22)

26

Let Jesus be

Violence has been a factor of social cohesion in all social formations until now. Violence is physical when aimed at harming the body, psychic when aimed at bending and taming the human spirit. In what follows we shall reflect on the way Jesus reacted to the problem of psychic violence.

The agents of psychic violence are social structures and their watchdogs. In traditional India, the structures that shaped the minds of people were primarily the joint-family, the caste, and the temple. With the advent of capitalism, their place is being taken by the work-place, the nuclear family, the school, the party, and the media. The impact of work-places like firms, factories, and government offices is more on the unconscious than on the consciousness of individuals. If you are a wage labourer in a factory, through some sort of unconscious symbiosis you appropriate the values of private interest, competition, efficiency, rationality, and so forth, without which no factory can work. In contrast, institutions like the school and the media directly appeal to people's minds and wills. In either case, one's sensuousness, thinking, and decisions are so shaped as to suit the interests of the status quo. It is by thus producing the right type of individuals required to run its economic, political, and cultural institutions, that the social system as a whole reproduces itself.

But, are we justified in qualifying the determinant influence of societal structures on persons as a form of violence? There is undoubtedly an element of violence here insofar as the spontaneous urges of human beings are either smothered or distorted. Take the case of little children. They know no distinctions of sex, colour, caste, or religion; they have a smile for all, are open to all; they suspect none, scheme against none, entertain evil thoughts against none. For them, life is a quest; a sequence of discoveries and inventions. But all this spontaneous humaneness and joy of living tends to wither away under the stultifying impact of social institutions. The violence done to the young is all the more evident in the way in which the educational system, political propaganda, and the media warp their minds and reduce them to mere sentient cogs in the machine.

Psychic violence is all-pervasive, vitiating the very air we breathe. But most people are either unaware of it or succumb to it unquestioningly. Only exceptional individuals choose to critically react to it. In any society, it is the dissenters who watch over mankind's authentic future. The price they have to pay for dissent is exposure to further violence from the watch-dogs of the Establishment. Let us call this secondary violence, that is, the violence of the violent meted out to those who resist all violence. It too begins with attempts to kill the soul but may end up destroying the body.

In Jesus' time, the agents of psychic violence were the family, the village community and the synagogue, and those who presided over them: the patriarchal father, the priests, the scribes, and the Pharisees. We know about the violence Judaism did to the human psyche less from any explicit discussion of it in the Gospels than from Jesus' resistance to it. The saying, "No one puts new wine in an old bottle", probably reflects his own self-awareness within the framework of a decaying Judaism. His search for meaning, beauty, and love could not come to fruition under the prevailing socio-religious conditions. But Jesus did not view this merely as a personal problem but as one that weighed heavily on the common people as well. And he felt it his mission to lighten that burden. Remember his words:

> "Come to me, all whose work is hard, whose load is heavy; and I will give you relief. Bend your necks to my yoke, and learn from me, for I am gentle and humble-hearted; and your souls will find relief. For my yoke is good to bear, my load is tight." (Mt. 11:29, 30)

Jesus' no to psychic violence comes into full relief in the criticism he directed against the endless muttering of inane prayers and petitions, the working out of the notion of ritual purity in everyday life, the interpretation of the law which dispensed one from having to care for one's own father and mother, and a practice of cult that had usurped the place of mercy. Resistance may be seen also in his practice of eating with social outcasts, doing good on the Sabbath, not eschewing physical contact with lepers, and journeying in the company of women. Particularly relevant here are the woes he pronounced on the doctors of the Law, who make up heavy packs and pile them on men's shoulders; who shut the door of the Kingdom of heaven in men's faces; who go about making converts but only to make the converted twice as fit for hell as themselves; who pay tithes of mint and dill and cummin but overlook the weightier demands of justice, mercy, and good faith; who, as true heirs to the tradition of their fathers, continue to murder prophets. (Mt. 23:13-33) Though these woes as formulated in Mathew may be reflecting the conditions in his own Jewish Christian community at the time when the Gospel was written, it is undeniable that their roots go back to the life-situation of Jesus himself.

How did the Jewish establishment meet the dissent of the young prophet from Nazareth? The chief weapon used by any society under such conditions is psychic violence in the form of ostracism, whether horizontal or vertical. Ostracism is horizontal when the dissenter is tabooed and segregated from the community as a threat to the normal functioning of social life. He is branded as deviant or even mentally deranged. Today the same purpose is served by attaching to such persons odious labels like Naxalites. revisionists, terrorists, and extremists. Vertical ostracism may take the form of either pushing the dissenter down to the nether world (Among the Hebrews the underworld of waters was the abode of Satan and his brood) or projecting him upwards to the overworld of gods and goddesses. Even a cursory reading of the Bible will show that Jesus was the object of ostracism in all the senses just explained. To begin with, he was looked upon by his relatives as mentally deranged, as we read in the Gospel according to Mark (3:21). He was also labeled by his adversaries a 'glutton', a 'wine-bibber', and a 'friend of publicans and sinners' (Mt. 11:19). Likewise, he merited the label of a zealot vowed to throw out the Romans by force. Further, he was accused of driving out devils with the help of Beelzebub, the prince of demons (Mt. 12:24), thereby implying that he belonged to the satanic nether-world. In the Gospels, we find also attempts to project him upwards to the world of gods by pinning on to him high-sounding religious titles. Significantly, here the lead is given by the demons. It is they who for the first time call him 'the Holy One of God', 'the Son of the Most High God' (Mk 2:25; 5:7). The demons thus prove to be the first theologians. The disciples, with Peter at their head, do the same. They hail their Master, 'the Messiah'. In every case, the response of Jesus is invariably one of anger. He told the demons, "You shut up" (Mk 2:25). To Peter, at Caesarea Philippi, his answer came like a thunderbolt: "Away with you, Satan" (Mk 8:33). Traditional exegesis holds that what provoked Jesus' anger was the premature revelation of his identity. I suggest that his words are to be taken literally. He is resisting the attempt on the part of demonic forces to rocket him into the outer space of gods, from where he would be allowed to come down to earth only when the magical rites of priests so bid him. His stance in regard to ostracism in any form may be paraphrased as follows: "I am not in league with the demons; nor am I mad; nor am I a god. I am just Jesus, son of Mary and Joseph the carpenter." The true divinity of Jesus is revealed precisely in this refusal to be segregated from the family of humans, to be anything other than fully human.

Where ostracism fails to silence dissent, the guardians of the status quo resort to physical violence, as happened in the case of Jesus. What they did not realize was that a prophet murdered has a million tongues, whereas, alive, he has only one!

(Anawim No. 36, *Jesus and Society*, Chap. 23)

27

Historizing and Historiology as Prophecy

History is generally taken to mean the story of the significant events - economic, political, cultural - in the life of a people. The sequence of events goes to form an objective process, and it is up to the historian to identify and formulate its internal laws of motion. Underlying this conception is a quantitative notion of time with its mutually exclusive moments of past, present, and future. Of these three moments, the past is set up as the specific object of the science of history. Time, in this perspective, is homogeneous and is the common element in which all beings from inorganic things to humans have their beginning and their end. This way of viewing time and history has its level of truth but fails to reveal the essence of history as a human phenomenon. Deeper reflection will show that time and history are grounded in the kind of Being which human beings have and are. In what follows, I shall try to show that the historical is constitutive of human existence and how it dovetails with prophetic vision and hope. In doing so, I shall draw largely on the seminal reflections of Martin Heidegger, though on many issues my line of thinking will be found deviating from his.

Temporality as the Ground of the Historical

All subhuman beings, whether organic or inorganic, have certain completeness in themselves. They are what they are at any given moment and nothing more. Not so human beings. These are essentially more than what they actually are; that is, they await their completion in the future. They exist ahead of themselves, from the future. In this sense human beings alone exist, that is, stand outside and ahead of themselves, in the *not-yet*. Living from the future is to be understood not psychologically in the sense of longing for some definite state of being but ontologically as constitutive of humanness itself. What is the point of arrival of this tending ahead? Death? In a fundamental sense, yes. For, with death humans find their outer limit in non-being. But death is not negativity pure and simple. It is not merely passion but also action. It is the act of surrendering all one has, to the generations yet to come. It is that definitive act of tradition (from the Latin verb *tradere* which means to hand over) which ensures the continuity of history. But if death is the final act of tradition, it is because life itself is a handing over and a handing down. For, no sooner is a human being born than he starts dying, than he starts handing down the power and the glory and the shame that is his. Every deed done, every word uttered, goes to swell the planetary stream of life for good or for bad.

What is true of the individual, is true of the community as well. What it has received from the generations gone by, it hands down to the generations to come. For the community, too, to live is to die, and to die is to give itself away, thus constituting the flux of history. Now, the question we raised earlier crops up again: What is that to which the human community is tending? The answer can come not from reason but only from hope. And hope will say that the human caravan has for its goal theandric plenitude, the full revelation of the Divine in the full revelation of the human. But theandric fullness can be the future of the human community, only if it gathers into itself the past, individual as well as collective.

Seen from this angle, every individual exists as a project, as a structured whole of possibilities, whose ultimate realization merges with the absolute future of mankind. But whence does the individual draw the possibilities that await maturation in the future? From the heritage, he was born with. Human existence stretches itself between two finitudes, those of birth and death. But just as by handing down what has been accomplished to coming generations, one transcends the finitude of death, so too by appropriating the heritage handed down, one transcends the retrospective finitude of birth. In drawing upon the possibilities handed down, one also accepts the limitations accompanying one's birth in a particular family, in a particular community, at a particular historical juncture. These possibilities and limitations are anterior to any choice on our part and go to make up our fate as individuals and our destiny as a collectivity.

Living from the future and taking over the heritage of the past, we comport ourselves in the present. The possibilities of the past are never taken over as they are found but subjected to a critique. That is why each generation has its own 'world', understood as the structure of meanings that mold our dealings with the environment of humans, implements, and nature. Correspondingly, each generation lets the earth reveal itself in a way unique to it.

It follows from the reflections that the three ecstasies of time - past, present, and future - are immanent in one another, thus constituting the temporality of human existence. This seems to be what T.S. Eliot meant when he wrote,

"Time present time past

Are both perhaps present in time future,

And time future contained in time past." (Four Quartets)

Where we live from the future and draw upon the heritage of the times gone by, we invest the present with a meaning that overflows the bounds of the *here-and-now* and render our being and acting at once redemptive and recreative: redemptive, in so far as we gather into, and save for, the future the authentic possibilities of the past; re-creative, in so far as we thus prepare the way for the full revelation of the human and the Divine. To live out in this manner the reciprocal immanence of the future, the past, and the present is to authentically historize. Historizing in this sense is at once fateful and free: fateful, because the possibilities we take over are not of our own making but pre-given; free, because we choose what we have inherited. This holds true of the community as well. In projecting a future, it has to rely on the possibilities the past has destined. Between the destiny and the destination (the realm of freedom) lies the way of the cross. In Heidegger's words,

> "Only in communicating and struggling does the power of destiny become free."

Fall From Authentic Historizing

Historizing can be inauthentic about the future, the past, or the present. And most people most of the time are inauthentic in one way or another.

One can be inauthentic about the future either by denying it or absolutizing it. Whoever denies the future does so for fear of death. One tries to flee from the prospect of death by imprisoning oneself in the *here-and-now*. Such a one lives by the motto, "Eat, drink and make merry, for tomorrow we die." This is to disown one's responsibility to future generations. For, instead of accepting death as the definitive handing over of oneself to the human community, one consigns it to the subconscious as part of the fate of the anonymous 'they.' The resulting loss of eschatological tension renders the person incapable of creative intervention in history.

Forgetfulness of the future often coexists with its spiritualization. This happens when the ultimate goal of life is conceived as an overworld of disincarnate souls, enjoying the beatific vision of an equally unfleshed divinity. A direct consequence of this is the devaluation of matter and all that is connected with it - body, sex, marriage, and the earth. What is more, civilization and history are debased to the level of a necessary evil to be transcended, a scaffolding to be dismantled, once the heaven above is reached. And creation's groaning in travail for the liberation of the children of God is frustrated. Angelism of this kind is what gave birth to the kind of "spirituality" that rules the hearts and minds of most Christians even today.

Regarding the past too, one can assume two contrary stances each leading to its form of inauthentic existence. The first consists of cultural amnesia, i.e. forgetfulness of the past in reaction to the traumatic experiences associated with one's birth, early childhood or lowly social origins, or in response to the colonization of one's mind by an alien culture. Whatever be the cause, the consequences are ruinous to the individual and the community. For, without the past, there is no incubation of the future nor any meaningful presence in the here-and-now. Where the umbilical bond with the past has been severed, creativity withers away. This explains the sterility of Indian Christians in the field of literature, drama, painting, music, sculpture, and so on. Shorn of their past, they have no unconscious reservoir of myths and symbols, without which no creation of the beautiful, no sensuous revelation of meaning, is possible.

The negation of the past often provokes its opposite, namely cult of the past which, in turn, manifests itself either as fundamentalism or as revivalism. Both are in full swing in contemporary India. Both look to the past for the supreme revelation of the human and the Divine. Every element of the tradition is seen as divinely inspired and, for that reason, valid for all times. Curiously, the cult of the past is, in effect, the negation of the past. For, the past is not allowed to be past, the dead is not left to remain dead but set up as eternally valid. In the bargain, the real challenges of the present are ignored and collective infantilism holds sway.

An inevitable consequence of the alienation of the past and the future is the estrangement of the present. Where the past and the future are glorified, the present exhausts itself either in chewing the cud of 'one's glorious past' or in dreaming up some illusory bliss yet to come. Both conservatism and futurism dehistorize the present. Another way of rendering the present inauthentic, is to absolutize it. This happens where the past and the future are repudiated and the individual or the community falls back on the present and encases itself in it. Delinked from memory and hope, the present becomes an end in itself and is valued in terms of the pleasure it can give. Human existence is, thus, reduced to a series of disparate experiences, some pleasing, others annoying. The resulting fragmentation of being and consciousness has become a universal phenomenon under capitalism which, on the one hand, destroys traditional cultures and, on the other, focuses on immediate consumption at the cost of humankind's global, futurul well-being.

From Historizing to Historiology

Having delineated the structured movement of historizing as constitutive of human existence, individual as well as collective, we are in a position to understand the nature of historiology or the science of history. "Every science is constituted by thematizing." To thematize means to render explicit what we are implicitly aware of. What historiology thematizes is the historizing of people. Its role is to disclose how a people, placing their hope in the future, draws upon the resources of the past and creatively lives out the *here-and-now*. This is something different from either discovering the universal laws of motion of history or describing and serializing past events.

But why disclose the historizing of individuals and communities that are no more? Because, to be in the future, one's own and that of the community, demands that each human being appropriates the traditions of his forbears to fulfill his task in the present. What everyone does unreflectively in virtue of one's historical essence, the historian does methodically and systematically. But he does so as one sharing his being with and representing the community. Through him, the community reaches back to the past generations, who in their day reached out to the future to hand down the wealth of what they had wrought in sound, wood, and stone.

It follows then that the historian is deeply involved in what he is trying to disclose. In disclosing the life of a people, he is appropriating his legacy as a sum of possibilities, which will go to shape his and his community's existential project. Which means the historian is part of the history he is trying to unravel. In other words, in unveiling history, he is making it. Here the familiar distinction between subject and object breaks down in favour of an encompassing primordial unity. This is what distinguishes historiology from the natural sciences where the scientist remains neutral to the object of his research.

From Historiology to Prophecy

The triune structure we have discerned in historizing and historiology also defines prophecy. The prophet is one who bears witness to the absolute future of humankind and places his hope in its coming. The Hebrew prophets spoke of that future in terms of the new heaven and the new earth where wolf and lamb shall feed together; Jesus, in terms of the Kingdom of God; the Buddha, in terms of the rule of *dharma*; and traditional religion, in terms of the heaven above. In prophetic vision, the future envisaged is also the fulfillment and recovery of the past. Underlying this is the conception that history is not necessarily a progression to ever more perfect modes of human existence but is in many respects a regression and so self-estrangement from an original state of wholeness and fullness. A clear instance is Jesus' pronouncement concerning the Mosaic law of divorce that it was made because of the obtuseness of the Hebrews and that "in the beginning, at creation", God had made humans male and female so that they join together and become one flesh. In fact, at the root of every significant breakthrough made by humankind in the past, one can find an attempt to recover some state of affairs that obtained "in the beginning". Anticipating the future and recovering the past, the prophet lives the present critically and creatively. Thus Jesus, the prophet par excellence, not only ruthlessly criticized the religion and society of his day but also initiated a counterculture and a counter-community.

Jesuit Presence in History

None would contest that as "companions of Jesus" the mission of Jesuits is to continue his prophetic intervention in history. But to be prophetic is to be historical in the fullest sense of the term, that is, so to live from the future hoped for that we, drawing upon the possibilities of the past, help usher in a new "world" and bring about a more primordial revelation of the earth.

But to be able to fulfill this task, Jesuits must tear themselves away from the inauthentic forms of historizing in which so many of them are caught up. Chief among such forms are angelism, cultural amnesia, and activism.

Angelism which projects the salvation of the soul as the ultimate goal of life has for its obverse side the devaluation of matter and everything material. The underlying dualism of matter and soul is foreign to the original Jesus tradition and is of Hellenistic provenance. To the Hebrew mind, the soul was nothing more than the dimension of inwardness specific to the human body. It is forgetfulness of this holistic conception of the human that led to the proliferation of 'spiritualities', not excluding the Ignatian. While claiming to save the soul, 'spirituality' spells doom for the earth. This is borne out by the ecological crisis we are facing today. The pursuit of matters spiritual served to legitimize the aggressive exploitation of the earth as a factor of production. The earth and the heavens were thus desacralized and disenchanted. Now the challenge is to reverse this trend and rediscover the divinity of the earth. This calls for dialogue with the fertility cults of old, which the Judeo-Christian tradition has from the time of the prophets denounced as incompatible with true faith.

Cultural amnesia has been the lot of Christians in all erstwhile colonies. Being a Christian means to have had one's being grafted on to an exotic tree that has not yet struck deep roots in the Indian soil. True, Christians are as much sons and daughters of the earth as Hindus. But, whereas the latter make their own the treasures the earth has handed down, the former disown and repudiate them as contrary to their faith. Tortoise-wise, the average Christian imprisons himself in encrusted beliefs and dogmas, which make him immune to the voice of the past. This holds true of most Indian Jesuits despite recent attempts at inculturation. They relate to their tribal, Dalit, or Hindu past only as an object of study. The past does not speak through their voice, becoming a 'subject' in and through them.

Activism: The end-result of angelism and cultural amnesia is a present devoid of meaning and creative tension. The estrangement of the present takes the form of cyclicism or activism. The first looks back to the past; the second to the future. Cyclicism characterizes the life of Jesuits working in institutions where they have to conform to the ever-recurring cycle of functions, rites, and festivals. Where it holds sway, one always ends where one began, and begins where one ended. Emptied of all uniqueness, the *here-and-now* offers nothing but boredom. Unlike cultural amnesia, activism is of comparatively recent origin. It is industrial-technocratic society's gift to religion. It is not so much a single malaise as a complex syndrome with varied manifestations. The activist Jesuit takes after the machine. He wants results and wants them immediately. To hell with the Kingdom and its glory.Also to hell with the promptings of the past. Salvation comes in the here-and-now in the form of tangible results. And producing results is a matter of technique. Hence the frantic search for ever new techniques psychological as well as para-religious: techniques of counseling and consoling, techniques of communicating and commanding, techniques of conjuring up and monitoring charisms. Mortally afraid of his techniques becoming obsolete and himself along with it, he must at regular intervals go abroad to the Meccas of technicized religion for updating sessions and refresher courses. Like his industrial counterpart, the activist Jesuits are acutely aware of the value of time. He knows that time is not only money but also favour with God and man. No wonder he is always busy, hopping from appointment to appointment. Tyrannized by the particular, he lives a life of means and no ends, of expertise and no wisdom.

(*Ingathering*, Chap. 21)

28

The Cost of Discipleship

We are disciples of Jesus. And our discipleship does not consist of saying long prayers, in scrupulous observations of rituals and rubrics. Nor does it consist of strictly following certain rules and prescriptions. It consists rather in making our own the faith, the hope, and the attitudes of Jesus. Our task is to recapture his authentic spirit and make it the principle of our action today.

For this, we must reinterpret his teaching and life in the context of *our* historical situation. Conversely, we should reinterpret our historical situation in the context of his life and teaching. In doing so we may arrive at conclusions that go beyond what Jesus explicitly taught. In other words, our discipleship has to be original and creative. It does not spare us the agony of searching, experimenting, correcting our failures, retracing our steps, and even taking risks. And the supreme risk which discipleship includes is that of being put to death by the enemies of the Kingdom as was the case with Jesus himself.

Prophets of Hope

Like Jesus, we must live in the hope that in the end, God will reign supreme, that he will gather us all into his household. This hope we must share with the Indian masses who for long have been victims of fatalism. The poor must realize that it is in their power to overcome misery and oppression and that God is on their side. They must learn to look to the future rather than to the dead past, to the future they have to shape in response to God. Only when people begin to look ahead and forward can they engage in responsible planning for development. Where hope is absent the masses either lapse into a passive acceptance of their lot or succumb to collective frustration. And where frustration reigns there we have revolt without reason and protest without goals. *Hence we need a pedagogy of hope.* Here the crucial point we have to keep in mind is that hope can be communicated less by preaching than by action. It is the experience of success in eradicating misery which kindles hope and keeps it alive.

Meeting the Secular God

To believe in Jesus is at the same time to believe in the reign of God as a *present* reality. And the God of the present meets us not only, nor even primarily, in the sphere of cult but also and above all in our ordinary secular life. Jesus too met his God in the context of secular life, in homes and streets, by the well-side and the lake-side at gatherings and weddings. His death too was a secular death which he incurred as punishment for an allegedly political crime. As the master, so the disciple. We should learn to discover God and his call in the concrete situations of life. These situations may be either individual or collective. The secular *present* is the moment of decision, the hour of salvation. To act on this principle is to opt for a spirituality, not of withdrawal but commitment. We may not ignore the world of industry, commerce, politics, and culture as irrelevant to the Kingdom.

Building Up the Total Man

The God who meets us in the secular context makes a twofold demand on us as He makes on Jesus: to discover and foster those factors and forces in society which announce the germinal presence of the Kingdom and to uproot those others which fulfill the authentic aspirations of man. For the glory of God is the perfection of man. God calls man to become what he *ought* to be, to grow into maturity, and reach up to his full stature. Hence values like freedom, justice, cooperation, solidarity, and concern for one another are not merely values of the world but also values of the Kingdom.

Hence we as disciples of Jesus and as men committed to social reconstruction must give priority to projects which embody and realize these same values. When for instance we organize a cooperative and thereby educate its members in mutual concern and collective responsibility, we are not only contributing to secular welfare but also promoting the interests of God's reign.

As Christians, therefore, we have an obligation to collaborate with all groups and organizations which have for their aim the realization of human values and the creation of a new humanity.

Uprooting and Destroying

But human values cannot grow where oppressive structures abound, structures which wound and mutilate man. These must be uprooted and destroyed. Where these structures are allowed to exist, projects for development will benefit only the privileged classes.

What is the meaning of helping farmers produce more if the surplus goes to fill the coffers of money-lenders and merchants? What is the use of building roads if these make it easier for the exploiters to extend their empire into the rural areas? What is there is in increasing the income of the poor, if the added income is again expropriated in the form of taxes and finally given as government loans to big business? If so, no development is possible without a revolution of structures. Hence the call of the Kingdom as revealed in our concrete historical situation is a call to revolt against structures of exploitation. To respond to this call is at the same time to express our solidarity with Jesus who had the courage to challenge the socio-religious establishment of his day, knowing full well that it meant certain death for him.

Not by Bread Alone

We have seen that the total development of man is of relevance for the Kingdom of God and is, therefore, a Christian concern. It would, however, be wrong to conclude from this that mere economic development understood as progress in technology and the availability of consumption goods equals the reign of God. In relation to the Kingdom, such material progress is essentially ambivalent. Take for instance the mass media. They have bridged the gulf between peoples and nations. They have made it possible for man to be conscious of all men in all places. In other words, they have created a universal consciousness, and thereby made universal love possible. But to make universal love possible does not mean realizing it. More, these same mass media could also be an instrument of universal hatred. What is true of mass media is equally true of all products of civilization. They may work for or against the interests of God's reign depending on the way man uses his freedom. Those who fail to recognize this cannot evade the conclusion that the Americans are nearer the Kingdom of God because science and technology have brought them nearer the moon.

Material progress contributes to the growth of the Kingdom of God only in the measure in which it fosters human values like justice, love, and fellowship. It is therefore not enough to dig wells, build roads, raise crops, etc.

What is more important is to make use of such projects to change the attitude, and values of the masses. What we should aim at in our social commitment is nothing less than a revolution of the spirit of man.

Commitment as Humanism

Our faith in Jesus impels us to commit ourselves to the total development of man. But would not such commitment lead to a diminution of our personality, to a loss of our beings? In trying to develop others are we not condemning ourselves to underdevelopment? By no means.

For it is in our commitment that we meet God. And in meeting the visage of God we recognize and realize our true visage. In working with and for Him we understand our true name and fulfill our true destiny. Besides it is in our effective concern for others that our authentic self unfolds.

The human in us will grow and bear fruit only if we strike roots in others of our kind. Therefore, he who lives only for himself will eventually end up as a stunted human being. The words of Jesus are still relevant,

"The man who loves himself is lost, but he who hates himself in this world will be kept safe for eternal life" (Jn. 12:25)

(Chap. 22, *Ingathering*)

29

The Present Cultural Crisis

Analysis and Prognosis

That we are in the thick of a cultural crisis all would readily concede. Many and varied are its symptoms: the all too frequent strikes, gheraos, and demonstrations; the recurrence of atrocities against the Harijans, repeated outbreak of communal violence, the arrogance and the callousness of the bureaucracy, the floor-crossings, and defections indulged in by the politicians, the shameless subservience of the intellectual elite to whoever happens to be in power, the ruthless pursuit of profit by traders and big business, and the cynicism pervading the nation as a whole. What is the nature of the malaise affecting the body-social? What are the social dynamics that led to its emergence? What is going to be the outcome of the crisis? These are some of the issues which I shall try to answer in this study. The crisis being truly continental in its sweep, and the forces at work so complex and fluid, it is impossible to arrive at conclusions applicable to every part of the country. All one can hope for is to define the basic contradictions underlying the present crisis. Much, therefore, of what I am going to say will be exploratory and subject to further revision.

Before we attack the theme itself it is necessary to clear up the ground by defining the conceptual framework used in this study. The key term is *culture*, by which I mean the system of ideas, beliefs, values, and hopes which shape the conduct of the members of a community. In other words, culture is the normative consciousness of a community inherited from the past and transmitted, with or without modifications, to the coming generations. But ideas and values do not hang in the air. They crystallize into myths, legends, folklore, cult, art, and literature. They body forth into specifically cultural institutions such as schools, temples, and the media. They inform also political and economic structures.

It is, therefore, impossible to define society outside of culture. However, the inner unity between culture and social structure should not blind us to the possible emergence of tension between the two. Tensions develop either because institutions fail to conform to the culture they are meant to embody; or, more importantly, because of the unequal development of both. Culture may lag behind institutions (feudal loyalties in relation to democratic elections) or *vice versa* (as when the rural youth who have undergone urban schooling return home to find themselves inserted in the traditional framework of joint-family and caste).

It follows then that culture has a certain autonomy *vis-a-vis* social structures and institutions. The former is never totally determined by the latter. On the other hand, all culture is conditioned by the social base, i.e. by social and political relations, just as these in their turn are moulded by culture. Does this mean that culture and social structures stand to each other in relation only to mutual conditioning? But such a purely circular causality does not explain how society changes, how the circular movement becomes spiral. The usual Marxist answer is that it is changes at the level of the mode of production that brings about cultural changes. But, all changes on the economic level *presuppose* a new consciousness, and therefore, cannot be adequately explained without reference to culture. More, it is in consciousness that we should see the decisive factor that enables man to effect a rupture in the social envelope and achieve a break-through into the future. Revolution of consciousness has, therefore, a certain priority over the revolution of structures. This, however, does not mean that the latter begins only where the former ends. All that is claimed is that significant changes in values and beliefs can be achieved even before the transformation of the economic and political system.

I shall now indicate the elements which go to make up culture, viewed both as a process and a system, by suggesting the main questions to be asked under each head. Admittedly, the following enumeration is to be taken more as an analytic tool than as an accurate mirroring of reality. For in concrete reality each element presupposes and is presupposed by all the others, as is the case with any organic whole.

Production: Who are the creators of culture? People as a whole or only a privileged class? Who owns the means of cultural production such as knowledge of the language, access to already written texts, etc? What is the content of the culture produced?

Circulation: How is culture disseminated in a community? Who controls the mechanism of cultural dissemination?

Consumption: How do people assimilate cultural products? Is culture consumed equally by all? Or is there an elitist consumption distinct from mass consumption? Is the appropriation of culture by the masses free or determined from outside?

Legitimation: How are people led to accept a culture as valid? In virtue of tradition, authority, legends, myths, or religion?

Closure: How does the community impose restrictions on the kind of culture to be produced, disseminated, and consumed by its members? Negatively, how does it ensure that a counterculture does not develop which would disrupt the status quo? Who are the persons that apply closure? The community as a whole? or only the privileged classes (the rich, the rulers, the teachers)?

Sanction: What is the system of rewards and punishments whereby strict adherence to the dominant culture is assured? Are rewards and punishments secular (economic, social, political) or religious? this-worldly or other-worldly?

Safety-valves: Which are the devices whereby pent-up frustration with the dominant culture can vent itself so that the social system returns to its original equilibrium without having to break up? Are these safety-valves secular or religious or both?

The elements enumerated above must be viewed from the point of view of the contradictions inherent in them. And the basic contradiction affecting all of them in all social formations hitherto is the *contradiction between the teachers and the taught,* between the intellectual elite and the masses. It consists of the fact that, though all may consume cultural products, it is a privileged minority that controls the production, circulation, and consumption of culture. This minority also controls the machinery of legitimation, sanction, and closure. In simpler terms, a few arrogate to themselves the right to decide what the rest of the community should think, how they should evaluate things and what they should live for. The contradiction between the teachers and the taught is at once the cause and the effect of two other contradictions: *the one between the rulers and the ruled* (political) and the other *between the rich and the poor* (economic). These three contradictions are equally primordial though at a particular historical juncture one may prevail over the others.

The Traditional Culture of Domination

Production

All cultural activity is based on a certain understanding of the world shared by all the members of society. Or, better, culture is the expression of a community's self-understanding in the world. This self-understanding is the horizon in which beliefs, values, and hopes emerge and crystallize into cultural patterns. Now, people of *all* races, castes, and classes interpret the world and let their interpretation assume concrete cultural forms. But not all races, castes, end classes are in a position to impose their culture as valid for all. In India, the dominant culture has been that of the dominant race (the Aryans) and of the dominant caste (the Brahmanas). In the Code of Manu, we read,

> "Teaching, studying, performing sacrificial rites, and giving away and receiving gifts — these he (*Purusha*) assigned to Brahmanas."[1]

Not having to work for a living, they could devote themselves to mental labour i.e. to the elaboration of religious, moral, and philosophical ideas, deemed normative for society as a whole. To a lesser extent, the warrior castes also engaged in cultural activities. In medieval and colonial India kings, not all of whom were Kshatriyas, were the patrons of art, literature, and philosophy. In contrast, the labouring caste of Sudras was debarred from the study of the Vedas, the chief means of cultural production.

> "The Lord has prescribed only one occupation for a Sudra, namely service, without malice of even these other three classes."[2]

Today, however, the Brahmana monopoly of culture is being challenged by the emergence of the intermediate land-owning castes as dominant castes. But the condition of the Sudras and the Harijans remains the same as before. Their role even today consists of passively conforming to the values and norms laid down by their masters. No wonder that the dominant culture serves the interests of the higher castes.

The same conclusion will be borne out by an examination of the content of the same culture, of its ethics, religion, and philosophy. But the limited scope of this study forbids such a venture. I shall instead dwell briefly on the caste system, itself a product of culture. The ethos permeating it consists of servility to those above, and arrogance, superciliousness, and paternalism in respect of those below. It combines in one the desire to dominate and the desire to be dominated. It creates in the social actors a sadist-masochist psychic structure, cutting across every rung of the social ladder. For even the outcaste, while recognizing the superiority of caste Hindus, will view himself superior to the other outcastes. The resulting division among the labouring castes prevented any organized revolt against caste domination. The bias in favour of the upper castes may be discerned also in the constituents of culture described below.

Circulation

Unlike Christianity, Hinduism did not develop into an institutional church distinct from the people. The social organization itself fulfilled the function of disseminating culture. Once the caste system became congealed into a rigid pattern, each caste became the vehicle not only of its own sub-culture but also of the dominant culture. However, within the macro-system of caste, two institutions stand out as the organs of cultural dissemination: the joint-family where the young were schooled in the values and beliefs of their elders, and the temple where the young and old assembled to listen to music, dance, drama, folktales, puranic recitations, etc. So long as the Brahmanas held a ritual monopoly, it was easy for them to use the temples for propagating their culture of domination. Since then the lower castes have won the right to have their own priests. However, even today the Brahmana hegemony over the interpretation and dissemination of traditional culture continues, though in subtler ways than in earlier ages. Besides new organizations have sprung up for the reproduction and propagation of traditional culture, such as the Ramakrishna and Chinmaya missions.

Consumption

The appropriation of any culture corresponds to the need people have for it. Now, it is obvious that the dominant culture was not created to satisfy any *spontaneous* need felt by the common folk. Rather it was imposed on them from above by the ruling castes. The priestly class also resorted to the strategy of co-opting elements of folk culture but not without distorting their original content to suit their own interests. In the course of time, the beliefs, values, and norms of caste hierarchy were internalized by the disprivileged classes. Without such internalization, the caste system itself could not have emerged. Herein lies also the explanation for the process of Brahmanization whereby the lower castes sought to raise their social and ritual status by imitating the customs and practices of the higher castes. The situation is fast changing in contemporary India with the low castes and outcastes trying to repudiate the culture of their erstwhile masters which they had been forced to accept as their own.

Legitimation

The higher castes realized early enough the need to fashion a system of legitimation. To this end, they created myths, legends, and scriptures. Where traditional texts did not lend themselves to the promotion of their interests, they were tampered with or distorted with additions and interpolations. Thus the *Purusha-sukta* of the Rigveda is probably a later interpolation to legitimate caste inequality. Probably, too, the *Gita* in the present form is the result of an attempt on the part of the ruling castes to provide scriptural legitimacy for caste exploitation. Krishna of the *Gita* claims he has created the caste system; he emerges also as the champion of violence when he urges Arjuna to embark on the extermination of the Kauravas, among whom were his own revered preceptors. Yet another source of legitimation was the authority of seers, saints, and members of the priestly caste. Legitimation was sought also in the antiquity of the tradition concerned. The older a practice or belief the greater was its normative value, its binding power.

Closure

In order to ensure that no counterculture emerged that might pose a threat to their supremacy, the priestly class closed the canon of the scriptures. Originally the Vedas alone formed the canon. Subsequently, with a view to domesticating the protest movements that arose around the sixth century B. C. it was expanded to include also the epics, the Puranas, and the Law Books. Later still, the writings of the Bhaktas in medieval India were integrated into the Hindu tradition, though not on a par with Vedas and Agamas. In the wake of successive foreign invasions, which put Hinduism on the defensive, the mechanism of closure became more and more rigid. Besides, economic dependence on the upper castes impeded the lower castes and the outcastes from producing a counterculture, particularly so, when the local rulers were hand in glove with the former. Today, however, under the impact of western education, the capitalist mode of production, and the politicization of the masses, the walls put up by the upper castes around the minds and hearts of the disprivileged are tumbling to the ground, and the cultural enclosures are thrown open to new ideas and questions.

Sanctions

The mechanism of closure was reinforced with a system of rewards and punishments. Punishments ranged from social ostracism to physical torture, mutilation, or even death. Understandably, the system of punishments favoured the upper castes, since, for identical crime, the lower the caste status of the culprit the severer was the punishment meted out. (Code of Manu VIII, 1-420) Worse still, punishment pursued the offender even after death. Here the popular belief in Karma and samsara came in handy as a stick to beat the poor with. These could hope to be born in a higher caste only if they scrupulously fulfilled their caste duties which consisted, by and large, in serving the upper castes. It should be further mentioned that in traditional India it was the duty of the king to enforce the law, in other words, see to it that each citizen fulfilled his caste duties.

Safety-valves

Popular discontent with the hegemony of the upper castes found an outlet in religious festivals, folk dance, and martial arts. The tension built up in the social organism by sexual repression found relief in ritual intercourse, erotic devotional practices, and occasional festivities (such as Pooram festival in Kerala) when the customary taboos were lifted and obscenity was sanctioned. For the down-trodden masses it was easy to let off accumulated resentment in ways provided by their own sub-cultures, which were granted such autonomy as would not harm upper-caste interests. By reenacting their origins in own cultural forms they could maintain the illusion of their greatness. The traditional culture of domination whose dynamics I have tried to explain, persists even today, though greatly modified by the invasion of capitalist culture. Space does not permit me to deal with Christianity and Islam which also have developed, each in its own way, ideologies calculated to enslave the minds and hearts of people.

The Capitalist Culture of Domination

Production

The capitalist culture did not emerge from within traditional society as it did in the west. Rather it was born in the west and subsequently imported to India by the colonial rulers. But soon there sprang up an indigenous class of ideological parasites — bureaucrats, lawyers, writers, journalists, teachers, etc, who either came from the wealthier classes or at least shared their interests. They became the votaries of the new culture. They did not so much create as circulate the cultural stereotypes which western capitalism had thrown up. Paradoxically, it is the traditional intellectual elite, the Brahmanas, who took to the new culture like fish to water. They managed to infiltrate the professions, the universities, journalism, politics, and, latterly, also business. In the course of time, the intermediate castes, too, began to assimilate the culture of the bourgeoisie.

And in what did the new culture consist? It proclaimed the primacy of rationality and science. It preached the value of private interest, profit-seeking, competition, aggressive self-assertion, efficiency, and consumerism. In contrast to a traditional society based on *quality* (in terms of ritual purity) the new culture taught the primacy of *quantity* in so far as everything — goods, honour, virtue, love, esteem, the favour of God and man — was reduced to a commodity to be bought or sold. It introduced social relations of personal indifference in the place of relations of personal dependence which marked earlier society. On the political plane, it gave rise to the notion of the abstract 'citizen' who, legally, is equal to every other citizen but in reality either belongs to the rich or the poor, rulers or the ruled.

A little reflection will show that this culture is eminently suited to promote the interests of the emerging bourgeoisie. The pursuit of private interest and profit makes sense only for those who own the means of production. Similarly, competition among unequals can only benefit the stronger in terms of wealth and power.

Efficiency in production helps capitalists to augment profits. Consumerism serves the same purpose by producing a consumer class who would buy the products marketed. The commoditization of everything helps the bourgeoisie to buy not only raw materials, machinery, and human labour but also honour, esteem, and political power. The impersonality of human relations under capitalism frees them from all feudal obligations which might come in the way of capital accumulation. The same judgement applies to the new political culture, which, in the name of democracy, politicizes the masses at the time of elections only to depoliticize them in the time between elections, which proclaims the equal rights and obligations of all as *citizens* but in truth degrades the poor to being subjects only of obligations and not of rights.

Circulation

The principal means whereby the bourgeois culture is disseminated is the educational system, itself imported from the west. Its aim is to instill in the young the sense of values (disvalues?) and the proper attitudes which would equip them to fulfill the roles required by

Capitalist economy and politics. The children of the poor are trained to become obedient and disciplined workers; the sons and daughters of the rich are taught to become technicians, executives, professionals, government servants. A second important vehicle of bourgeois culture is the mass media, comprising newspapers, radio, television, films, and advertising. Rare exceptions apart, the values and ideas these communicate, are germane to capitalism. For instance, in films, the popular hero is usually an example of conspicuous consumption, or if he is not already such, destined to become one. He is also an example of aggressive self-assertion. The systemic violence of capitalism is reflected in the cult of violence that marks the more popular films. As for newspapers, the version they give of events is the one that emanates from the guardians of the Establishment and the ideologues of capitalism. This is not in the least surprising; for, after all the media are controlled, if not owned, by the ruling classes. What is true of the media is true also of most political parties, cultural organizations, and trade unions. The values of capitalism are disseminated also through institutions and structures that in themselves have nothing directly to do with the production or circulation of culture. Thus one cannot work in a factory or firm without appropriating the scale of values and the patterns of thinking, acting, and reacting proper to it. By merely going through his routine functions the worker learns to discipline himself, to produce more in less time (efficiency), to produce more than others (competition), to blindly obey his boss, to maintain impersonal relations with his peers and to view himself as a mere unit of production and not as a person.

Consumption

First, there is an elitist consumption centred upon the cities, indulged in by the upper and middle classes educated in the west or in the public schools within the country. For them, cultural entertainment consists of pop music, western dance, discotheque, cabarets, night clubs, parties, and a bit of social service as a convenient covering for conspicuous consumption. The Mecca of this elite is the centre of international capitalism, the United States. The neo-colonial culture they represent is steadily percolating to the lower strata of society, thanks to the film industry and the radio. It is held up as life's supreme goal accessible only to the elect. In places where the labouring classes still maintain social relations of dependence they too appropriate this culture by identifying themselves with their masters. Wider still is the appeal of consumerism. Capitalism weaves myths around commodities, by projecting them as symbols of status, good taste, high living, and sophistication. As a result, the consumer sees in such products not merely objects meant to satisfy a certain physical need but also a cluster of meanings. That is why their consumption is not only an economic but also a cultural phenomenon. True, the commodities in question are such as can be bought only by a privileged minority. But the impact of this sort of culture is noticeable also among the very poor.

Thus, for instance, a slum dweller may even forgo necessaries of life in order to save enough and buy a nylon shirt or a wrist-watch. What is dehumanizing about this mode of cultural consumption is that it is not spontaneous but engineered and artificially induced by means of advertisements. It nurtures the need for gadgets and kills the need for beauty, freedom, and genuine sociality.

Legitimation

The new culture of the masters has created its own secular myths for self-legitimation. Such indeed are the myths of progress, modernity, and individual freedom. I call them myths because they throw a veil over the concrete reality of people's lives, which for the most part is characterized by barbarism, stagnation, regression, and loss of freedom. Similarly, on the political plane, the sovereignty of the few over the many is legitimated by the slogans of democracy, socialism, and the sovereignty of the people.

Closure

The required closure is effected in a number of ways. Developing capitalism has an in-built tendency to suppress critical reflection on the part of the working class in so far as it denies them the necessary pre-conditions for such reflection, like the satisfaction of the minimum material needs (food, housing, clothing, medicine, etc.), a modicum of leisure, knowledge of the language, and access to existing texts. There are also deliberate attempts on the part of ruling classes to prevent any cultural awakening among the exploited masses. For instance, there has been in the last decades a decline in the funds allotted to primary education while the allotment for college education has shown a marked rise.

More importantly, closure is imposed by strictly controlling the media of cultural dissemination. This is done, first, by screening the personnel who man educational institutions, the press, the radio, and television. Besides, only such works are chosen as text-books for schools and colleges which do not pose any serious threat to the Establishment. Articles and books deemed 'unsafe' are confiscated and their printers and publishers taken to task by the Government. Government officials and the police keep a close watch both in towns and villages on anyone who may spread 'subversive' ideas. Terms tike 'socialism' and 'revolution' are all right for politicians to bandy about because in any case, they do not mean what they say. If you, the ordinary citizen, utter the same words and *mean what you say,* you are likely to find yourself in a prison house. Screening and censorship are resorted to also by private agencies that have a stake in the growth of capitalism in India, such as religious leaders, newspaper editors, and heads of publishing companies.

Sanctions

Sanctions are directed against those who either fail to conform to the prevalent ideas and values or violate the closure by smuggling in other ideas and values detrimental to the interest of the ruling classes. A subtle form of sanction is *margination,* whereby those who refuse to conform are labeled crazy, deviant utopian, pathological or even mad, and 'excommunicated' from the company of 'decent' people. The guardians of the status quo employ also cruder forms of sanction such as harassment, economic discrimination, and brute force. Not infrequently, labeling, and use of force go hand in hand. In some parts of the country, anyone who dares challenge the local landlord is labeled a Naxalite and taken to prison, if not shot dead. Significantly, the system of sanction is so devised as to work to the advantage of the privileged classes. If politicians, bureaucrats, and capitalists swindle crores of public money or unleash violence against the poor, the law professes helplessness. But the same law will come down heavily upon the poor wretch who steals a few coins wherewith to buy some food. Prostitution is tolerated if carried on in five-star hotels for the benefit of tourists and the indigenous rich but will be severely dealt with if resorted to by a poor woman who has no other way to make a living. The nudity of the rich is fashion; of the poor is obscenity. The lying and the dishonesty of the 'haves' are virtues; of 'have nots' vices.

Safety-valves

Strikes, demonstrations, and protest marches serve also as safety-valves whereby the working class gives vent to their resentment and are for that reason tolerated by the ruling classes, so long as they do not transgress the prescribed limits. The same purpose is served - this time by way of sublimation — by sports, karate, and films depicting violence. By identifying themselves with the exhibition of violence in sport and in films, the onlookers or the audience, as the case may be, satisfy their urge to pit violence against the violence of the social system.

Thus far I have tried to delineate the structure of the traditional and the capitalist cultures of domination. But the two do not run on parallel lines. Now it remains to see how they interact and whether the present cultural crisis can be explained on the basis of that interaction.

The Dialectic of Traditional and Capitalist Culture

At first sight, it would appear the traditional and capitalist cultures are diametrically opposed and, as such, can in no way co-exist. Which is probably true if we view things in the long run. But at the present stage of capitalist development in India, there seems to be no significant conflict between the two. Rather they seem to get along well, constituting what may be called conflictual harmony or harmonizing conflict. However, it is important to remember that they relate to each other not as equal but as unequal partners. Of the two, capitalist culture is the more dominant one, because it has an ever-expanding economic and political base, whereas traditional culture exists today without the corresponding economic and political relations, in other words, without the pre-conditions for its own reproduction. That is why in the long run it will be superseded, but not before having profoundly influenced the emergent culture of the bourgeoisie. With these preliminary reflections let us take a closer look at the interaction between the two cultures.

Group interest versus private interest

In itself, the pursuit of private interest which is the mainspring of capitalism is opposed to the traditional stress on group interest (the interest of family, caste, or village). But in reality group interest is made to serve private interest. It is a well-known fact that heads of firms and factories favour their own caste in the matter of recruitment and promotion. Politicians know that they can have a share in power only if they at least give the appearance of promoting the interests of their caste, community, or village. On the other hand, traditional communities take on the nature of corporate persons, each seeking its own private sectional interest and competing with similar communities. In consequence, traditional institutions become imbued with the spirit of capitalism which in turn assumes features of traditional culture.

Simplicity versus consumerism

Considered abstractly, the two run in opposite directions: the first requiring the minimization of wants; the second their maximization. Traditionally, simplicity was cultivated by the higher castes as a virtue; for the lower castes and the outcastes, it was a social necessity. With the introduction of the capitalist mode of production, the habit of self-imposed limitation on consumption helped the bourgeoisie to accumulate capital. On the other hand, the *induced* simplicity of the labouring castes made it easy for the former to extract more surplus value by decreasing wages to the minimum. But this was only at the initial stages. Today the bourgeoisie is beginning to realize that conspicuous consumption is itself a means to maximizing profit, in so far as it promotes business contacts and enhances the prestige of their firms. The organized proletariat for their part is demanding a greater and greater share of the cake, spurred on by the example of their employers. However, the unorganized poor by and large remain wedded to the traditional value of simplicity.

Inequality versus equality

The equality that capitalism embodies is twofold: the equality of exchange and the equality of all as *citizens*. The first consists of this that, whether you are rich or poor, Brahmana, or pariah, your one kilo of rice will exchange for the same quantity of any other commodity. The second means that, whatever be your position in the hierarchy of wealth or power, legally you enjoy the same rights as any other citizen. But it is obvious that both these types of equality are sham, without real content. For the equality of exchange has for its basis inequality in respect both of the number of goods you can offer exchange and of your capacity to purchase the goods you need. Similarly, the equality of all citizens is contradicted by the unequal sharing of power. Therefore, on the deeper level, capitalism too is a system of inequality Thus caste inequality dovetails with class inequality. The poor whom tradition had taught to look upon *caste* inequality as natural have little difficulty in accepting *class* inequality. More, where the higher castes are also economically and politically privileged, caste and class reinforce each other at least in rural areas.

Personal dependence versus personal indifference

Under capitalism, each individual is concerned about his own interest and is indifferent to those of others. If he relates himself to others, to society, it is only indirectly i.e. through impersonal market relations. This is just the opposite of what obtained in a traditional society where the labouring castes and their masters had some concern for one another, though within certain prescribed limits. Under the onslaught of the market economy, traditional relations of personal dependence are fast disintegrating. But where they persist they seem to subserve capitalism. They help the bourgeoisie elicit from the workers, feudal type of loyalty and obedience. The relations between the employer and the employee in capitalist enterprises tend to resemble that between the upper and lower castes. This prevents the coalescence and the integration of the working population on the basis of class interests, which too suits the bourgeoisie. In rural areas, too, relations of personal dependence tend to harmonize with capitalism, as is clear from the prevalence of capitalist agriculture on the basis of bonded labour.

Similar social relations prevail in the world of bureaucracy. Government officials treat their subordinates as Brahmanas did the Sudras and outcastes. The upper bureaucracy is the new 'Brahmanas' whose relations with the rest of society are governed by taboos not very different from the traditional ones concerning social intercourse, commensality, and connubium. This explains their unashamed exhibition of arrogance and callousness towards people. Just as the Brahmanas of yore used their knowledge of ritual technology to exploit the ignorant masses, so, too, the 'neo-Brahmanas' use the intricacies of bureaucratic ritualism to confound, bully, browbeat and swindle the common man. Not any better is the attitude of Politicians and intellectuals. In all these cases we are witnessing the working out of traditional caste mentality within the framework of non-traditional institutions.

Circulation of traditional and bourgeois culture
What we have here are not two parallel processes that never meet. On the contrary, capitalist culture uses traditional means of circulation as traditional culture uses the more modern ones. Let us consider the three institutions which disseminated traditional culture, namely, the temple, the family, and caste. Of course, generally, these do not explicitly propagate capitalist ideas and values. But they do so indirectly, that is, through their concrete mode of functioning. Temples, for instance, besides being centres of commerce in the ordinary sense of the term, are also places where money is exchanged for divine favour. More than any other place, the temple and the church witness to the quality of money as the *universal* equivalent. The nuclear family, unlike the traditional joint-family, is the owner of private property and is engaged in competition with other families. This is true, though to a lesser degree, also of caste, since the relation of any one caste to other castes is determined by private interest, competition, and aggression.

If thus, tradition serves the dissemination of bourgeois culture, the reverse also is true. The culture of the traditional masters is today propagated through the radio, television, the Press, and films. This shows that in respect of circulation, too, there is no real antagonism between the two cultural currents.

Intercultural relation at the level of consumption

As the bourgeois culture extends its dominance from town to village there is less and less demand for traditional culture. This is already verifiable in the case of ideas and values. For instance, the magico-mythical attitude is slowly giving way to the scientific; blind obedience to rationality; status by birth to status by wealth; resignation to revolt. But as far as aesthetic-religious culture is concerned the more dominant trend seems to be one of the coexistence of tradition and modernity. Magico-mythical practices go hand in hand with the hankering after the new Indo-western bastard culture represented by films, radio, and television. The average educated Indian is a split personality, part attuned to the culture of the west, part steeped in cultural forms inherited from tribal days.

Traditional versus secular legitimation

Here, too, the opposition is only apparent. For tradition, on the whole, tends to reinforce the ever-expanding bourgeois culture. The scriptures which taught caste was divinely ordained have conditioned the minds of people to extend the same legitimacy to capitalist exploitations as well, the belief in karma and the spirituality of resignation it generates make the unorganized poor accomplices to their own liquidation. The individualism of traditional religious quest — which itself was probably compensation for the suppression of individuality in real life — well accords with the bourgeois concept of the individual and his rights. This power of inherited religious belief to legitimate capitalism is more and more recognized by capitalists and politicians. Proof for this provided by their religious exhibitionism, by their munificent donations to temples and churches, by their patronizing of gurus, swamijis, and saints. Religion in their case is the fig leaf used to cover the obscenity of conspicuous consumption and the no less obscene lust for power. In the bargain, magic, superstition, and religious obscurantism are given another lease of life.

Traditional versus capitalist closure

What earlier foreign invasions could not do, the onslaught of capitalism has done to tradition. It has torn down the age-old mechanisms of closure. The very interaction we have observed at various levels would not have been possible but for the failure of traditional closure. Hinduism has proved itself particularly vulnerable in this respect since it, unlike other religions, has no organized magisterium to regulate the belief and practice of its members. Besides, in the measure in which the lower castes and Harijans become economically independent, the traditional closure imposed by the higher castes becomes ineffectual. Hence the insecurity and fear that haunts the guardians of tradition. Hence also the fanatical attempts by organizations like the RSS to build up a militant Hinduism in the name of loyalty to our cultural heritage.

However, the collapse of traditional closure is not uniformly verified in the case of all castes. The spread of capitalist agriculture in rural India shows that the land-owning castes have come under the spell of the culture of private interest and competition. But the same castes want the low castes and the Harijans to be confined within the mental enclosure tradition has imposed on them, and to that end seek the help (which is readily available) of the police and the bureaucracy. This is because they find that the traditional attitude of subservience on the part of the labouring castes offers less resistance to capitalist exploitation than would be the case if they were unionized.

Here capitalism reinforces traditional closure. The reverse process also is noticeable. The watch-dogs of tradition strengthen capitalist closure by preventing the infiltration of socialist ideas into the Hindu fold. (See, for instance, Bhagvan Rajnish's booklet, *Beware of Socialism*)

Safety-valves: traditional versus modern

Does mass resentment against capitalism expend itself through traditional safety-valves? The organized working class has little need for the traditional safety-valves provided, above all, by religion since, as noted earlier, the ritual of strikes and agitations fulfill that function. In contrast, the unorganized urban proletariat consisting of workers in small enterprises has to resort to exhaust mechanisms deriving from traditional and bourgeois culture. As for the rural proletariat, who are mostly unorganized, the chief means to let off pent-up frustration with feudal, as well as capitalist exploitation still consist in customary religious ceremonies, festivities, folk dances, etc. Our analysis shows that the impact of capitalism on traditional culture is not uniform. Certain elements of tradition wither away; certain others co-exist with capitalist culture either in their original purity (e.g. religious beliefs and practices) or as transformed by capitalist ethos (e.g. caste relations); in either case, they serve the interests of expanding capitalism. Still, others are reinforced in the process (e.g. the individualism of traditional religious quest) but not in any manner that is detrimental to the growth of capitalism. In sum, capitalism has managed to domesticate traditional culture and use it to serve its own ends.

The Nature of the Present Cultural Crisis

It follows from our reflections thus far that the present crisis is not due to any antagonism between traditional and bourgeois culture. Might it then be that it is the result of conflict between bourgeois culture and a socialist counterculture? For an answer, we have to examine the nature and extent of socialist consciousness in India.

The non-socialist character of the crisis

In the wake of the Russian revolution, there was a widespread socialist awakening in the country, particularly among the elite. The example of the proletarian uprising in the Soviet Union had a tremendous impact in vernacular literature especially in Kerala, West Bengal, and Andhra Pradesh. For the first time in the history of our country, the life of the masses became a worthy theme for literary creations. Plays, short stories, and essays appeared in the various languages romanticizing the poor, holding up the vision of a classless society, and calling for the overthrow of the existing social order. Indian communism was in the vanguard of this cultural movement. But in course of time, the heralds of revolution retraced their steps, made peace with their consciences, and found each for himself a comfortable niche in the Establishment or tailored their radicalism to suit the pursuit of private interest and power. Socialist thinking has since congealed into stereotypes, into eternally valid dogmas, with predetermined answers to predetermined questions. There have been some notable exceptions to this such as the speeches and writings of Rammanohar Lohia and Jayaprakash Narayan. In the field of historical research as well there has been some original contribution by scholars like Kosambi and Chattopadhyaya. But, by and large, what circulates in the country in the name of socialism are ideas imported from countries like the Soviet Union, China, and Britain. In any case, what little socialist thinking there is influences only certain petty-bourgeois circles and has not percolated down to the masses, except in the States mentioned earlier. Besides, unlike capitalism which has penetrated every aspect of Indian tradition and uses it as a means for its own reproduction, the main current of Indian socialism represented by the Communist Parties still remains a foreign body in relation to our cultural heritage and for that reason is doomed to sterility and impotence. Clearly, then, there is no powerful current of original socialist thinking in India capable of stemming the tide of capitalist ideology.

Nor may we interpret the prevailing social unrest as the index of an emerging socialist counter-culture. Take, for instance, the growing industrial unrest. What inspires it is not any longing for a classless society but the private interest of individual workers or the interests of the already better-off sections of the working class. Like the bourgeoisie, trade-unions, too, are competing with one another, each for its own advantage and to the detriment of the unorganized workers and the unemployed. Trade-unionism has created a labour aristocracy with a vested interest in maintaining the less privileged in their present condition. This shows that it, too, derives its motive force from the bourgeois culture of private interest and competition. The same culture underpins also student unrest. What students want is not the demolition of classes but secure employment in firms, factories, or government service. In other words, what bothers them is their possible margination from the mainstream of capitalism and their exclusion from the world of conspicuous consumption. Understandably so, since the values they imbibe from school or college are those of private interest, competition, and individualism. If they had ever demonstrated in favour of the poorest of the poor, that would have been a clear indication of their socialist aspirations. To my knowledge, no such things have ever happened in the history of student agitations in India.

Nor may we interpret the conflict between castes as symptoms of a socialist upsurge. Within the pre-capitalist framework, the lower castes and the outcastes accepted the subordinate role custom assigned to them. But today they do not. Besides, universal suffrage has put in their hands a powerful weapon to fight the higher castes. Their struggles, therefore, are directed against traditional caste domination and capitalist exploitation. They do not have for aim the abolition of castes and classes, as is clear from the fact every caste seeks to improve its position even to the disadvantage of those others that are poorer than they.

What of the current political unrest? In my view, there is nothing socialist about it. All attempts to explain the extent of defections by people's representatives, their frequent change of loyalties, and their total unconcern for the needs of the people, on the basis of the conflict of ideologies are unconvincing. The changing pattern of alliances cut across all ideologies. Irreconcilables become reconciled; incompatible become compatible. Equally unsatisfactory is all explanations in terms of the economic interests of the social strata represented by the parties. For there is no significant and consistent correlation between the economic interests of the constituencies (not in the sense of area but of sections of the population) and the political stance of the elected representatives at any given moment.

I would suggest that the real explanation is to be sought in the working out of the *culture of private interest in the sphere of public interest,* i.e. in the political sphere. For the average politician whatever is meant to promote the common good - whether it is party, legislature, judiciary, or bureaucracy — is but a means to further his own private interest, which is gain or power or both. So are also the people. That is why the politician is without lasting loyalties or abiding friends. Not less blatantly private are the interests of that despicable, parasitical brood bearing the name of public servants, who use the governmental machinery (i.e. organs of public interest) to harass, humiliate, and fleece the common citizen. Already enjoying the lion's share of national revenue they, too, are organizing themselves in order to secure higher salaries and better emoluments!

A crisis internal to capitalism

Clearly, then, the symptoms of crisis enumerated earlier do not spring from any threat capitalism faces from an emerging socialist counterculture. They can be explained on the basis of the concrete working out of the capitalist culture of private interest and competition. In this sense, the present cultural crisis is internal to capitalism.

But how is it that we do not find such unashamed play of private interest, competition, and individualism in the West where capitalism originated? Of course in the West people are experiencing ever new forms of human alienation resulting from the capitalist system of exploitation. Nevertheless, one finds a certain humanism pervading social relations. Outside periods of the strike, the labourer does his work well. Merchants do not resort to crude forms of cheating as they do here; sales-persons are courteous and helpful. So are the police and government officials; before them, you feel accepted as a person (so unlike their counterparts in India who by their very arrogant look reduce you to the position of a contemptible worm meant only to be trampled upon). More importantly, one is impressed by the efficiency of service provided at railway stations, airports, and Public offices.

All of which goes to prove that capitalism need not necessarily assume the brutal form it has done in our country. Why this difference? The reason seems to be two-fold: one having to do with the uneven and retarded development of Indian capitalism, and the other with the cultural-historical context in which capitalism functions here.

First, capitalism is driven by its own inner logic to disseminate its culture far and wide to reach every section of the population and permeate every social institution. But the universality of its culture is contradicted by the limited possibilities it offers to people of putting it into practice. Let us consider a few examples. Capitalism proclaims the primacy of private interest but millions of people have no private interest to promote, deprived as they are of the minimum means of subsistence. Again, all are taught the virtue of competition but only a minority has the means — be it raw materials or instruments of production — to compete with. Not even labor-power is competitive since it is available in plenty whereas employment is limited. In consequence, millions in our country are marginated from the game of competition and are either unemployed or underemployed. Similarly, capitalism creates needs and arouses expectations universally, but it can satisfy the needs and aspirations of only a minority. The majority sink into frustration, resentment, and bitterness, all instinct with violence. This means that the masses who have internalized the values of their masters find themselves deprived of the means to realize them. The situation is quite different in the West. There the basic needs of people have already been met, thanks to the expansion of productive forces, the exploitation of the colonies, and recourse to unjust trade relations with the so-called developing countries.

Second, the contradiction we have just described is further accentuated by the cultural-historical context into which capitalism was inserted. In the West, the emergence of the bourgeoisie was brought about by the French revolution which overthrew the feudal system of privilege and heralded a future of freedom, equality, and brotherhood.

True, under the bourgeois relations of production freedom, equality, and brotherhood could be realized only in an alienated form. But the realization, even in an alienated form, of these values is better than their repudiation. Besides, the same ideas fulfilled the function of an ideal project, of a myth. But myth has a truth and a power of its own to shape the minds and hearts of people. The myth of equality, freedom, and brotherhood had, in fact, its roots in the humanism of the Judeo-Christian tradition. It kept alive the hope in an age of total fulfillment that Jesus and the prophets before him had proclaimed. Implied in it was also a *universal* morality based on the human person as such, irrespective of caste, colour, race, or distinctions of wealth and power. This humanist tradition softened to some extent the ethos of private interest inherent in capitalism.

In India, on the contrary, capitalism was not accompanied by any socio-cultural upheaval comparable to the French Revolution. The slogans of liberty, equality, and fraternity did not issue forth from an indigenous tradition and are even at variance with the ethics of caste, based on inequality, domination, and social fragmentation. Nor had the dominant Hindu tradition projected any hope in the collective historical destiny of man. More, under the system of caste, no universal morality based on the dignity of man as *man* could have emerged. In consequence, the average Indian tended to view his neighbour as inferior or superior, as impure or pure, as belonging to a particular caste or colour, but seldom, if at all, as a human being worthy of respect in his own right. Quite different would have been the situation if the original teachings of the Buddha were allowed to bear fruit on the Indian soil. For, long before Jesus of Nazareth and around the same period when the prophets of Israel were preaching the universal liberation of man, Gautama preached a message of equality, cosmic compassion, and universal brotherhood and thereby laid the foundation for a universal morality. He also envisioned a collective destiny for mankind which he called 'the kingdom of righteousness'. Unfortunately, his liberating message was smothered, and the movement he initiated domesticated by an all too militant Brahmanaism. Since then, in spite of the revolt of the Bhaktas in medieval India, the ethics of segregation proper to caste has reigned supreme, preventing the birth of an ethics of concern and communion. No wonder that, reflected through the prism of caste, the evils of capitalist economy and of bourgeois politics have assumed demonic features unparalleled elsewhere.

Prospectives

Any crisis implies that society has reached a stage where the status quo cannot continue, that it has come to the parting of ways. Which are the ways open to society and where will they lead us? The answer would depend on the free decision of millions of social actors. Therefore, no certain prognosis is possible. Still one may reasonably envisage two alternatives.

The first is the way of dictatorship whereby the privileged classes will suppress the aspirations of the masses, break their will to resistance, and enforce discipline by means of the repressive machinery of the state and through cultural indoctrination. This will admirably suit the interests of national and transnational capitalism. It would also accord well with the psychic structure produced by the caste system of subordination and super-ordination. The emerging constellation of political forces today seems to portend such a future.

The alternative to fascism would be a collective option and struggle for *a* socialist society, i.e. a society in which people themselves will control the economic, political, and cultural processes. But is this alternative — the only one that will give both bread and freedom to the masses — a viable one? Are there socio-cultural forces that would prepare the ground for such a radical restructuring of society? I shall try to answer these questions in a subsequent issue of Socialist Perspectives.

(Socialist Perspectives, January 1980; *What the Thunder Says,* Chap. 4)

30

Values in Crisis
A Socio-philosophical Analysis
of the Indian Situation

Our country is going through a crisis. Its symptoms are many and varied: the phenomenal rise in prices of even essential commodities, the increase in unemployment, the breakdown of law and order, the cynicism of the common man regarding political parties, his loss of faith in the government in power, the prevalence of corruption as a way of life and the widespread frustration among the masses. Though the existence of a crisis is beyond question, there is little concerted attempt made either by the government or by the intelligentsia to detect its deeper causes and suggest remedies.

No claim is made to attempt a competent scientific analysis of the present crisis. The aim is rather modest, namely, to provide a few tentative reflections on the valuational aspect of the crisis. In this, the basis is primarily the observation of the social and ideological trends and forces around us. Naturally, no one views the world from a position of absolute neutrality. One is always involved in one's world and approaches it from a particular standpoint which is itself conditioned by one's understanding of what man in society ought to be. Such involvement is quite legitimate on condition that one does not read into reality what is not there and is prepared to criticize one's presuppositions at every stage of the investigation.

Value and Values

At the outset, it is necessary to define what we mean by value. By value, we mean any socially desired goal. That values are socially desired implies that they are not to be considered in themselves but in relation to the well-being of man, and this relationship is dialectical in character. It is human persons who constitute values and meanings. In fact, each person constitutes his own world of values. What is valuable to one person may not be so to another. To a *yogi* wealth is a disvalue, not so to a businessman. So too the importance attached to the same value may vary with persons. A work of art may mean much to one, but little to another. If it is true that each person forms his own world of values, it is equally true that values in their turn make persons. A person cannot be defined in isolation without any reference to what he values. That is why the quality of a person can be judged by his system of values.

Though values are essentially related to individuals they have also a social character. If the values of one person have nothing in common with those of others he will not be able to enter into any meaningful relationship with them. Communication and social interaction are possible because all members of society, or at least significant sections of it, recognize certain things as values though all may not aspire to them in the same way or to the same degree. Values are therefore not only personal but also inter-personal realities. In other words, they are socially desired goals.

Values are essentially related to men and to their well-being. Depending on the dimension of human life to which they correspond, they may be grouped under various types. First of all, there are material values like food, clothing, housing, and medicine, which have a special reference to man's bodily existence. Then there are social values like association, recognition, and prestige; aesthetic values like education and books. There are also religious values that either embody or mediate man's relation to the ultimate ground of all. Finally, there are moral values like equality, justice, and honesty. This last category comprises all attitudes, actions, and patterns of behaviour which contribute to the total well-being of man in society.

Values have different modes of existence. First, they exist at the level of articulate consciousness as in novels, poems, newspapers, films, etc. Secondly, they have an existence at the level of praxis i.e. of man's dynamic, active-passive relationship to the world of things and persons. Thus we find them embodied in economic and social life. For instance, the mode of corporate production in factories is the concrete manifestation of a system of values like hierarchy, co-ordination, efficiency, private interest, and competition. No factory can function where these values have not been internalized by the participants. This is true of all social institutions. The functioning of the bureaucracy and the judiciary, the procedure of elections, the mode of decision-making - all these represent so many ways in which values become crystallized. Thirdly, values exist also in the form of concrete products of artifacts. Take for instance any traditional Muslim house in Kerala. Its facing Mecca is the expression of a religious value. The absence or paucity of windows shows that the inmates, especially the women-folk, consider being seen by outsiders undesirable. The arrangement of rooms is indicative of the value attached to the segregation of sexes. Finally, the material structure as a whole is meant to embody a special type of aesthetic valuation.

All this points to the fact that values are intimately interwoven with praxis especially with socio-economic praxis. Praxis not only embodies values but also mediates between them and the members of a community. It also forms the basis for the articulate formulations of theories. Articulated values in their turn consciously influence the socio-economic base. The relation between value-systems and praxis too is dialectical. It forms a constant unity in tension.

It follows from what we have said, that any significant change at the level of praxis brings about a corresponding change in the value system of a people. Changes in the mode of production, distribution, and consumption condition, more than anything else, the emergence of new values. In this process factors like contact with alien cultures and ideologies also play an important role. In the initial stages, it is only a small minority that usually adopts the new values. This dissenting minority finds itself in conflict with the masses who hold on to the old values. Eventually, the new trend gathers momentum and confronts the old from a position of strength. In this process of dialogue and confrontation, each side becomes influenced by the other, reformulates its position, and thus arrives at a synthesis. It can also happen that some old values completely succumb to the new ones and eventually become extinct.

Values in Transition

In light of these general reflections let us focus our attention on the concrete ways in which values change in our country.

Values are like plants. Uprooted from the soil, from the socio-economic infrastructure, they die. Thus many of the traditional values have become extinct. Time was when Nair women in Kerala considered it a privilege to bear children to lovers from the Brahmana community, for the Brahmana was considered a god on earth. This is no more the situation today. The same fate has befallen the collective mode of living represented by jointfamilies. There are many other values that are on the way to complete extinction like arranged marriage, caste status, the observance of ritual purity, and blind submission to authority. On the basis of controlled observation of social behaviour over a fairly long period of time, it is possible to distinguish those values, that are destined to perish from others which are likely to persist though in a modified form. This brings us to another kind of valuechange. That is, certain values become in course of time demoted and begin to occupy an inferior position in the scale of values. For instance, temples which were at one time highly valued have become less so, as is clear from their neglected appearance today in the countryside. This is true also of landed property, religious knowledge, cult, certain traditional forms of art, like drama, religious story-telling, etc.

Transference is yet another mode of change affecting values, by which we mean the process which detaches a value from its original bearer and attaches to a new one. The personal loyalty which the poorer classes formerly showed to the feudal landlord is, at the initial stages of industrialization and democratization, transferred to the factory manager, to the political leader, or to the government official. Closely resembling transference is the process of the transvaluation by which certain values, while preserving their traditional linguistic garb, take on a new meaning. Consider for example justice. Justice to slaves in ancient society meant nothing more than respecting their minimum rights which were themselves determined by their masters. In feudal society, justice meant the fulfillment of the obligations deriving from the relationship of personal loyalty on the part of the vassal and his lord. In the capitalist society, the same term carries a different meaning, namely the observance of the respective rights of the employer and the employee. In none of these societies is the question ever raised whether the systems of slavery, serfdom, and wage-labour respectively were just. This radical question is posed today by those who believe in socialism. In the eyes of Marx, capitalist justice is the worst form of injustice, of alienation. True justice can be realized only with the abolition of wage-labour and of its presupposition, the accumulation of the means of production in the hands of a few. What we said of justice is true also of other values like equality, freedom, participation, love, etc.

Finally, we come to the secularization of values. In traditional society, every aspect of life was determined by religious belief. Only what conformed to religious prescriptions was considered a value. This held good not only of moral but also of material, aesthetic, social, and ideational values. In this sense religion was the mother of all values. Such a sacral society could exist only on the basis of a pre-scientific socio-economic praxis. In the pre-scientific world, man found himself subject to the forces of nature as well as to social institutions. Not yet conscious of his power over his environment he naturally attributed to God what he could not dominate. But with the advance of science and technology, he became aware of the fact that the world of things, persons, and institutions around him had its own inner nature and was subject to its own immanent laws, which could be investigated and known through scientific reasoning. This led to an explosion of rationality. People began less and less to appeal to religious faith in order to discover the meaning of things. In consequence, the various domains of knowledge gained autonomy from religious conceptions, and secular systems of values came into existence.

We have indicated some of the ways in which values undergo change. But not every change constitutes a crisis. Change becomes a crisis when it reaches a situation of conflict which can be resolved only through a radically new orientation. That such a crisis has affected the values of our society none can deny. However, it is difficult to identify its internal dynamics. For we see in India, the co-existence and interaction of different systems of values operative in varying degrees in different parts of the country. First, there are feudal values that still influence socio-economic and political life. We have also the capitalist system of values, comprising private interest, competition, aggressive self-assertion, efficiency, etc. Finally, there is a socialist system of values represented by the political parties of the Left.

The Capitalist Spectrum of Values

The fundamental value of capitalism is private interest which has its economic basis in private property. It implies a philosophy that reduces society to the position of the means to individual well-being and thereby denies man's social dimension. Where private interest reigns supreme, the other becomes either a means to one's economic ends or a rival. Competition is thus installed as an important value. In competition, only one can survive who asserts oneself aggressively. As a result, aggression, whether physical, moral, or psychological, becomes even socially respectable, and the law of the survival of the fittest determines the whole of social life. Within this frame of reference, freedom is understood as the possibility to pursue one's individual ends unhindered by others. In reality, it is nothing more than the freedom of the few rich to exploit the many poor. Capitalism also regards equality as a value but understands it as an equal opportunity given to physically unequal competitors in the same race. It is a type of equality in which some are more equal than others.

The fundamental value of private interest consists in the relentless pursuit of profit, and of production for the sake of it. He who produces more, irrespective of what he produces and how is projected as a model for others. One produces in order to make a profit and makes a profit in order to consume. Thus consumption installs itself as the be-all and end-all of life. The richer classes give the lead in the acquisition of more and more gadgets, of more and more refined comforts. And the masses follow suit. With this, a new concept of happiness emerges. Your happiness consists of your having something which your neighbour does not have, and your unhappiness, in not having something which your neighbour has. Your value as a person is equated with what you have and not with what you are. And you can have whatever you want if you have money, the equivalent of all commodities. Money, therefore, assumes the character of a universal value. It is the 'sanctifying grace' of capitalism.

A critical observation of Indian society will show that its essential determinants are private interest, competition, aggression, consumerism, money, and other values and attitudes germane to capitalism. Initially, these values held sway only amongst those who owned the means of production. In the course of time, they seeped into the lower strata of society. Though alien to Indian culture, they became progressively internalized in varying degrees by the masses. They made their impact felt first among the industrial working class and subsequently also among the rural population.

However, the internalization of the new values was not spontaneous but manipulated. Capitalists make a profit only if their products are sold. And the products will be sold only if they meet a corresponding need in the people. Where this need does not exist, it has to be artificially created. This is done with the help of advertisements, posters, exhibitions, and the like. To this end, capitalists make use of all the media of communication: radio, television, the press, and films. They prostitute sex, womanhood, family, religion and even God to generate new needs among the unwitting masses. They weave myths around commodities and project them as symbols of status. The prospective customers are told, for instance, that foam cushions will give them 'the rest of their life', that 'odorono' will help them 'make love without having to share body odour', that 'to live on love and Limca' is one of the in things of the day. Through these and other methods of psychic coercion, the capitalist system is manipulating and deforming not only the psychology of our people but also its somatic substructure. It thus produces not only goods for consumption but also consumer classes. The masses are thus degraded to the level of mere byproducts of the economic system.

Capitalism versus Feudalism

How is it that the capitalist value system was able to make headway in spite of the fact that it did not come into being as the result of the internal development of traditional society, but was imported from outside and imposed on our people? The answer seems to be that in its confrontation with capitalism the feudal system of values played an ambiguous role.

In the initial stages of its development, capitalism found an ally in many of the traditional attitudes. The masses, psychologically attuned to the collectivism of joint-family and caste, both of which subordinated the individual to the group, had little difficulty in adapting themselves to the collectivism of firms and factories. It was easy for them to work for goals in the choice of which they had no say. Centuries of psychological conditioning by the hierarchy of caste facilitated transition to the hierarchy of functions and authority inherent in capitalist production. Accustomed to considering wealth and status as associated with birth, the working class saw nothing unjust in a few people concentrating in their hands the means of production, agricultural as well as industrial. The division of labour characteristic of a caste society found its counterpart in capitalism. Traditional conceptions regarding the superiority of the Brahmanas as repositories of knowledge and bearers of economic privileges dovetailed with the capitalist assumption of the superiority of intellectual over manual labour. Thus through a process of transference, feudal values contributed to the growth and expansion of capitalism. However, in serving the ends of capitalism the same values and attitudes themselves underwent a change. They could survive only by assuming new content and meaning. In other words, they went through a process not only of transference but partially of transvaluation.

But the struggle between feudal and capitalist value systems is one between unequal partners. With the breakdown of traditional structures like caste and joint-family, the former was deprived of its social basis. It therefore could survive only in the consciousness and habits of the people. The capitalist value system, on the other hand, was firmly rooted in an ever-expanding economic praxis. The economic praxis produced not only consumer goods but also the media of communication like radio, newspapers, and films, which in their turn, helped the diffusion of the same values. In this context, we should keep in mind that capitalism, in the process of domesticating feudalism, took on certain features. This is particularly true of its initial stages and is clear from the way that caste, kinship, and communalism influenced the location of factories, the recruiting of workers, and the promotion of employees. But soon capitalism reasserted itself in its original purity. Capitalists realized that the maximization of production was possible on the basis of accommodation to feudal values and concerns. This victory of capitalism sowed the seeds of its own defeat or at least the frustration of its own avowed goals.

A Diagnosis of the Present Crisis

The dissemination of capitalist values would not have led to the present crisis if the ever-increasing needs of the people could have been satisfied in some measure. This is not what is happening in India. The economic system generates needs in all but can satisfy the needs only of a few. Even the poorest man in India is told of the advantage of foam mattresses, but those who can afford them constitute no more than five percent of the population. In other words, capitalist propaganda artificially generates needs that capitalist praxis is unable to satisfy. The result is frustration among the masses. The mood of frustration is deeper among educated youth, who are more exposed to the world of advertisement. The present economic system breeds, in this manner, collective resentment and envy. It is in this light that we should view the widespread student unrest and agitations which have become so much a part of our social life.

The student protest all over the country is not so much against the capitalist system as the conditions which make it impossible for them to satisfy the needs that the same system creates in them. What students aim at is not the eradication of exploitation but to terminate their exclusion from the circles of exploiters. No wonder, the moment they get a secure job which guarantees them the benefits of the system, their protest dies out. The same holds true also of the organized working class, industrial as well as agricultural. They organize strikes and demonstrations primarily to secure more and more benefits in the form of a higher salary and better working conditions, in other words, for advantages within the system. What motivates them is not common but private interest. It is not even the good of the workers as a class that is at issue. Workers join trade unions in order to make use of them to secure their individual ends. In fact, private interest determines the behaviour of the working class so much that they become divided into opposing groups, each trying to promote its interests and privileges even to the detriment of other groups. Hence the competition between worker groups.

What is striking is that even political parties professing socialist ideologies have become infected with capitalism. Most politicians and legislators representing the Left engage in politics mainly for the sake of their economic interests. They use the masses as a means for capturing political power and use political power to amass wealth. Thus we have the paradox of communists fighting capitalism in the name of capitalist values. Such straggles will in the long run only serve to reinforce the existing exploitative system.

It is clear, from what has been said, that the present crisis does not consist in the conflict between feudalism and capitalism or between capitalism and socialism. It is essentially a conflict between capitalist values and capitalist praxis. Its roots lie in the inability of capitalism to satisfy the needs it generates. In other words, the conflict is internal. However, feudalism has played a role in accentuating the crisis in various ways. Feudal attitudes associated with fatalism, other-worldliness, detachment, non-involvement, etc. dampen the popular urge to revolt, and breed conformism. The particular loyalties nurtured by family, kinship, community, and race divide the oppressed classes into opposing groups and thereby make it easier for the oppressors to pursue unhindered the policy of exploitation. All this creates frustration among those sections of the masses who want to revolt. It is not surprising that in these conditions splinter groups emerge which resort to violence. Like feudal attitudes, socialist propaganda too has served to aggravate the crisis. The present atmosphere of frustration and unrest is due not a little to the political parties which draw inspiration from Marx. Their leaders preached the new heaven and the new earth of the classless society, while they themselves settled down comfortably in their own heaven of conspicuous consumption. By widening the gulf between expectation and fulfillment, they too sowed the seeds of frustration.

Where Are We Tending To?
Regarding the outcome of the crisis, one thing is certain. There will be no return to feudal, pre-capitalist society. The march of history is dialectical, and in it, nothing repeats itself. There is no hope either that the crisis will automatically lead to a truly socialist society. A struggle against capitalism that is motivated by capitalist values cannot give birth

to socialism. Besides capitalism has been able to tame not only feudalism but other forms of Indian socialism. Indian socialists have become so much infected with the ethos of capitalism that even the new society they project bears capitalist features. They think of a socialist society either in terms of state capitalism in which every citizen is reduced to the status of an employee or in terms of distributionism in which every citizen is made an owner of private property, i.e. a capitalist. The present crisis has therefore little in its internal dynamics which assures transition to socialism. Does this mean that the crisis will continue indefinitely? I do not think so. The continuation of the crisis will only issue in total chaos, and this will go against the interests of capitalists themselves. They, therefore, may in the decades to come, accede to the minimum demands of workers by increasing their ages and improving their working conditions. They may also try to widen their circle of supporters among the ideological classes like teachers, lawyers and religious leaders, and the well-paid workers, by conferring on them still more economic privileges. To achieve this end, they may also try to strengthen their hold on the bureaucracy and on politicians. There is also the possibility that the Government may turn Fascist and usher in an era of repression.

The Christian Challenge

The capitalist system of values is essentially dehumanizing. It denies the dignity of man in so far as the masses are made tools to promote the welfare of the privileged few. It reduces the working class to the position of accessories in the machine, of mere byproducts of a system. It denies also the sociality of man by subordinating the common good to private interest. It releases the hidden powers of aggression in man, inasmuch as it makes competition the principle of social life. It is also essentially materialistic. For it sets up money as the supreme value, the value of all values. For these reasons, the believer in Jesus cannot but oppose it tooth and nail. For the same reason, he cannot be wholly unhappy about the present crisis. For capitalism completely stable and at peace with itself is a more dangerous foe to deal with than one that is in crisis. Seen from this angle, the value crisis of today gives us more reason for hope than the situation a few decades ago. Yet the present social unrest, being motivated by the values of capitalism itself, cannot lead us to socialism. Capitalism may even regain its equilibrium by further taming its internal and external foes. Hence the challenge that faces all men of goodwill is one of giving today's crisis a qualitatively different orientation, of rendering it pregnant with possibilities for a truly socialist future. This means we have to work for a cultural revolution.

Such a revolution will demand the transformation of all the values of today. What is needed is nothing less than the creation of a new society that sets up the person in the community as the primary value, one in which the good of all will consist in the full flowering of each person, and the good of each person in the well-being of all. It will have to be a society in which co-operation will replace competition, love will replace aggression, quality will have primacy over quantity, the aesthetic will subsume the useful. In that society freedom will be realized, not in spite of, but through one's fellowmen, justice will determine not merely interactions within a given system but the system itself, commodities will take on the quality of gifts, the products of labour will have value only in the measure in which they are sacraments of human togetherness, and the materialism of consumption will give way to the humanism of communion. In that society, each man will be open to another, and in that openness become also open to the Absolute, to the dimension of transcendence.

A cultural revolution of this type cannot be brought about without a radical restructuring of the entire social system. New values demand new structures. The scope of this paper does not allow discussion of the methodology of such a revolution. One thing needs to be stressed. For those who believe in Jesus of Nazareth and in the reign of justice and love he preached and died for, the time for a radical choice has come, for a choice against the capitalist system of values and the economic praxis in which it is embodied, and in favour of a truly socialist future in harmony with the message of the Gospel. The organized Church is not yet ready to make that choice, for its praxis, if not also its theory, is still governed by the values of capitalism. Individual believers, therefore, will have to carry out their choice in collaboration with genuinely revolutionary groups and movements in India. To refuse to make such an option is to follow the way of the priests and elders of old who stood by approvingly while the Son of Man was crucified.

(Jeevadhara, 5, 1975; *Jesus and Culture*, Chap. 12)

Notes

Chapter 1

1.Marx-Engels 1976, p.67. **2.** Kenelm Burridge, "New Heaven, New Earth: A Study of Millenarian Activities", quoted by Gager 1975, p.1. **3.** Karl Marx, "The Eighteenth Brumaire of Louis Bonaparte", in Marx-Engels 1970, p.96.

Chapter 2

1. Lohse 1976, p. 25. **2.** Hengel 1974. p. 310. **3.** Lohse 1976, pp.15-47 **4.** Hengel 1974, p.194. **5.** Mt 13:33; Mk 2:22; 4:31-32; Lk 7:22-23; 11:20. **6.** Mt 5:11; 6:33. **7.**Mk 3:35. **8.** Mt 13:44-46. **9.** Mk 10:25; Mt 6:24. **10.** Mt 5:3; Lk 6:20. **11.** Mk 10:29-30. **12.** Ibid. 10:42-44. **13.** Chapter 17 **14.** Lk 13:30; 14:11 **15.** Miranda 1971, pp.44-52 **16.** Mt 11:25. **17.** Ibid. 5:8. **18.** Dt 24:1. **19.** Mk 10:9. **20.** Ibid. 12:25. **21.**Ibid. 3:34 ff. **22.** Jn 4:27. **23.** Lk 10:38-42. **24.** Ibid. 8:1-3; Mk 15:40-41. **25.** Jeremias 1971, p.226. **26.** Gn 38:34. **27.** Lv 20:9. **28.** Mt 19:14. **29.** Ibid. 10:35-37. **30.**Mk 3:21; 6:4. **31** . Cf. Doughlas 1978; Also, Belo 1974, pp.62-92. **32.** Belo 1974, op. cit. p.119. **33.** Ibid, pp.86-92. **34.** Ibid, pp.69-71. **35.** Ibid, pp.86-92. **36.** Mk7:1-23. **37.** Mt7:12. **38.** Mk2:27 **39.** Ibid. 7:21-23. **40.** Ibid. **41.** Ibid. 3:14. **42.** Ibid. 1:20; 6:7-13. **43.** Ibid. 1:20. **44.** Ibid. 7:1-6. **45.** Ibid. 2:23-24. **46.** Lk8:1-3. **47.** Kee 1977, pp.162-163 **48.** Acts 4:32-35. **49.** Gager 1975, p.35. **50.** Ibid. p.82. **51.** Kee 1977, p.148. **52.** Gager 1975, p.35. **53.** Ibid. p.82.

Chapter 3

1. Gager 1975, p.39. **2.** 2 Pt 3:34. **3.** Ibid. 3:8. **4.** Acts 10:38. **5.** Perrin 1963, pp.60-63. **6.** Gager 1975, p.126. **7.** Marx-Engels 1975, p. 275. Also, Gager 1975, p. 94; A. H. M. Jones, "The Social Background of the Struggle between Paganism and Christianity", in Momigliano 1963, p.17ff. **8.** John G. Gager, "Religion and Social Class in the Early Roman Empire", in Stephen Benko 1972, p.113. **9.** Gager 1975, p.108. **10.** Ibid, p.113. **11.** Cf. Grant 1978, pp.13-44. **12.** Theissen 1978, p.117. **13.** Marx-Engels 1975, pp.275-276. **14.** Gager 1975, pp.76-78.

Chapter 4

1 . For a Marixst interpretation of Indian history see Kosambi 1977 and 1962. On Indian Philosophy, see Chattopadhyaya 1959 and 1964.   **.2** Kosambi 1977, pp.78-79. **3.** Zaehner 1969, 2:31-37. **4.** *Rig Veda*, 10:90, translation adopted by Bary 1963 **5.** Gita, 4:13; 18:41-48. **6.** Quoted by Kosambi 1977, p.87. **7.** Hiriyanna 1960, p.17. **8.** Kosambi 1977, p.87. **9.** Ibid. **10.** Ibid. **11.** *Brihadaranyaka Upanishad.* I, iv.2. **12.** Hiriyanna 1960, pp.23-24. **13.** Kosambi 1977, pp.100-101. **14.**Quoted in Ibidem. **15.** *Samutta Nikaya,* 5:421 ff. **16.** *Digha Nikaya,* 2:99ff: Bary 1963, p.113. **17.** Aloysius Pieris, "Towards an Asian Theology of Liberation", Paper presented at. the Asian Theological Conference, Colombo, 1979. **18.** *Digha Nikaya,* 2:99ff. **19.** *Dhammapada,* 1:5: Bary 1963, p.122. **20.** *Sutta Nipata,* Bary 1963, pp.120-121. **21.***Khuddaka Patha,* 8: Bary 1963, pp. 119-120. **22.** *Kutadanta Sutta* in Ling 1981, pp.89-99. **23.** *Sigala Vada Sutta,*Ibid, pp.136-139. **24.** *Samanna-phaia Sutta,* Ibid, pp.21-23. **25.** *Sutta Nipata,* verse 136: Bary 1963, verse 136: Bary 1963, p.143. **26.** *Majjima Nikaya,* 2:147ff: Bary 1963, p.144. **27.** Kosambi 1977, p.111. **28.**Ibid, p.103. **29.** Ibid, pp.170-171. **30.** R. N. Dandekar, in his introduction to ch. X of Bary 1963, pp.217-218. **31.** John Arackal, "The Indian Ideology - Remarks on Manu's Defence of the Caste System", *Jeevadhara,* January-February, 1976, pp.148-159. **32.** *Manu Smriti,* 8:413. **33.** Ibid. 10:45. **34.** Kosambi 1962, p.32. **35.** C. Parvathamma, "Religion and Social Change: A Study of Tradition and Change in Virasaivism", in Sreenivas 1978, pp.243-252; Ramanujam 1973, introduction. **36.** *Bhagavata Purana,* in Bary 1963, p.337. **37.** Ibid, p.357. **38.** Ibid, p.362.

39. *Bhagavata Purana*. IV. 31.21. 40. Ibid. X. 60.14. 41. Ibid. VIII. 16.56.
42. Thomas J. Hopkins, "The Social Teaching of the Bhagavata Purana",
in Singer 1968, p.21. 43. Kosambi 1962. pp. 33-34. 44. Ibid. p.34. 45.
Fuchs 1955. 46. Chapter 29

Chapter 5

1. Vatican II, "Church in the Modern World", 58. 2. Vatican II, "Decree
on the Missionary Activity of the Church", *22*. 3. Vatican II, "Church in
the Modern World", 44. 4. Vatican II, "Decree on the Missionary Activity
of the Church", 22 5. Vatican II, William Stewart, *Christian Presence
and Modern Hinduism*, SCM, London, 1964, pp.62-64. 6. Ibid., p.84. 7
Quoted by Thomas 1976, p.76. 8. Ibid, p.79.   9. Ibid., p. 180. 10. Ibid.,
p.151. 11. Ibid., p. 116. 12. An instance is Magdalena Mariam (Mary of
Magdalene) by Vallathol, Poet-Laureate of Kerala. The new-wave poems
in Malayalam by Satchidanandan, Kadammanitta, Chullikad and others
abound in Christian symbols and motifs. 13. Vishnu Purana, 1,7. 14.
Eliade 1952, pp.62ff. 15.Is 33:14. 16. Brihadaranyaka Upanishad, 3.1.5.
17. Ibid., 1.3.28. 18. Svetasvatara Upanishad, 2.1.5; also Gita, 13:24, 26.
19. Mundaka Upanishad, 3.2.5. 20. Brihadaranyaka Upanishad, 1.3.8.
21. Mundaka Upanishad, 3.2.28. 22. Gita, 6:9. 23. Brihadaranyaka
Upanishad, 1.3.28. 24. Gita, 13:34. 25. Ibid., 2:29; 9:28. 26. Ibid., 6:24.
27. Ibid., 6:23. 28. Ibid., 2:71. 29. Ibid, 2:64. 30. Ibid., 2:70; 4:39; 5:12.
31. Ibid., 5:21. 32. Ibid., 5:7. 33. Ibid., 5:24; 6:27; 14:26. 34. Ibid, 8:5;
13:18. 35.Kappen 1977, pp.53-67. 36. Zimmer 1962, pp.13-16. 37.
Kappen 1977, pp. 60-64. 38. O'Flaherty 1975 39. Quoted by Thomas
1976, p.70. 40. Damodaran 1970, pp. 81-82. 41. Kappen 1977, pp. 97-
98. 42. Gita, 12:13-20. 43. Mascaro 1978, p. 50. 44. Mt. 6:30. 45. Bary
1963, pp.111-112.

Chapter 14

1. For historical information on the condition of women in Jewish
society, I have drawn largely upon Hanna wolf, *Jesus der Mann*, Radius,
Stuttgart, 1979

Chapter 15

1. In writing this piece, I have derived much inspiration from the audacious work: Belo 1975

Chapter 29

1. Code of Manu, 1:88 **2.** Ibid, 1:91 **3.** Ibid, 8:1 **4.** See, for instance, Rajneesh 1984

Bibliography

Bary, Wm. Theodore (1963), *Sources of Indian Tradition,* Motilal Banarsidas, Delhi

Belo, Fernando (1974), *Lecture Materialiste de Evangile de Marc,* Cerf, Paris

Benko, Stephen and John J. O. ed.(1972), *Early Church History,* Oliohants, London

Chattopadhyaya, Debiprasad (1959), *Lokayata: A Study in Indian Materialism,* People's Publishing House, New Delhi

- (1964), *Indian Philosophy,* People's Publishing House, New Delhi

Damodaran, K. (1970), *Man and Society in Indian Philosophy,* People's Publishing House, New Delhi

Doughlas, Mary (1978), *Purity and Danger. An Analysis of the Concepts of Pollution and Taboo,* RKP, London,

Eliade, Mircea (1952), *Images and Symbols,* London

Fuchs, Stephen (1955), *Rebellious Prophets,* Asia Publishing House, Bombay

Gager, John G. (1975), *Kingdom and Community - The Social World of Early Christianity,* Prentice-Hall

Grant, Robert M. (1978), *Early Christianity and Society,* Collins, London

Hengel, Martin(1974), *Judaism and Hellenism,* I, SCM Press, London

Hiriyanna, M. (1960), *The Essentials of Indian Philosophy,* Allen and Unwin, London

Jeremias, Joachim (1971), *New Testament Theology, The Proclamation of Jesus,* Scribners, New York

Kappen, S. (1977), *Jesus and Freedom,* Orbis Books, Maryknoll, New York.

Kee, Howard C. (1977), *Community of the New Age,* SCM, London

Kosambi, D. D. (1977), *The Culture and Civilization of Ancient India,* (abrev. Culture), Vikas Publications, New Delhi.

- (1962), *Myth and Reality* (abrev. Myth), Popular Prakashan, 1962

Ling, Trevor, ed. (1981), *The Buddha's Philosophy of Man: Early Indian Buddhist Sources*, Everyman's Library, London

Lohse, Eduard (1976), *The New Testament Environment*, SCM Press, London

Marx-Engels (1970), *Selected Works*, Progress, Moscow

- (1975), *On Religion*, Progress, Moscow

- (1976), *The German Ideology*, Progress Publishers, Moscow

Mascaro, Juan tr. (1978), *Dhammapada*, Penguin Classics

Miranda, Jose Porfirio (1971), *Marx and the Bible*, Orbis Books, New York

Momigliano, ed. (1963), *The Conflict between Paganism and Christianity in the Fourth Century*, Oxford University, New York

O'Flaherty, Wendy Doniger tr. (1975), *Hindu myths: A sourcebook* , Penguin Classics.

Perrin, Norman (1963)*Rediscovering the Teaching of Jesus*, SCM, London

Rajneesh, Bhagwan Shree (1984), *Beware of Socialism*, 2nd Revised edition, Osho International Foundation

Ramanujam, A.K. (1973), *Speaking Siva*, Penguin Classics

Singer, Milton, ed., (1968), *Krishna: Myths, Rites, and Attitudes*, ed. University of Chicago Press

Sreenivas, M. N. ed. (1978), *Dimensions of Social Change in India*, Allied Publishers, New Delhi

Stewart, William (1964), *Christian Presence and Modern Hinduism*, SCM, London

Theissen, Gerd (1978), *The First Followers of Jesus, A Sociological Analysis of Early Christianity*, SCM, London

Thomas, M. M. (1976), *The Secular Ideologies of India and the Secular Meaning of Christ*, C.L.S. Madras

Wolf, Hanna (1979), *Jesus der Mann*, Radius, Stuttgart

Zaehner, R. C. tr. (1969), *The Bhgavad Gita*, Oxford University Press, London

Zimmer, Heinrich (1962), *Myths and Symbols in Indian Art and Civilization*, Harper Torch Books, New York

Sebastian Kappen's Books

- *Jesus and Freedom* (1977), intr. Francois Houtar, Orbis Books, Maryknoll, New York, Edition 2: Notion Press, Chennai, 2019

- *Marxian Atheism* (1983a), self published, Bangalore.

- *Jesus and Cultural Revolution - an Asian Perspective* (1983b), BILD, Bombay

- *Jesus Today* (1985). AICUF, Madras

- *Liberation Theology and Marxism* (1986), Asha Kendra, Punthamba

- *The Future of Socialism and Socialism of the Future* (1992), Visthar, Bangalore.

Posthumous Publications

- *Tradition Modernity Counterculture – an Asian Perspective* (1994), Visthar, Bangalore.

- *Spirituality in the New Age of Recolonisation* (1995), Visthar, Bangalore

- *Hindutva and Indian Religious Traditions* (2000), ed. Sebastian Vattamattam, Edition 2: Notion Press, Chennai, 2019

- *Divine Challenge and Human Response* (2001), ed. Sebastian Vattamattam, CSS, Tiruvalla

- *Jesus and Society* (2002a), ed. S Painadath S. J., ISPCK, Delhi.

- *Jesus and Culture* (2002b), ed. S Painadath S. J., ISPCK, Delhi

- *Towards a Holistic Cultural Paradigm* (2003), ed. Sebastian Vattamattam, CSS, Tiruvalla

- *Marx Beyond Marxism* (2012), ed. Sebastian Vattamattam, Voice Books, Manjeri.

- *Ingathering – Autobiographical Writings and Selected essays* (2013a), ed. Sebastian Vattamattam, Jeevan Books, Bharananganam

- *What the Thunder Says – A poem and selected Essays* (2013b), ed. Sebastian Vattamattam, Jeevan Books, Bharananganam

Books in Malayalam

- *Viswasathil Ninnu Viplavathilekku* (1 9 7 2) , e d it i on 3: Pusthaka Prasadhaka Sangham, Kozhikode, 2019

- *Nalathekku Oru Laingika-sadacharam* (1973), Edition 3: Pusthaka Prasadhaka Sangham, Kozhikode, 2019

- *Paristhithi Samskruthi* (1988), (Co-author: Sebastian Vattamattam), Edition 2: Ascend Books, Kottayam, 2014

- *Marxian Darsanathinu Oramukham* (1989), tr. of Marx Beyond Marxism by Sebastian Vattamattam, Edition 2: NBS, Kottayam, 2012

- *Kalasrushtiyude Uravidam* (1991), tr. of Martin Heidegger: Der Ursprung Des Kunstwerkes, DCB, Kottayam

- *Pravachanam Prathisamskruthi* (1992), Yatra Publications, Kottayam

- *Socialisathinte Bhavi* (1993), Manusham Publications, Ettumanoor

- *Akraistavanaya Yesuvine Thedi* (1999), Current Books, Kottayam, 2005

- *Irupathonnam Noottandinoru Prathisamskruthi* (1991), tr. of Tradition Modernity Counterculture, Yatra Publications, Kottayam

- *Yesuvinte Mochanam Sabhakalil Ninnu* (2012), Dr. Bishop Paulose Mar Paulose Foundation, Thrissur

- *Daivathinte Maranavum Manushyante Jananavum*, (2015), tr. of Marxian Atheism, Media House, Calicut

About the Editor

Sebastian Vattamattam is a retired professor of mathematics and a writer. In Malayalam he has authored the books: *Ecology and Culture* (with Fr. Kappen), *Language and Power, Unconscious Travels of Language – From Freud to Lacan, Ideology and Symbolic Revolution, Sigmund Freud*. His books in English are *Book of Beautiful Curves* (Math) and *What Dreams Tell Us – Lacanian Interpretations*. Vattamattam has compiled, edited, and published many books of Fr. Kappen.

Contents of the Six Volumes

8. The Dialectical Method II

9. Man - A Dialectical Being

10. Alienation and the Dialectic of History

11. The Materialist Conception of History

12. Indian Communism and the Challenge of Cultural Revolution

13. The Goals of Revolution

14. Revolution: For What? By Whom?

15. Consciousness and Reality in Marxism

16. Dialectic of the Psycho-structure and the Social Structure

17. How not to be a Revolutionary

Volume III

Part 1: Jesus and Cultural Revolution
Foreword

1. The Dialectic of Culture and Prophecy

2. Jesus: the Prophet of a Counterculture

3. The Decline of Prophecy

4. Countercultural Movements in India

5. Jesus and Transculturation

6. Communities for Countercultural Action

Part 2: Essays
7. The Prophet of Hope

8. Towards Theandric Fullness

9. The Not-yet and the Already

10. The Future: A Gift and a Task

Volume IV

Part 1: Liberation Theology and Marxism

3. For a Contextual Theology of Liberation

4. From Religious Ideology to Prophetic Religiosity

5. Towards an Ecumenism without Domination

6. Church, Liberation Theology, and Marxism

7. The Marxist and the Christian Dialectics of Liberation

8. Marxist Christian Dialogue

Part 2: Essays

9. The Spirit Descended Upon Him

10. Jesus beyond Jesus

11. The Man Jesus: Rupture and Communion

12. A Lesson in Socialism

13. Table-fellowship as Socialist Praxis

14. Christians and Class Struggle

15. Church a People's Movement

16. Between the Church and the Reign of God

17. Church as the Bearer of New Values

18. The Asian Search for a Liberative Theology

19. A New Approach to Theological Education

Volume V

Part 1: Hindutva and Indian Religious Traditions

1. The Materialistic Conception of History and the Indian Religious Tradition

2. Religious Ideologies and Political Change Hindu-Christian Relations in India

2. Culture and Class Domination

3. Towards a Revolution of Symbols

4. Countercultural Perspectives

5. Vedic Orientations for a Relevant Ecosophy

6. The Emerging Paradigm of Vision and Values

7. Art and Social Consciousness

8. Towards an Alternative Cultural Paradigm

Part 2: Essays

9. Beyond the Cult of the Dead God

10. The Dialectic of Faith and Unfaith

11. Spirituality in the New Age of Re-colonization

12. The Prophetic Role of the Christians in Contemporary India in the World of Art

13. Jesus and the Elections

14. Towards an Indian Model of Socialism

15. The Future of Socialism and Socialism of the Future

Part 3: A Poem and Autobiography

16. What the Thunder Says

17. Ingathering

www.ingramcontent.com/pod-product-compliance
Lightning Source LLC
LaVergne TN
LVHW092345170726
843489LV00001B/40